The
Intemperate
Engineer

Isambard Kingdom Brunel
in His Own Words

The
Intemperate
Engineer

Isambard Kingdom Brunel
in His Own Words

Adrian Vaughan

Acknowledgements

All 'Rail' documents are to be found under that catalogue number at the National Archives at Kew. Nearest railway station is Kew Gardens on the District Line. The other major source of information is the collection of Brunel papers and artefacts held in the Special Collections Department of Bristol University Library, Tyndal Avenue, Bristol. All the letters and pictures from that collection are produced with the permission of the University of Bristol Library Special Collections. I must express my sincere thanks to the Archivist of the Special Collections, Hannah Lowery, Special Collections Librarian, Michael Richardson and Assistant Librarian Anna Rigg for their great kindness over many years. Also Nick Lee, Special Collections Archivist, now retired, who supported me when he was at work and with generous lodgings after that. At the Institution of Civil Engineers, One Great George Street, Westminster, I could always rely on the co-operation of librarian Robert Heffernan and Archivist Carol Morgan. At Ian Allan Publishing, I would like to thank Nick Grant, Mark Beynon and Alan Butcher for their good work on the book.

Adrian Vaughan
Barney, 2010

First published 2010

ISBN 978 0 7110 3280 4

Published by Ian Allan Publishing

an imprint of Ian Allan Publishing Ltd, Hersham, Surrey, KT12 4RG
Printed in England by Ian Allan Printing Ltd, Hersham, Surrey, KT12 4RG

Distributed in the United States of America and Canada by BookMasters Distribution Services

Visit the Ian Allan Publishing website at www.ianallanpublishing.com

CONTENTS

Author's Note

My purpose in writing *The Intemprate Enginer: Isambard Kingdom Brunel in His Own Words* is to gain a feeling of closeness to him. I hope that by reading all these letters anyone can gain a strong impression of Mr Brunel. I want to feel and I want the reader to feel that he is standing next to him while he works at his desk, travelling with him, knowing the detail of his worries and feeling his tensions, and to realise his humanity – his genius and his fallibility.

There is an *ocean* of research available and I have concentrated on his early diaries, his work in planning and constructing the Great Western Railway, and his relationships with assistants and contractors, enemies and close friends, and relations. There is some reference to other railways but I have not gone into his great works with ships, and it should always be remembered when reading this book that on top of all his worrying activity on the railway he had as much of that again in dealing with his ship experiments and designs.

I have also included some letters not written by Isambard Kingdom Brunel. Some are by his father, Marc Isambard, because these relate to I. K. Brunel's very early life and domestic affairs of middle age, and a couple by his trusted assistant, John Hammond, because they show how those close to him understood their master's drives.

I have deciphered and typed out Brunel's words accurately and what he wrote is printed in the *italic* typeface and the text indented. Where I have been unable to read a word I have inserted [...]. My comments within letters are also enclosed in [brackets]. Brunel occasionally emphasises a word or words by underlining and I have copied this. Where I want to make an emphasis in the course of his words I have used **bold** text.

The 'PLB' and 'DM' prefixes to reference numbers refers to letters housed in the Special Collections section of Bristol University Library. The 'Rail' prefix refers to letters housed at the National Archives, Kew.

1 : Early Days

'Our Young Man'

When Isambard was 11½ his father sent him to a tutor in Paris. The identity of the 'Mentor' is not revealed in this short note, which perhaps little Isambard would carry with him and hand to the Mentor. However, the later letters strongly suggest that the Mentor was the greatest clockmaker of the age, Louis Breguet. This note (DM 1282/1) asks that Isambard be tamed, brought to order and made to learn. Note that, contrary to Rolt's 'definitive' biography, Isambard had not 'mastered Euclid by the age of six', but had only just started learning it at the age of 11.

DM1282/1
Le 2 Sept 1817

My Nephew [Mon Neveu]
*I entrust my little boy to you as he needs a Mentor. I don't believe
I could make a better choice than in imploring you to moderate the
impetuosity of his youth. He is a good little boy but he doesn't care
for his books – except mathematics for which he has a liking. He
has started Euclid. Use it as much as you can. You must not let him
sit an excessive examination as he often becomes exhausted. As he
is not in the best of health he sometimes needs to take a small dose
of rhubarb which he carries with him.
He must not be allowed to drink cider.*

I am always to you your uncle,
Marc I. Brunel

Monsieur Louis Breguet
Quai a l'Horologe
Paris

28 November 1820

Monsieur,
Monsieur Melin brought me a letter from my son and informed me

at the same time of your good disposition towards him. You have already given me proof in his last stay in Paris three years ago when he was still a little schoolboy. I hope that you'll find him more reflective and much less importune/vexatious/troublesome. I know that he had got much more inclination towards useful recreation and instructions to go to the theatre or other public amusements and besides, as Sundays are the only days that he can give you, I've told him what your cousin told me on your behalf – that he was to inform you when he did not have any invitation for that particular day.

I would really have liked to have gone with my family to Paris and to have received your amiable Father and Aunt but I was more occupied than ever with the discovery which is connected with a new process of stereotype which Isambard will be able to explain to you with the greatest precision as he has now been my collaborator for several months. I have found him not only very useful but of unflinching perseverance. He never gets tired even though we work till after midnight. As a draughtsman he surpasses me and is first class not only by his exactitude with which he copies but he is of a rare frame of mind and he loves work particularly that which holds his attention and involves his hands. He cannot find a better way of occupying himself than by working with you and is persuaded that he will be recognised by it.

I have instructed him to make the best use of your experience and expertise.

Will you accept the assurance of my feelings of gratitude which Madame Brunel and Mme Hawes share with me with all their hearts and with great sincerity,

Your devout servant,
Marc Brunel

Early in 1821 Marc Brunel's bankers failed. He was deeply indebted to them and was now insolvent. On 14 May 1821 he was committed to the Marshalsea debtors' prison. This must surely have been very unsettling for young Isambard, studying theory and practical sciences. Marc's debt was paid for him and he was released early in August 1821.

Monsieur Louis Breguet
Quai de l'Horologe
Paris

19 November 1821

[There is no opening greeting to this letter.]
*Mrs Brunel and I can't thank you enough for your attention my
dear monsieur, in dispersing the worry in which we were with
regard to our young man. We were really determined to make him
return to Ms Massin when Mlle Dumergue coming by chance to
our house with Mde Necholion [?] they have spoken such a eulogy
of Isambard that we are asking you for an expiry date we
promising you to return our party immediately on that date.*

*We have received the letter from Ms [...] speaking of a teacher
Ms Massin who must take on some pupils. I have told Isambard
to get the information on terms of the boarding house. By all
accounts it would be a better place for Isambard.* [Better than
staying with Breguet?]

*We can't thank you enough for your good attentions towards
him. He shares also the feeling with us for he does not stop
repeating to us how highly you regard him and with what pleasure
he spent the day with you. He sent us his journal in which he tells
us the way in which he uses his time and those things that really
interest him. You figure there often. He doesn't want the honour
of sitting next to you at dinner at Mlle Dumergue.*

*Your good advice will not be lost, I dare to flatter myself,
concerning him especially as he is so honest and that he makes
himself amenable to all that is demanded of him.*

*Ms Navier who has been recommended to me by your Ms [...]
must be coming back from Paris. He has promised to inform us
how our young man's attempts at entering the Ecole Polytechnique
are progressing.*

*When you write you can give your letter to Isambard who will
send it on to us – the bridge between you and us in London.*

Your devout servant,
Marc Brunel

Isambard does not appear to have taken lodgings at the boarding house.

Monsieur Breguet
Quai de l'Horologe
Paris

19 February 1822

My Dear Sir,
My interesting [Mon interessant] Isambard reiterates how <u>lovely it</u>
<u>is at Ms Breguet's house</u> that I cannot delay any longer writing to
you to tell you just how much we are recognising and how much
we are congratulating ourselves that he has merited your esteem
and your friendship. Nothing can [...] from a separation so long
that [...] to know he is in such good hands and that he has been so
careful to write to us every week.

We see with a great interest that he is behaving himself as he
finds himself now in the first place amongst the best of his time
[concurrent redoubtables]. He has all he needs for his admission to
the Ecole Polytechnique next August and he will not be put off
under any circumstances. I look forward with impatience to what
could be the success of the exam [by which he will be admitted to
the Polytechnique] while he must be scared stiff of the result. If he
has the good luck to acquit himself well he will not only be more
sure of himself that of which must decide his lot.

I implore you to be my close interpreter and to express to him
just how much I appreciate the real advantage of having such a
friend as Ms Breguet. I [...], Monsieur your son with whom I share
the same feelings of gratitude of really wanting us to say/tell us
with the same honesty that he did before that he now thinks of his
little friend as his pupil. Can you really thank on our behalf Mlle
Breguet for all her attention to him.

Will you please accept, my dear, Ms Breguet, the assurance of my
feeling of gratitude and of my devotion and accept my sincere
cordiality,

Yours sincerely,
Your respected friend,
Marc Isambard Brunel

PS from Sophia Brunel
Mr Brunel charges me to thank and compliment your son and
Mlle Breguet and to assure you that she is being very helpful.

Unfortunately, or maybe not, Isambard failed to qualify for the
Polytechnique. The exam was in French, which was not his first
language, and there were 600 men for 100 places. He came home to
London on 21 August 1822 bringing with him the priceless experience of

three years training in the greatest clockmakers' works in the world. His training in civil engineering began in his father's office near the gold-filled vaults of the Bank of England – slightly ironic, given Marc's continuous lack of money. Marc pursued his inventive genius without regard to money. He invented and patented a large number of useful things, including the first truly precise machine tools; expanding piston rings; a tall dome for steam collection on a boiler; and a mechanical stoker for those boilers. And, of course, the tunnelling shield.

Isambard Kingdom Brunel began his private diary on 22 April 1824.

On 2 March 1825 work commenced on sinking a brick shaft at Rotherhithe from which Marc's tunnelling shield would advance below the bed of the Thames to Wapping. Marc was paid £5,000 in advance and this was swallowed by his overdraft. On 9 March Isambard wrote: *'I am most terribly pinched for money, should barely receive enough to pay my debts and am this moment without a penny. We keep neither carriages nor footmen and only two maidservants.'* Clearly they were without a penny as well.

Isambard was kept out of the tunnel – because the conditions were so vile – until in April 1826 his father and the Scots engineer employed to assist Marc were so ill that Isambard was appointed. He loved the challenge and the terrible dangers and earned the huge respect of the miners and bricklayers by leading from the front and cheering them on with his youthful enthusiasm.

But Isambard also used a management technique that remained with him all his life – he refused to pay wages as an incentive for the men to work harder. The money was held hostage against good behaviour the following week.

Isambard had been told to expect fame and fortune as an engineer and he threw himself into this work, toiling for great fame in a subterranean hell-hole.

His diary contains references to his fear of not achieving his ambition. On 19 October 1827 he wrote:

As to my character. My self conceit and love of glory vie with each other which shall govern me. The latter is so strong that, even of a dark night, riding home, when I pass some unknown person I catch myself trying to look big on my little pony. I do the most silly, useless things to attract the attention of those I shall never see again. My self conceit renders me domineering, intolerant and even quarrelsome with those who do not flatter. My ambition – it is more than the mere wish to be rich – is rather extensive – but still – I shall not be unhappy if I do not reach the rank of Hero and

Commander-in-Chief of His Majesty's Forces in the Steam or Gaz Boat Division. Make the Gaz engine work, fit out some vessels, of course a war is required, get employed by government contract – command a fine fleet and fight – take some fortified town – Algiers or something of that style. Be at last rich. Be the first Engineer and example to all others.

On 19 October 1827 he wrote:
Sunday night – 10pm. West parlour Rotherhithe.
A new broom sweeps clean! The second night and again at it! I have been today to Mr Sweet about agreement but I did not see him –

   When thinking of this journal whole volumes crowded in on me – my character, my 'chateau d'espange' – now I am quite without an idea.

   I wish I had kept this journal while we were at work on the river. What a dream it now appears to me – going down in the diving bell finding and examining the hole – standing on the corner of No 12! The novelty of the thing, the excitement of the occasional risk attending our subaquatic excursions, the crowds of boats to witness our works all around – The anxious watching of the shaft – seeing it full of water rising and falling with the tide with the most provoking regularity – at last by dint of claybags, clay and gravel – a perceptible difference we began pumping at last reaching the crown of the arch – what sensations! – standing on the arch – the engine rattling away – my father more cautious certainly foresaw the consequence of too quick pumping – but we prevailed –

   NB never <u>will</u> I then be prevailed upon by others to do what I think imprudent.
At last water below the arch – nearly down to the plynths [sic] traverse under the arch for some distance.

   I go to an evening party at Greenwich – rather an anxious evening return all right. Go down 200ft with Sophie Buy … and Sarah – go to bed am awake by nurse – something the matter. Jumps up. Dress – run to the shaft – full!

   Altho' to others I appear in such cases rather unconcerned and not affected [proud] the internal anguish I felt is not to be described. I thank God however I rather returned thanks that it was no worse then grumbled [sic] – I am an optimist I hope in deed as well as word – 11½pm I will lie down on the rug a little and then go below.

November 4th

I have been to day to London Bridge am full of my skeme [29 December 1827] for a 300ft arch metal joints – sketching centring for arch. My father's negotiations with the French may yet turn out something.

What will become of me? To go to France I to lose my connection and damage my prospects here yet to stop here at my age [21] I cannot expect to be employed.

A Tunnel at Gravesend or Liverpool? Mr Pitt was only 22 Prime Minister and for the first time in his life!!! [At 22 one would not have expected it to have been his second term in that position.]

I may be said to have almost built this tunnel having been active resident Engineer. What Castles!!

My Gaz engine – a tunnel – tunnels.

What a field – yet I may miss it –

5 November, 3am

Am sitting up writing my journal. Kemble drunk. Millwrights gone home. Just written to Mr Wilks to wait till Directors can come. Am just recovered from a serious thing. Fell into the river water well and hurt my knee – intend giving a dinner next Saturday in commemoration or as a thanksgiving for our having completing [sic] 20ft since the grand water battle – which we shall have please God at that day.

I must make some little Indian ink sketches of our boat excursions to the frames – the low, dark, gloomy, cold arch. The heaps of earth almost up to the crown hiding the frames and rendering it quite uncertain what state they were in and what might happen. The hollow rushing of water, the total darkness of all around rendered distinct by the glimmering light of a candle carried by ourselves – crawling along the bank of earth a dark recess at the end – quite dark – water rushing from it in such quantity as to render it uncertain whether the ground was secure. At last reaching the frames – choked up to the middle rail of the top box – frames evidently leaning back and sideways considerably – stave in curious directions bags & chisel rods protruding in all directions reaching No 12 the bags apparently without support and swelling into the frame threatened every minute to close in with side brickwork – all bags – a cavern huge, mis-shapen with water cataract in full coming from it – Candles going out.

21 November, Wednesday evening.

Returned from town put on my fighting dress having given some directions at Smiths shop screwing gauge for new long jacks.

Having in fact smelt the cold frosty night air on entering my parlour a nice blazing fire my table before it paper books etc nicely arranged thereon the whole inspired such a feeling of comfort that I could not resist sitting down and imparting my sensations to this book as to a friend.

As long as health continues, one's prospects tolerable and <u>present</u> efforts whatever they may be tolerably successful then indeed a bachelor's life is luxurious. Fond as I am of society '<u>selfish comfort</u>' is delightful. I have always felt so. My chateau d'espange have mostly been found on this feeling. What independence! For one who's ambition is to distinguish himself in the eyes of the public such a freedom is almost indispensable but on the other hand in sickness or disappointment how delightful to have a companion whose sympathy one is sure of possessing. Her dependence on you gives her the power to support you by consolation and however delightful may be freedom and independence still we find that certain restraints are necessary for the enjoyment of pleasure.

I have always wished and intended to be married but have been very doubtful on the subject of ———- children ——————— it is a question whether they are the source of most pleasure or pain. I have had as I suppose numerous attachments if they deserve the name each in its time has appeared to me <u>the true one</u> E H—- [Ellen Hulme of Manchester] is the oldest and most constant now however gone by. During her reign, nearly 7 years!!!, several inferior ones caught my attention.

I need hardly remind myself of M'selles CD – OS and numerous others –

With E————e it was mutual and I trust the present feeling is also mutual in this case. The sofa scene etc must appear now to her as to me rather ridiculous. She was a nice girl and had she improved as a girl of her age ought to have done.

This entry was written on the left-hand page of the journal. Brunel's note at the foot of the page concludes the entry because the right-hand page, upon which he would have continued freely reminiscing about his girlfriends, was very carefully cut out of the book, probably by Mrs Mary Brunel. Thus the right-hand page facing this entry is lost, together, of course, with what was on the other side of it, and the girlfriend recollections of 21 November conclude with:

> *...have served me right if I had been spilled in the mud – certainly*
> *a devilish pretty girl, an excellent musician and a sweet voice – but*
> *I am afraid those eyes don't speak a very <u>placid temper</u>.*

29 December, Saturday 5 pm

> *I always feel inclined to write in this journal when I am alone. I*
> *feel so comfortable that I wish to perpetuate a small portion of the*
> *luxury I enjoy.*
>
> *Beamish and Gravatt are both in town nothing in particular*
> *going on below. [Seven shorthand symbols follow] all quiet and I*
> *at desert – <u>alone</u> – how luxurious! I am getting monstrous orderly*
> *now and have got a rage for instruments excellent ones in their*
> *kind at least. I have now some very pretty electrum drawing tools,*
> *have ordered a super excellent electrum 4 inch pocket sextant of*
> *Simms. I now only want a good level with telescope that can see*
> *through a brick wall and then a good 9 inch or 10 inch theodolite*
> *– double telescope – low and snug above deck – (only 15 or 20*
> *degrees of elevation all these in electrum if I find it answer and*
> *nothing superior is invented). The first however will cost £25 to*
> *£30 and the second £70 to £80 – say £100 the two – therefore*
> *'attendons un peu' [let's wait a while].*
>
> *My father and mother at Lady Spencer's Althorp – should like*
> *to have been there.*

There were four contradictory parts to Isambard Kingdom Brunel's character: he was the risk-taking lover of danger; the insecure and defensive; the mathematician engineer; and the romantic, artist and dramatic actor.

The river broke into the tunnel at 6.00am on 12 January 1828 when Brunel was at the tunnelling face. It was only by the most astonishing freak of good luck that Brunel escaped with his life (see page 25 of my *Isambard Kingdom Brunel: Engineering Knight-Errant* [John Murray, 1991]).

22 April 1828

> *Here I am in bed at Bridge Ho. I have now been laid up quite*
> *useless for 14 weeks and upwards ever since the 12 January. I*
> *shan't forget that day in a hurry. Very near finished my journey*
> *then. When the danger is over it is rather amusing than otherwise.*

While it existed I can't say the feeling was at all unsatisfactory. If I was to say the contrary I should be near the truth. In this instance while exertions could be made and hope remained of stopping the ground it was an excitement which has always been a luxury to me when we were obliged to run I felt nothing particular I was only thinking of the best way of getting us out and the probable state of the arches when knocked down. I certainly gave myself up but I took it very much as a matter of course which I had expected the moment we quitted the frames for I never expected we should get out.

The instant I disengaged myself and got breath again – all dark – I bolted into the other arch – this saved me by laying hold of the rail rope – the engine must have stopped a minute – I stood there for nearly a minute. I was anxious for poor Ball and Collins who I felt too sure had never risen from the fall we all had and were as I thought <u>crushed</u> under or in the stage – I kept calling them by name to encourage them and make them also (if still able) come through the opening –

While standing there the effect was <u>grand</u>. The roar of the rushing water in a confined passage and by its velocity rushing past the opening was grand, <u>very grand</u>. I cannot compare it to anything – cannon can be nothing to it. At last it came bursting through the opening. I was then obliged to be off – but up to that moment as far as my sensations were concerned and distinct from the idea of the loss of those 5 poor fellows whose death I could not then foresee except this the sight and the whole affair was well worth the risk and I would willingly pay my share, £50 about, of the expenses for such a 'spectacle' – reaching the shaft I was too much bothered with my knee and some other things to remember much – If I had been kept under another minute when knocked down I would not have suffered more and I trust I was tolerably fit to die.

If therefore the occurrence itself was rather a gratification than otherwise and the consequences in no way unpleasant I need not attempt to avoid such –

My being in bed at present tho' no doubt arising from the effects of my <u>straining</u> was immediately caused by my returning to a full diet at Brighton. Had I been properly warned of this I might now have been hard at work at the Tunnel but all is for the best.

I have formed many plans for my future guidance which I verily believe I shall follow and if so my time will not have been lost –

This record of a few of them will thus serve to keep me in check as I cannot then deny them.

1st Rules as regards my health

I will (if I can) go to bed at such time as to be able to rise early for instance I think I <u>could</u> always go to bed at 12 or 1 and get up at 5 or 6 this would agree pretty well with my shift duties and I should then get an appetite for breakfast at 8 and eat a substantial one. I could then when I wanted go to Town pretty early – oh that I had a gig or a horse!!

I would dine at about 4½ or 3½ according to circumstances have tea at 8½ and a <u>light</u> supper at 10½. This arrangements is peculiarly suited to my occupations for instance all dietists seem to agree in one point viz – that after a meal one should remain quiet (not asleep however) for one, two or three hours – as I have remarkably good digestion 1 or 1½ hours would be sufficient after this period exercise is <u>necessary</u>.

Now my duties below will be best performed by visiting at the end of the shift then giving directions for the ensuing shift and going down in the middle to <u>find fault</u> etc etc and again at the end as before – this middle visit should alone be ever dispensed with – the duties above ground would require attention more particularly before breakfast and then at any time –

By rising early I can go below to see the end of the night shift give directions for the next – then attend to above ground & at 8 eat a hearty breakfast. After breakfast write letters – draw – attend to any sedentary business – if anything particular go below at 10½ or so then attend again to active business going below again towards 1½ giving directions for the other shift – then dine at 3 (on these regular days).

After dinner <u>write my journal</u> (standing) – read – Etc draw – attend to office business always having Morgan Orton etc into me [sic]

NB. This will save me a great deal of time.

If nothing particular below – continue these <u>amusements</u> till tea at 8. Going below again at 9 about – shift changed etc come into a comfortable supper at 10½ reading and <u>enjoying myself</u> till 11½ or 12 – go below – come up write my journal and go to bed.

Now as I have a habit of eating quick reading at my meals will be a pleasant and excellent thing but having a bad memory I must take notes another very good habit.

I shall thus eat slower which P- says is the way not to eat too much and enjoy my meals –

Another thing is always to have my Journal – a memo book and general sketch book at hand (Locked up tho').

NB In writing my journal I will always open at once an index at the end and also to refer to the page of my sketch book – My memo book to enter everything as it strikes me and then have a pocket one to carry with me –

My sketch book will I think be one of Hawkins letter books – then by drawing on <u>whole</u> foolscap sheets pinned as a drawing board I can enter them afterwards. All calculations I will enter <u>arranged</u> into my <u>miscellany</u>.

I will have a desk which I <u>can raise</u> high enough to stand to. Q. How? Make a sketch –

I will write my journal whenever I have the opportunity.

I must try and introduce order in everything. I am decidedly improved in that respect within the past two years –

As I have a bad memory for words or phrenologically, a Deficiency of Language [is this why he uses so many words, so many asides, that sometimes he loses the thread of what he is writing about?] I must make up for it by writing and sketching everything I wish to remember – but I will also try to improve the faculty.

6 May 1828

Here I am again – 12½ am – Wednesday 7th May.

Smoking some excellent canaster J. Hulme [Ellen Hulme's brother?] has left me. He went to Manchester today having spent a day in Town on his way from Berlin. Poor fellow he has had some unfortunate <u>downs</u> as well as others – It makes me rather blue devilish to think of it and since I am very prone to build airy castles I will now build a few blue ones which I am afraid are likely to prove less airy and more real –

Here are these Directors damming the tunnel as fast as they well can. If they go on at this rate we must certainly stop – and then – by jove we shall stop – payment – where the devil money is to come from in that case I know not. Tawney is sneaking – we must not expect much from that quarter after a short time. What money we may get from the Battersea concern will produce at most £300 a year most likely not £200!! – The Gaz we may never realise – even if we find success to prosecute the experiment difficulties may arise to render the ultimate success doubtful nay perhaps impossible – where then will be all my fine castles – bubbles – well if it was only for myself I should not mind it – I fear if the Tunnel stops I shall find all those flattering promises of my friends will prove – friendly wishes –

The young Rennies whatever their true merit *[this is an odd comment to make of George and John Rennie, capable, engineering sons of the engineer Sir John Rennie. Does it indicate Brunel's jealousy of them?] will have built London Bridge the finest bridge in Europe and have such a connection with government as to defy competition – Palmer has built new London docks and thus without labour has established a connection which ensure his fortune, while I – shall have been engaged on a tunnel which failed – which was abandoned – a pretty recommendation. All the engineers glad enough of publishing that it was my father's debut almost in engineering. I have nothing after all so very transcendent as to enable me to rise by my own merit without some such help as the Tunnel – It's a gloomy perspective and yet bad as it is I cannot with all my efforts work myself up to be downhearted. Well it's very fortunate I am so easily pleased. After all let the worst happen – unemployment – untalked of – penniless [sic] (that's damned awkward) I think I may say depend upon a hoe at Benjamins. My poor father wd hardly survive the Tunnel – my mother wd follow him – I should be left alone – here invention fails what wd follow I cannot guess – a war now and I would go and get my throat cut and that would be foolish enough – well 'vogue la galerie' very annoying but so it is.*

I suppose a sort of middle path will be the most likely one – a mediocre success – an engineer sometimes employed sometimes not – 200 or 300 a year, that uncertain. Well I shall then have plenty to wish for and that always constituted my happiness. May I always be of the same mind and then the less I have the happier I shall be.

I'll turn misanthrope. Got a huge meerschaum as big as myself and smoke away melancholy – and yet that can't be without money and that can't be got without working for it. Dear me, what a world this is where starvation is an expensive luxury – but damn all croaking. The Tunnel must go on it shall go on – by the by – why should I not get some situation? Surely I have friends enough for that?

Q2. Get a nice, snug little berth and then a snug little wife with a little somewhat to assist in housekeeping. What an interesting situation! –

19

No luxuries. None of your enjoyments of which I am tolerably fond – oh horrible – and all this owing to the damned Directors who can't swallow when the food is put into their mouths – here is the Duke of W——n speaking as favourably as possible offering unasked to take the lead in public meeting and the devil knows what and they let it all slip by as if the pig's tail was soaped – Oh for Sir E here now he'd give it them – but they are all asleep.

Hawes and all alike

If the Tunnel does go on no thanks to them well then for a good four years yet I'm pinned down and when finished all the 'éclat' will be gone all the gilding tarnished and I shall find as I saw before all my fine castles – gone – well it's all for the best it may damp a little my vanity – make me a better fellow and who knows tempers may turn up again I'm sure we've no reason to complain yet whenever we've been worn off something good has come.

8 June 1828, 1am

I have not opened this book for a long time to record my old attachment. Who would have thought I should ever have lost anything from over-modesty? It appears that I really might have had A B——w a fine girl, plenty of accomplishments and £25,000 – no joke. S R——s assures me of it. W——s saw it and B——s also. Well its all for the best again. It would never have done to have married then – quite absurd – so young and when it came to the point I should have found too late what I now find – every day I return to my old love – Ellen is still it seems my real love. I have written her a long letter yesterday – her answer shall decide. If she wavers I <u>ought</u> to break off for I cannot hope to be in a condition to marry her and to continue with this state of suspense is wronging her. After all I shall most likely remain a bachelor and that is I think best for me – my profession is after all my only fit wife.

Oh that I may find her faithful to me – how time and events creep on. Next Wednesday is the public meeting. Shall we get the money? To be or not to be? If we don't – why? And the works suspended – it can only be temporary – they will be secured and opened as a show and in the meantime we must try and get the government to begin borings at Gravesend. This wd after all not be so bad – Oh Ellen, Ellen if you had kept up your musick and can even only play tolerably we might be very happy yet – and starve – it won't do – however, we'll see – If the tunnel stops our main hopes must be on Gravesend. My father [...] of going abroad

for a time will never do. All the other business. Oxford canal &
sundries etc wd alone support us and Gravesend with what little
salary I get from the Tunnel for they must have a resident engineer.

If I had married A B—w I should certainly have been
independent to a certain degree tho' I should hardly have liked
depending on my wife she'd have made a good one tho', I think –
but it wd spoil all my future prospects I'm to marry so early.

Oh for a lighthouse. I must find some places where one is
wanted. If we can get anybody to go on with the gaz machine. Oh
dear many many irons and none hot! If it was not for the thought
of Benjamin [Hawes] I really should be blue. Dear fellow, he's a
good fellow and has but one fault and that's more than I can say
for any other being I know – Well I know I shall take offence at
him whatever happens .

Damn it Ellen how you keep creeping on me how I am thinking
of you again – Well, until have your answer I cannot form a view
on the subject and therefore it is no use thinking of you.
My father is gone to Towcester. Gravatt in the country – Beamish
working away at the Tunnel – [some code follows] I still Brw p.
W— working at Mathematics – intend going to Cardiff next week
– Am now almost <u>quite better</u> after nearly five months pull pretty
well I think.

13 June 1828

No answer yet from E—-n and I'm afraid when it comes it will be
a quizzing one without any decisive answer – a shocking habit that
of quizzing it at last prevents a person from thinking seriously.

I'm almost afraid of an answer however for to marry wd be
painful and I fear that I ought not to marry unless I find a wife with
a fortune.

A Bachelor's life is a very happy one I shall have every advantage
of introduction into the best society and a wife unless she is of that
class in her own right becomes a bar.

As a bachelor I may be sure of living tolerably at my ease while
with a wife I have every prospect of starving.

If I have anything like an answer it will probably decide my state
for life.

17 August 1828

Tunnel

The last time I wrote I appeared to be thinking of nothing but my answer from Ellen. We are now in correspondence but I do not putting the thing home [sic] I am half afraid of my old attachment binding me and yet I have not the heart to break it off.

The Tunnel is now <u>blocked up</u> *at the end and all work about to cease. A year ago I should have thought this terrible and not to be born [sic] now it is come, like all other events it is only at a distance that they appear to be dreaded, time present seems to me* <u>always</u> *[sic]* <u>alike</u>. *To a person who only looks at the future or the past the present situation is quite disregarded like a traveller enjoying a beautyfull [sic] landscape or admiring a fine view the mere spot on which he stands never enters into the picture. If the prospect before him is more dismal than that through which he has passed he looks behind him – he may thus always have something to admire – just at this moment that the Tunnel ceases to be a resource the arbitration the Battersea concern is likely to be terminated and thus most opportunely supply ways and means. I have always found it so either we are peculiarly favoured or else the misfortune must consist more in discontent that in reality.*

The poor Hulmes are in a very unfortunate situation I wish I could go down and see them indeed, I need to go soon for other reasons.

Beamish is gone to Ireland. Adieu to him. [Beamish returned and became Marc Brunel's right-hand man in the long and painful completion of the Tunnel, while Isambard left to pursue his fame with the Great Western Railway and steamships.]

We shall soon all break up. I shall recommence our work on the Gaz. I am rather anxious about the specific heat of the liquid now if this also should fail down go a good portion of my castles in the air. Well can't be help it. I wish only that I was the only one concerned.

The last entry in his private diary was made on 16 April 1829 but this is confused because at the end of the entry he includes a letter to his dearest friend, Benjamin Hawes, and this is timed and dated 4.00am on 8 April 1829 – not a good time of the day to be writing anything seriously personal. Matters always look better in daylight.

16 April 1829

Why the lock's almost grown rusty so long since I have opened this book – a new system of dating too – the March of Intellect.

Here I am at Rotherhithe renewing experiments on Gaz – been

getting apparatus up for the past six months!! Is it profitable? A
1/40 of the remainder of my life – the life of a dreamer – Am always
Building castles in the air what time I waste – I have refrained from
several indulgencies by making up my mind and making a sort of
vow why should I not do the same with respect to castle building
for it may increase till it will become a sort of madness –
    I have had a long correspondence with Ellen which I think I have
managed well I may now consider myself independent.

It is obvious that, at 4.00am, he was feeling horribly low. All his
engineering hopes had died – and he had even given up the love he had
for Ellen Hulme. In this Gothic epistle to his closest friend he expresses a
deep love to Benjamin that perhaps he was really feeling for the lost Ellen.
It is a desperately unhappy, insecure, Isambard who wrote this. He even
announces that he is aware that he is capable of self-deception – a trait
that might account for some later engineering failures.

8 April 1829, 4am
    I had always intended that this book should perish with me ... but
having decided to make my will I found how poor I was and how
unable I was to leave you anything which could give you an idea
of my attachment to you. The greatest proof I could imagine was
to leave you this – my private journal and if you could form an idea
of my secretiveness, of my horror of telling anybody that which I
wish to be secret, you would be able to value this mark of my love.
    I conceal things from myself and it was to get rid of this load of
secrets I had to keep, that I imagined this staunch friend. Yet I
always have my fears. I keep the key always about me, the book
itself in a strong box with a secure lock but when from home I am
always afraid. My dear Benjamin, ever since I have known you I
have esteemed you and now my attachment is as strong and perfect
as I think possible on earth. My passions are not warm but they
are staunch and true and unchangeable.

Adieu my dear Fellow,
Yours in death,
I. K Brunel

And it was from that low point that he climbed to become the Engineer
of the Great Western Railway – and much else besides.

2: THE GREAT WESTERN RAILWAY

'Promoting my Skeme'

After his near death experience in the Thames Tunnel, Brunel spent a few days in bed and was then, according to his doctor, sufficiently recovered for a convalescence in Brighton. There he kept in touch with civil engineering work but also indulged his love of the theatre, attending plays and escorting actresses. On 4 February 1828 he wrote in his diary: *'Pleasant company. Very comfortable. Strolled on the pier smoking my Meerschaum before breakfast – breakfast at noon. Rode about visiting works* [a sea wall was under construction]. *Dined at 7.'*

On the 8th disaster struck and he had to write: *'Violent haemorrhage after riding horse.'* He was still bleeding on the 11th, and on the 15th he wrote, *'Still ill and retrieved by Beamish in a hired chariot.'* The shaking he received travelling over the rutted London road brought on more bleeding and he arrived back in Lambeth in a very bad state. He was confined to bed until 4 May 1828. During that time he was subjected to 'bleeding' by his doctor and to being dosed daily with 'sugar of lead'. Nowadays this is called lead acetate; it is toxic and was used to increase the octane rating of petrol until it was banned in the 1990s. It is, however, sweet, and Isambard put it in his wine.

On 7 May the work of bricking up the Thames Tunnel, entombing the tunnelling frames, began. Isambard was doubtless carrying out light work for his father. On 12 July he took ship for Plymouth, a voyage of five days, then took a ten-day holiday with his Kingdom grandparents and cousins, the clockmaking Mudge. In October, the tunnelling project dead and walled up, Marc and Sophia Brunel departed for Paris, leaving Isambard in charge of the tourist attraction that the tunnel had become. It was 600 feet long, with a mirror on the far end wall to give an impression of the full length. Stalls selling souvenir knick-knacks were permitted and the public was admitted at a shilling a head. Isambard was ticket-seller, while he read about other young men engineering railways in the North of England.

The Brunel family were together for Christmas, and in January 1829 Isambard Brunel set off for Paris. On his return his father introduced him to the project of a bridge across the Avon Gorge at Clifton, Bristol.

Between them they made designs for a suspension bridge. Coming to Bristol in 1829 brought Brunel into friendship with several important Bristolians – the lawyer Robert Osborne, and the merchants/factory-owners Nicholas Roch and Thomas Guppy. Brunel obtained the job of designing a dredger for Bristol Floating Harbour. This was a 'drag boat', winched along the harbour with a bulldozer-like blade scraping malodorous filth along the bottom to a sluice, where it was discharged into the river.

So it was that, when the businessmen of Bristol decided they wanted a railway line to London, Isambard Kingdom Brunel was in the right place. Page 22 of his diary records:

BDC [Bristol Docks Co]
20 February 1833

Went to dinner at Frenchay. I found on my return a long tirade from Mr Teate and summons to a committee to answer Mr T.'s objections at 10 this morning – warmed a little on the subject – wrote to Mr Osborne my opinion – 21/2/33 – of Mr T. – I wrote a note to Cookson pressing him to be there. I wrote these notes overnight and slept upon them – Cookson's I softened but sent Osborne's as it was. Yet even with these precautions I now find that I was needlessly hasty – it is time my note to Osborne was shown to the others and therefore produced a certain effect – Called Roch – found him at the Institution and walked to Osborne's with him – entered into all the points of Mr Teate's paper and fully exposed the absurdity of all his positions to the entire satisfaction of the Directors who expressed their determination to abide by my plans – my attention was called and my opinions required on several other points.

Mr Cookson afterwards saw Mr T. and pacified him by giving him the assurance that in anything that was done, his suggestions would be fully acknowledged.

Rode over to the Cumberland Basin – dragging going on well – came back in search of Mr Roch – he came to Mr Osborne and informed me in his presence that a sub-committee was appointed for the purpose of receiving offers from me in conjunction with Townsend and probably also from Brunton & Price as to what terms and in what time we would make a survey and lay down a line and on what terms we would afterwards undertake to lay out a line etc for Parliamentary plans –

Mr Roch then went with us to Townsend and made the same

communication to him – Townsend made some difficulties which Roch would not listen to – we then parted – I had a little chat with Townsend and agreed to see him tomorrow – How will this end? We are undertaking a survey at a sum by which I shall be considerably a loser – but succeeding in being appointed Engineer. Nous verrons – Dinner at Osborne's – went in the evening to Mr Bush's – large party – Mr Cookham invited me to his.

22 Feb 1833

Brunt called – went down to the Steam Navigation Company's wharf followed Lamble [?] to Cumberland Basin – and went with him over steam boats – William IV, Killarney, Victory – The first had a Greenock engine of 150hp, the second a 160hp Winwood and the third a Fawcett 150hp. The latter very pretty really I think fully equal to Maudslays –

Went to Brunt's according to appointment to see designs for Portishead cottages.

Went to Osborne – explained to him the necessity of stirring up Townsend – Osborne was of the opinion that unless I took the whole management & only left T. to nominal survey and a little of this end of the line we should never get through it. He promised to speak to Townsend.

Robt Osborne walked up to Clifton with me. We explored Clifton woods – sent a note to T. I to tell him to call on Osborne. [Osborne had walked with Brunel back to the Clifton hotel in which he was staying.] While we were at tea Townsend came – In conversation I entered (intentionally) upon the impossibility of two engineers pulling together in a business of this sort – Osborne **happening** *to leave the room, T-d asked me to explain frankly what I thought would be the relation between us two – I said that altho' I had no wish to be otherwise than as gentlemen perfectly on an equality yet as our standings would distinguish us he having generally acted as a surveyor I as an engineer there would be no fear of our interests clashing and therefore we could pull together. He said that <u>he did not aspire to stand on an equality with Mr Brunel</u> that he of course was not known in London and thus altho' he felt himself quite capable of understanding such a work <u>yet he should not pretend to put his opinions in opposition to but should yield to me</u>. He seemed to think Brunton does not possess friends in this sub-committee – if so we may secure the ground to ourselves –*

How the devil I am to get on with him [Townsend] *tied to my neck I know not.*

Osborne remained after Townsend had gone – we discussed the various ways of entering Bristol – Temple Meads is my present idea.

Mr George Whatley was a Birmingham solicitor with whom Brunel had stayed for a few days in November 1832 when he had been commissioned to make a survey of a route for a railway between Birmingham and Gloucester. Brunel wrote to that company asking for a letter of recommendation because he thought that the Birmingham & Gloucester Committee owed him a favour. The letter is undated, but must have been written on 24 February 1833.

Dear Sir,

A survey is about to be made of a line of railway between Bristol and London – I hope to be employed in making it. The Committee meet to decide the question on Wednesday next. Of four gentlemen who comprise the sub-committee there are two – both of the Society of Friends – to whom I am only known by reputation and not personally – It is possible that Mr Stourge who took an active part in our Glo'ster & Birmingham Railway may be acquainted with them and if Mr Stourge formed a favourable opinion of my activity on that occasion his writing to those gentlemen may be of great use to me – their names are Mr J. Harford of Harford & Davies wine merchants – and Mr Tothill. The letter to be of real use should be by return of post altho' the next day would be better than never – I have the less hesitation in asking as I think your Committee owe me some consideration – in asking you to exert yourself for me I must trust to your kindness.

Yours truly,
I. K Brunel

Brunel also wrote to the mysterious Mr Sweet (see letter of 19 October 1827) hoping to recruit his assistance in forming a supporting party in London.

24 Feb 1833, Sunday
Dear Sir,
You may remember some time ago I suggested to you the

probability of something being undertaken to forward the skeme [sic] of a Bristol to London railway – The Southampton railway party have been constantly agitating the question here and an Engineer of the name of Brunton has by making surveys set the thing going – a Committee formed of deputations from the principal public bodies of Bristol has been sitting for some weeks – money is raised for making the necessary survey for coming before the public and going to 'Parliament' – a survey is immediately to be undertaken – Brunton as first in the field has been applied to but I having much more influence here have within the last week succeeded in causing that I am also applied to and on Thursday the point between us is to be decided – The result will be either that we are both employed to make surveys in competition with each other in which case I shall eventually succeed – or as I have still hopes tho I am rather late in my application I shall at once [...] him and be employed alone – In either case it is of importance to form a party in London which would co-operate in promoting my skeme. I have an idea that the entrance of the railway into London may be on the south side – and that at whatever expense it must be brought to the river either at Rotherhithe or Lambeth – in the latter case to Waterloo & Vauxhall bridges ... and Landowners on that side must be interested [?] and would I should think advocate the measure.

My object of course is to be the first to form such a party & the question only is in what way can this safely and best be done. I think the time has arrived when it is worth turning the matter over in your mind.

I shall be in Town in the middle of the week but only for a few days and should wish to consult you about it.

On 19 August 1833 Brunel was introduced to Mr Charles Saunders. Saunders was then the newly appointed Secretary to the London Committee of the 'Bristol Railway'. He was an exceptionally capable and gifted manager. He was vital to the birth and development of the railway, raising large sums of money by travelling the West Country and interviewing the right people. He gave excellent advice and guidance to the GWR Directors regarding the arcane world of Parliamentary Committees, as well as on legal and organisational matters regarding the railway. As important, but behind the scenes, he immediately became Brunel's great friend, counsellor, confidante and consoler. Brunel was to rely on him for friendship and moral support throughout his career.

In September 1840 Saunders was appointed Company Secretary and General Superintendent (General Manager) of the Great Western Railway. He retired in September 1863 and the extent of his work was so great that three men had to be appointed to replace him – his nephew, Frederick Saunders, who had been Secretary to the South Wales Railway, took over as GWR Company Secretary, G. N. Tyrrell became the first GWR Superintendent of the Line, and James Grierson became the first General Manager.

Charles Saunders was probably the most highly respected of the railway officers of the 19th century. On his retirement Queen Victoria sent him a gorgeous silver centrepiece for his dining table in recognition of the friendship that had developed between them after Saunders had attended her on scores of Royal Train journeys. The GWR took the unprecedented step of granting him a pension. Saunders lived just one year to enjoy it, dying on 19 September 1864.

Subscriptions to the railway project were not sufficient to create the Parliamentary deposit – 10% of the estimated capital required to build the line – which money had to be deposited before a Bill could be accepted into Parliament for discussion and final acceptance as an Act. Brunel, with Charles Saunders in agreement, recommended to the Provisional Committee that they give up the central part of the railway in their first application to Parliament so that, with only the Reading-London and Bristol-Bath sections applied for, there would be enough money for the Parliamentary deposit.

1 September 1833

DISCONTINUANCE OF SURVEY BETWEEN BATH AND READING
The Board of Directors of the Great Western Railway Company have this day come to a resolution to discontinue the survey of that portion of the line between Bath and Reading & I am therefore under the necessity of informing you that your services will no longer be required.

17 Cornhill,
London
7 Sept 1833

THE LONDON COMMITTEE RESOLVED
'That this Committee do concur therein and recommend that Mr Brunel be instructed to commence without delay the

Parliamentary survey in such manner as may insure the completion by 30 November not exceeding the expense of £6,000 to be incurred under the authority of this Resolution.

From the outset, the Great Western was groomed by Brunel to be the politest railway in the Kingdom – the 'Gentleman's Railway' as Daniel Gooch called it in his recollections. This Brunellian ethic was not always lived up to, even when Brunel was alive, but it was his aim; indeed, the 'gentlemanliness' of the railway was still extant in 1962 as the Western Region of British Railways, as Gerald Fiennes – coming from East Anglia – complained when he became General Manager at Paddington.

Below are the orders Brunel gave to all his surveyors, telling them how they must behave while out 'in the field'.

53 Parliament Street.

In conducting that portion of the Survey of the Great Western Railway entrusted to you it is particularly desirable that you should ascertain the names of the owner and occupiers of any lands to be passed over and as early as possible to obtain their sanction to making the survey. It will of course be very often impracticable to obtain this information until you have actually entered upon the land but if you make the application as early as you can I think you will not find any vexatious opposition thrown in your way. You will at all time afford every information to persons interested in the property likely to be affected by the Railway and you will consult them as to the manner in which the line may be carried so as to be most advantageous to their property explaining to them at the same time if necessary any circumstances which from the nature of a Railway may render such a direction difficult or impracticable in order that as far as is consistent with the absolute requisites of a public work of this description the line ultimately selected may be adapted to existing interests.

You will be particularly careful that all persons employed by you shall conduct themselves with propriety and civility that no damage be done to the hedges or fences and that they do not unnecessarily encroach upon gardens or enclosed grounds or otherwise annoy the inhabitants.

I. K. Brunel

With the proposal reduced to just the two ends of the line – Reading to the Thames at Vauxhall Bridge and Bristol Temple Meads to Bath – the

Bill was, perhaps not surprisingly, thrown out on 25 July 1834 as being 'neither "Great" nor "Western" nor yet a "Railway"'. The loss of the Bill would have cost in the region of £50,000 – a loss to the subscribers to the project. But, remarkably, the evidences given in Parliament seem to have sparked a greater public support and more money was quickly raised.

The proposal in the 1834 Bill for a Thames-side terminus had required the destruction of too much recently built and very high-class property, and this, as well as the peculiarly fragmented nature of the asked-for railway, had contributed to the failure of the Bill. The 1835 Bill was for the whole route with an eastern terminus at Euston, the GWR proposing to join the London & Birmingham Railway roughly where the present-day Queen's Park station stands. Brunel was, of course, the main witness for the GWR and appeared before Parliamentary Committees of the House of Commons and House of Lords over a period of 11 days, his evidence running to 225 foolscap pages. Below are some extracts of Brunel's evidence to the House of Lords Committee taken on 23 and 24 June 1835. Their pay being by the minute, the lawyers made the interrogation last as long as possible. The questions begin as if Brunel is involved in something criminal. As the questioning proceeds confusion sets in until Brunel and the Committee seem to be talking at cross purposes. Occasionally the questions are simply stupid.

House of Lords Committee on Great Western Bill 1835
Isambard Kingdom Brunel Esquire is called in and examined as follows:

Mr Sergeant Ludlow: Be so good as to tell their Lordships your Christian names.
Isambard Kingdom.

Are you a Civil Engineer?
I am.

Do you remember, in or about February 1833, being applied to by the Provisional Committee at Bristol to investigate the Practicability of making a Railway between Bristol and London?
I do. I received a letter from them upon that subject.

Was the application to you to make a survey or to state the terms upon which you would make the survey?
The first application was to state the terms I should require if directed to make the survey.

And did you afterwards give them an answer?
Yes I did.

Were you afterwards directed to make a Survey?
Yes. In the following week I was directed to commence a survey.

Up to the time of your having this Application made to you by the Provisional Committee had you any Communication with any solicitor or any other party to suggest this measure?
Not at all. I arrived at Bristol on Tuesday morning without any knowledge that such a Committee was sitting and on the next day I received a Communication.

Was the Connexion between you and the Provisional Committee sought for by them?
Yes, entirely.

Have you reason to know that the Solicitors and other Officers connected with the Proceedings had not then been appointed?
I knew for a considerable time after I was at work on the Survey that no Officers were appointed and I was the only provisional Person employed by the Committee.

[This sequence of events is not what Brunel wrote in his diary on the day that the survey was first mentioned to him. Brunel had also forgotten that he was, from the outset, employed in partnership with William Townsend. As we have already seen, in his diary for 22 February 1833 Brunel wrote, 'He (Townsend) did not aspire to stand on an equality with Mr Brunel … he would not pretend to put his opinion in opposition to mine but would yield to me. How the devil am I to get on with him tied to my neck I know not.']

Have you selected, in your judgement, the best Line of Communication?
Of course the line I have selected I consider the best.

Your Line is this described by the Red Line? [On a map provided by Brunel.]
Yes.

From Bath to the next Tunnel?
It is a distance of some miles. In going out of Bath we pass through Sydney Gardens and we have made an arrangement with the proprietors of the Gardens to cover the line in passing through.

It is not a Tunnel?

No. It is a covered Cutting. It will be made an open Cutting and covered.

(By a Lord) With brickwork?
A part with brickwork and part with a wooden roof and skylights.

What is the length?
230 yards.

That is done with the consent of the Proprietors of the Gardens?
Yes it is.

That Tunnel you talk of in Sydney Gardens, will it be dark?
I have stated most likely there will be skylights at a part of it. We have undertaken to make any opening for light and air ornamental.

Can you make it light?
Yes.

So as not to have the disadvantage of a Tunnel?
Yes.

(Mr Sergeant Merryweather) This is not in the Section?
No. It is laid down as an open Cutting and it is an open Cutting which we have agreed to cover over. It would be impossible to show it on the Section in as much as the Arrangement has been made since.

(Mr Harrison) You do it by cutting?
Yes. And we have a certain time to cover it in.

You cut through instead of boring?
Yes.

(By a Lord) That is done by the consent of the Proprietors?
Yes.

[Brunel now had the opportunity to explain his ideas about gradients and locomotive power. He intended very slight gradients so as to have smaller, cheaper engines of modest power and low fuel consumption and to have only one or two steeper 'inclinations' where an more powerful assistant engine could be stationed.]

Did you think it an advantage to make your railway upon such a Plan as to have no steeper gradient than 11 feet in the mile? [1 in 480]
The lower the maximum can be kept upon a railway the better because the power of the engines or in other words the load that the same engines can draw will be governed by the inclinations over which they have to take that load.

At any one part of the Line?
Yes. Except it is very short indeed. But if there is any extent of inclination at 16 feet per mile the engines must have an assistant engine or be calculated to ascend it and it is therefore important to keep the inclinations as low as possible. The nature of the country along the Line we have taken is so favourable as to allow us to have a Line of Railway exceedingly level all the way from London to Bristol and it could easily be kept at 11 feet per mile as a maximum except in those nine miles which would be 16 feet per mile which is 1 in 330. To have passed this inclination of nine miles either the engines for the whole distance must be of sufficient power to overcome it or have their loads reduced or have some assistance given. It would be a serious loss to have engines upon the whole Line able to get over 1 in 330 for that nine miles and it [therefore] became important to have assistant power of some kind. If that Plan is used it is better to have the Line steep at that part and have the full assistance of that [extra] power and leave the rest of the line as nearly as possible level. There is nothing new in that theory.

[The questioning moves on to include Box Tunnel.]

What is the height of the Tunnel?
Thirty feet.

And the width?
Twenty-five.

Is it such ground you can ventilate it by shafts?
Yes. I should make it and ventilate it by shafts. In that hill are the principal quarries and some of the best Bath-stone in the neighbourhood of Bath. A considerable length of the Tunnel would be in Bath-stone and another in the Corn Brash, the Bath-stone and the end next to Bath in clay.

The inclination there is 1 in 107?
Yes. I took 1 in 107 particularly so as to have it a little less steep than the Inclined Plane known to be worked by locomotive engine every day upon the Manchester and Liverpool – that is 1 in 96.

Having the experience of a Railway before you in existence you took something easier than that?
Yes.

Have you any means of showing that?
I have had a model made. (The same is produced and exhibited to their Lordships.)

[Their Lordships seem to become confused by the model.]

I had these sides put for this purpose. It is supposed by some that, besides any mechanical effect of the Inclined Plane, there would be an effect produced upon the passengers by the knowledge they were descending something precipitous. The descent of 1 in 107 is considerably less than the descent from the houses at the corner of Parliament Street to the Parliament Houses. It is about half as steep as the Burlington Arcade and exactly the same as the Lowther Arcade and therefore as regards any appearance of steep descent there can be none. But as the appearance of the Inclination of the Line is considerably less on the surface of the ground I believe that to a person standing upon any part of the Inclined Plane the inclination would appear to be considerably the other way and any gentleman who has stood upon a Line of Railway entering a cutting would be aware that the level cutting appears to fall and that was the reason that the slopes were put to it [I suppose Brunel is referring to the side walls of the model Inclination], but in removing that and the Inclination being seen, the one end is three-quarters of an inch higher than the other.

The base upon which it is placed is supposed to be a level?
Yes.

(By a Lord) Is the whole upon a scale?
Yes, upon a Scale of Rise. That is a rise on 1 in 107.

Upon what scale is it? How many inches to a mile?
It was not made with that view. It is about four feet to an inch. It would make about 330 feet run of Railway.

In order to make the Committee understand it perfectly, how many Yards of Road would that represent?
About 110 yards. Of course I do not mean to say that the appearance of that model is to be any guide as to the effect upon the engines because all these acclivities are nearly imperceptible. I have had that made to show that the imagination of the passengers could not be affected by the appearance of the steep ascent.

You have said you were to make this Tunnel by means of shafts from above?
Yes.

How many shafts shall you have in the course of that mile and three-quarters? [The approximate length of Box Tunnel)

Four shafts for working. We shall make more for air, probably.

These shafts being left open would communicate a good deal of light?
Yes. Light enough to see when you were in the tunnel. [Yet the tunnel is and always was pitch dark throughout...]

Do you intend to light it by any other means?
I think not. If there was any desire on the part of the public for it we could easily light it with gas. They are but five or six minutes going through it.

What is the depth of the shafts?
One is as much as 220 feet. That is the deepest part of the whole hill. Another would be 90 feet.

Will the shafts be so constructed as to allow smoke to escape?
The principal object of the shafts is for ventilation.

What length of time would be occupied in passing the Tunnel?
Six minutes the slowest.

Is the whole Tunnel Bath-stone?
It is Bath-stone down to 120 feet.

That Bath-stone is easily cut?
Yes. And we should be very glad to get it.
[I once tried to cut Bath-stone in the subterranean quarry inside Box Hill. The energetically wielded pickaxe bounced off the stone.]

It is easily cut?
Yes. Until it is exposed some time. There is an establishment of sawmills in the neighbourhood to cut Bath-stone into blocks and slabs.

Is there not some danger of the atmosphere being rendered noxious by the passage of the engines?
I think not.

Would it not increase the smoke if you increase the power?
There would be more smoke with two than with one but the goods I should propose to take up by one locomotive engine and by a stationary engine.

Is there any other Tunnel a mile long?
[Brunel goes into one of his difficult-to-understand answers.] *There is one near Leicester that is nearly a mile long but that is only 12 feet high and they burn coals which causes a great deal of smoke but it is used and persons go through it but it is a low tunnel and they burn coals. If there*

was an assistant engine used so as to carry the train up at full velocity you have two engines at one time and one of those is behind the train of passengers and they do not fire in the next train [sic]. Coming down the engines do not work at all. You would have only the same quantity of coals burned and nearly the same effect upon that part of the Line as upon the other. The passengers would be rather gainers than otherwise.

Have you been under the Tunnels at Liverpool?
Yes, but not with locomotive engines. There is no effect produced by the inclination further than I mentioned just now of requiring two engines at one time but not on returning.

(By a Lord) How would you let it go down?
[Brunel gets into a description of firing technique.] *They must shut off steam and put in the damper.*

If they were to be the steam engine that were afterwards to convey the waggons upon the level Line – they must keep up the fire?
Yes, but if for a few minutes they neither add fuel to the fire and they shut the damper, the effect is very different indeed. It is heated air but not smoke going out. The effect is very different in sound and everything else in going down upon the Manchester and Liverpool Line.

(Mr Harrison) Have you visited a Tunnel upon an Inclined Plane near Canterbury?
[This was the Canterbury & Whitstable Railway, engineered first by William James, then by George Stephenson, who sent first a youthful Joseph Locke then John Dixon to complete the works. The line opened in 3 May 1830 and was 6 miles long, most of it on very steep grades. The first 2 miles out of Canterbury rose at 1 in 76/41/47/56/49, with an 828-yard-long tunnel on the 1 in 56. The 1 in 49 was followed by a mile of near level, then falling grades at 1 in 63/31/28 for a mile, a mile of near level, then falling at 1 in 57/50/82. Stationary engines were used to haul trains up the inclined planes.]
Yes, I went there on purpose.

What is the length of it?
Two miles.

All Tunnel?
No. There is a Tunnel half a mile in length, 12 feet wide and 12 feet high.

And you propose this 30 feet high?
Yes.

What is the Inclination of that at Canterbury?
One in forty-five.

(By a Lord) Is that for a Railway?
Yes.

(Mr Harrison) Did you go up and down it?
Yes, several times. I knew the railway had been in existence but evidence was given in the House of Commons that there was no Instance of a Railway [sic] of this length and that it was impractical. I knew there was an Inclined Plane that worked by a rope and I went down and spent some time upon the Railway.

That was with a view to the question of the rope more than anything else?
With regard to the Inclined Plane and the engine and the safety of running down it [the inclined plane].

Is there any necessity for the use of a rope?
No. I have stated several times in the course of my evidence there was nothing that absolutely required a rope on this Inclination. I believe the foundation of the statement that a rope was necessary arose from this – that in answer to a question on cross-examination, whether a stationary engine was necessary I said I believed we should have one for a time.

(By a Lord) Do you allude to the Railway between Whitstable and Canterbury?
Yes.

How long is this Plane at this Tunnel near Canterbury?
Near two miles.

All the way [1 in] 45?
Yes. I have been down that Plane twice without a rope in the carriage alone, with nothing but a break [brake] to check the carriage and after allowing it to run at full velocity by the break it was stopped in 60 yards.

How many passengers were in the carriage?
Five only. Of course I did not try an experiment of that sort with many passengers.

[Just before the examination of 23 June was concluded for the day, when the subject under discussion was the numbers of people that could be served by the GWR, Brunel was asked about this by the barrister, Mr Sergeant Mereweather, who, from his occupation, one would have thought was an intelligent man...]

(Mr Sergeant Mereweather.) You have spoken of two Lines – one to the North of the Marlborough Downs and one to the South. If you were a conjuror and could conjure the whole of the population on the North of the Marlborough Downs to the South, which line would you recommend?
I really cannot say. I should prefer the Southern Line. It is a pity people live on a part of the land so high, but choosing to live there, they must take the consequence.

Supposing there was no great town on the Northern Line and you considered the Connexion [sic] between Bristol and London only, which would you choose then – the Northern Line?
Yes.

Did you state that the levels were also a great deal better [on the northern line]?
Yes.

The Witness is directed to withdraw.
The Counsel and Parties are directed to withdraw.

While Brunel was so deeply embroiled in the machinations of getting the Act of Parliament for the GWR, he was also the designer and engineer of the Monkwearmouth Dock in Sunderland. He had appointed Michael Lane as his Resident Engineer and entrusted much to that great man – who became Engineer. Michael Lane had been a foreman bricklayer in the Thames Tunnel construction when Brunel was one of the Resident Engineers. This letter is to Michael Lane, not written by Brunel but by John Hammond. Hammond had worked as Marc Brunel's assistant but went on to work for Isambard following the suspension of work on the incomplete Thames Tunnel. Hammond knew Isambard well and he seems to have had a habit of making friendly 'in-joke' digs at his master. I include the letter (Tyne & Wear Archives, Ref DX1269/2) because of that.

53 Parliament Street
27 July 1835

Dear Sir,
Yours of 25th inst I have duly received also a specification for the excavation of the Dock and in answer to this latter you will find my letter of 25th will contain all you require.

I regret that your situation does not improve. I had hopes you would have been more comfortable after the truth of annoyance [sic].

Mr Brunel and myself are coming down by means of the new ship 'City of Aberdeen' which leaves London at 2 o'clock tomorrow afternoon then if we are 30 hours in reaching Sunderland we shall be there about 8 o'clock Wednesday evening. You will therefore come out and meet us with one of the fastest steamers of your Port and in order that we may know you put a flag on your bow, if dark put a lantern with a good light which you can prepare for the purpose.

Mr B thinks this is necessary as the 'City of Aberdeen' is a new vessel and may not be familiar to your port. I find in the sheet of the specification I sent you anything omitted of course you will add it – I think I should have made some provision about the wells being kept clean.

Yours truly,
J. H. Hammond

PS
In case anything should occur the prevent our going as I have informed you will have a line to that effect by Tuesday – tomorrow's post.

When you come out to meet us in case the 'City of Aberdeen' should hesitate about stopping Mr B wishes that you should provide a pair of your best men with boats as in such a case he should not hesitate to jump overboard. I leave it to you to pick him up.

3: BROAD GAUGE

'A deviation from the dimensions adopted'

The Royal Assent was given to the Great Western Railway Bill on 31 August 1835, and the construction of the railway was now a matter of the law. However, the route that had been authorised was not entirely to Brunel's liking, and once he had got his Act he started to make changes, or to attempt to make changes, to ease curves and lessen gradients – and, of course, the very much more famous object – the use a broader gauge than that which had generally become accepted in Britain.

PRO 1149/2
53 Parliament Street,
3 September 1835

Great Western Railway

I have received instructions to set out the line between Bath and Bristol, London and Reading, and have written to Mr Townsend to obtain immediately permissions to cut sufficiently through the small but thick underwood in Brislington and that neighbourhood will you have the goodness to assist him in obtaining leave from the different proprietors there is no need of asking the Duke of Buckingham we know he will consent his servant Fox is the only person to consult as to Gore Langton if he is in Town I will see him but his agent must also be seen – the operation is absolutely indispensable before we can get out the land wanted we shall have our flags flying over the Brent valley tomorrow I should not wish that Bristol should fancy itself left behind – I shall be down there on Tuesday or Wednesday.

Yours very truly,
I. K. Brunel

Brunel was the first person to realise that railways could become the perfect method of high-speed overland passenger travel. He deliberately set out to create a high-speed railway between Bristol and Paddington and, indeed, to Taunton. He told the Gauge Commissioners in 1846:

'Looking to the speeds which I contemplated would be adopted on railways and the masses to be moved it seemed to me that the whole machine was too small for the work to be done and that it required that the parts should be on a scale more commensurate with the mass and velocity to be obtained. I think the impression grew upon me gradually so that it is difficult to fix the time when I first thought a wide gauge desirable but I dare say there were stages between wishing that it could be so and determining to try to do it.' (*History of the Great Western Railway*, E. T. MacDermot, Volume 1, p17)

Brunel's broad gauge was based on an over-reaction to two bright ideas, the first that the larger the wheel, the more readily it overcame the constant friction in the axle bearing, and the second that a low centre of gravity was required for a high-speed railway. In the latter case, it is a matter of opinion as to what constitutes 'low'. Brunel's mind was fixated on these two points – this was a Brunellian feature – and as a result he was blinded to the consequences of his fixation; he did not look at the wider picture. His original designs for carriages, based on his fixation, were impractical and, indeed, outlandish. The desire to reduce the effect of friction in axle bearings was, of course, laudable, but he could have saved everyone a great deal of money and inconvenience if he had been aware, as he ought to have been – since he prided himself on keeping abreast of scientific inventions – that ball-races for axle bearings had been patented by Philip Vaughan in 1794 (Patent No 2006 of that year).

A relic of Brunel's original idea concerning a low centre of gravity can be seen in the relatively low brick arches over the many parts of the GWR main line; several still exist between Taplow and West Drayton. Having the wider gauge could have brought about proportionately taller carriages, but Brunel's lowest over-line bridges have about the same overhead clearance as the lowest on the London & Birmingham Railway (L&BR). Bridges on the L&BR and GWR were both of 30-foot span and the arch was 15 feet over the outer rail of each track. This was because Brunel intended to carry his carriage bodies within the space between the wheels, so higher-pitched arches were not needed. Brunel writes below of 'inconveniences', and in his proposals for removing them he introduces other inconveniences and, indeed, impracticalities. I have copied exactly from his letter to the GWR Directors.

This letter (Rail 1149/2) does not show to whom it was written, but I guess it is Mr George Frere, Resident Engineer of the Bristol Division. It is the order to start the great project.

His proposals to the GWR directors were as follows (Rail 250/82 p7):

53 Parliament Street,
Westminster.
15 September 1835

To the Directors of the Great Western Railway

Gentlemen,
I beg to submit the following observations upon the subject of the width of the rail as explanatory of the grounds upon which I have recommended to you a deviation from the dimensions adopted in the railway hitherto constructed.

The leading feature which distinguishes railways from common roads is the great diminution of that resistance which arises from friction at the axle trees [axles] and more particularly from obstruction on the road. The latter is almost entirely removed in a well-kept surface of a railway and friction may be considered as the only constant resistance.

The effect of gravity when the load has to ascend any inclination is of course the same whatever the nature of the road and depends only on the rate of inclination.

In the present state of railways and railway carriages the constant resistance which we will call friction amounts generally to about 9lbs per ton although under favourable circumstances it may be reduced to 8lbs. Assuming the latter as being the least favourable to the view I propose to take of the necessity of further improvement I will apply this to the case of the Great Western Railway.

Upon the GWR from Bristol to Bath and from London to the Oxford branch, a total distance of about 70 miles including those portions upon which two full thirds of the traffic will take place there will be no inclination exceeding 4 feet per mile which will cause a resistance of only 1lb and seven-tenths per ton, calling it an even 2lbs while friction is taken at 8lbs it appears that the latter will constitute 80 per cent of the whole resistance. The importance of any improvement upon that which forms so large a proportion is obvious but nevertheless according to present construction of railways a limit has been put to this improvement which limit is already reached or at all events great impediments are thrown in the way of any material diminution of the friction and this serious evil is produced indirectly by the width of the railways.

The resistance from friction is diminished as the proportion of the diameter of the wheel to that of the axle tree is increased there are some causes which in practice slightly influence this result but within the limits of increase which could be required we may consider that practically the resistance from friction will be diminished exactly in the same ratio that the diameter of the wheel is increased we have therefore the means of materially diminishing this resistance.

The wheels upon railways were originally much smaller than they are now as the speed has been increased and economy in power became more important the diameters have been progressively increased and are now nearly double the size they were but a few years ago even upon the Liverpool and Manchester Railway I believe they have been increased nearly one half but by the present construction of the carriages they have reached their limit.

The width of the railway being only 4ft 8 inches between the rails or about 4ft 6 inches between the wheels the body of the carriage or the platform [of a wagon] on which luggage is placed is of necessity extended over the tops of the wheels and a space must be left for the action of the springs the carriage is raised unnecessarily high while at the same time the size of the wheel is inconveniently limited.

If the centre of gravity of the load could be lowered the motion would be more steady and one cause of wear and tear both in rails and carriages would be diminished.

*By simply widening the rails so that the body of the carriage might be kept entirely with the wheels the centre of gravity might be considerably lowered and at the same time the diameter of the wheels be **unlimited**.*

*I should propose 6 feet 10 inches to 7 feet as the width of the rails which would I think admit of sufficient width of carriages **for all purposes** I am not by any means prepared at present to recommend any particular size of wheel or even any great increase of the present dimensions. I believe they will be materially increased by my great object which would be in any possible way to **render each part capable of improvement** and to remove what appears as an obstacle to any great progress in such a very important point as the diameter of the wheels upon which the resistance which governs the cost of transport and the speed that may be obtained so materially depends.*

The objections which may be urged against these alterations are 1st. The increased width required in the cuttings, embankments and tunnel and consequently the increased expenses.

2ndly. A greater amount of friction in the curves.

3rdly. The additional weight of the carriages.

4thly, the inconvenience arising from the junction with the London and Birmingham Railway.

1st. As regards the increase of the earthwork – bridges and tunnel – this would not be so great as would at first sight appear – the increased width of each railway does not effect the width between the rails or on either side as the total widths of the bodies of the carriages remains the same and as the slopes of the cuttings and embankments are the same the total quantity would not necessarily be increased above 1/12th [8%] and the cost of the bridges and tunnels would be augmented about in the same ration and such addition has been provided for in the estimate.

[A double-track 7-foot-gauge railway with a 6-foot space between the up and down tracks in total would require a width of 20 feet, irrespective of the footway along each side. A double-track standard gauge (4ft 8½in) railway with a 6-foot space between the tracks would require 15ft 4in. The broad gauge would therefore require an overbridge to be 25% wider than a standard gauge bridge. Brunel's overline bridges had the same span – 30 feet – and about the same height over the outside rail of each track, 15 feet, as those on the London & Birmingham, so, relative to the gauge, the overbridges of the London & Birmingham Railway were wider and taller than those on the GWR broad gauge.]

2ndly. The effect of friction upon small curves. The necessary radius of curvature will be increased in the ratio of the width between the wheels, viz: as 5 to 7, but the portions of the total length which is curved to such a degree as to render this effect sensible [noticeable] is so small (not being above 1½ miles of the whole line except immediately at the entrance of the depots) that it is not worth considering where a great advantage is to be gained upon a total distance of 120 miles.

[But where the broad gauge was extended into the country north, south and west of the original main line, the curves would become so sharp as to significantly increase the friction between flange and rail.]

3rdly. The additional weight of carriages. The axle trees alone will be increased and they form but a small part of the total weight of the carriage. The frame will indeed be simplified and I believe this will fully counterbalance the increased lengths of axle trees. If the wheels are materially increased in diameter they must of course be stronger and consequently heavier but this weight does not effect the friction at the axletrees and not sensibly the resistance to traction while their increased diameter affords the advantages which are sought for.

4thly. The inconvenience of effecting the junction with the London & Birmingham Railway. This I consider to be the only real obstacle to the adoption of the plan – one additional rail to each railway [he means 'track'] must be laid down. I do not foresee any great difficulty in doing this but undoubtedly the London and Birmingham Railway Company may object to it and in that case I see no remedy but the plan must be abandoned it is important that this point should be speedily determined.

I am, Gentlemen,
Your obdt. Servant,
I. K. Brunel

Brunel does not inform the Directors that there will be 'inconvenience' at every place where the incompatible gauges meet, involving complexity of track and transfer of goods and passengers from one gauge to the other. In a later report he suggests that there should be several different gauges to suit the topography of the country through which the railway runs. Brunel was the Engineer of the Taff Vale Railway, which would connect the South Wales coalfield with the docks at Cardiff and would inevitably have to bring traffic to the railway he intended to build from Swindon to Gloucester and South Wales. He made the Taff Vale a 4ft 8½in-gauge railway because of its curvature, while the Gloucester-Cardiff route, which in places was as curved and as steep as the Taff Vale, was built at the 7-foot gauge because it was an extension of the GWR. Brunel could not have a 'break of gauge' within his own system, but did not mind having this inconvenience where his railway met another. All the coal coming down the Taff Vale for onward transport to the towns and cities on the Great Western system had to be unloaded and reloaded from one railway to the other.

The route of the GWR that was passed into law on 31 August 1835 was never meant, by Brunel, to be the definitive line. Furthermore, the powers granted by that Act for the GWR to use the L&BR line from a junction approximately at the site of the existing Queen's Park station into Euston, was a huge weakness in the Act, which Brunel realised at the time – because that route could only be used if the L&BR made a friendly, accommodating agreement with the GWR. Brunel knew about that problem and also about all the deviations he laid out during the time that he was convincing Parliament that he had chosen the best route for the GWR. Even the changes he details in the following report to the Directors were not his final word on deviations.

PRO 1149/2
To the Directors of the Great Western Railway.
53 Parliament Street
October 8th 1835

Gentlemen,
The time is now arrived when it becomes necessary to decide upon any question which involves an application to Parliament in the coming Session and I beg to lay before you the following deviations or alterations in the Line of Railway which are either absolutely necessary or which I should recommend to be adopted as improvements upon the old line.

The first and most important of these deviations is at Acton – it is rendered necessary by the arrangements made with the Messrs Wood and involves an alteration in the line from Hanwell to the Junction with the London and Birmingham Railway, a distance of about 3½ miles. All the circumstances of this arrangement and the steps which have been taken to obtain the consent of the landowners upon the line of deviation are well know to the Directors.

The next deviation is at the crossing of the river at Maidenhead which I should propose to carry about 120 yards higher up the River. The line was carried as far north as it could be without actually destroying an Ornamental Cottage and Fishing House and Gardens belonging to a Miss Payne. [It is possible that she was related to Mr William Payne, the representative of the Thames Commissioners with whom Brunel was soon to be exchanging much correspondence. The original embankment and approach viaduct were to have been to the south of her house and, being so close, would have cast large shadows upon it for much of the day.] *I have reason to believe that this Lady would not object to the line passing altogether on the other side of the house which would be an improvement to the line and diminish the curve at that point and render the crossing of the River square instead of being slightly oblique.*

The deviation would not exceed 120 yards at any point and would I think pass through only 2 fields of landowners not in our present Book of Reference. And if Miss Payne who is the only person really affected by it consents I should recommend this deviation to be adopted.

The deviation by which the Purley Tunnel might be avoided I fear must remain undecided at present as Mr Storer the owner of the house and ground through which the line must be carried is I believe still abroad and I do not think it would be advisable even to give the Notices for such an alteration without the previous consent of this Gentleman.

The next deviation which I have to bring under the consideration of the Directors is the most important and requires the most consideration as affecting the character of the whole line – The object is to improve very materially the general levels of the line by the introduction of a second Inclined Plane at Wootton Bassett. By the present line I should be able to keep all the gradients between London and the Oxford branch and thence to Oxford and between Bath and Bristol under 4ft per mile.

Upon the intermediate portion of the line the gradients may be kept under 6 feet 6 inches per mile and with the exception of 19 miles which vary between 8 feet 6 inches to 11 feet 6 inches per mile.

By the introduction of an Inclined Plane of 1 in 106 and of 1 mile in length at Wootton Basset all the gradients may be kept under 6 feet 6 inches per mile and probably under 6 feet.

The expense of construction would be rather diminished than increased by this alteration and the line improved in point of curvature. The great importance of reducing to the utmost extent of general gradients of the line upon which locomotive engines are to run without assistance can fully be appreciated by anybody. When it is considered that an inclination of only 11 ft 6 inches per mile causes such an increased resistance that while an engine of a power of 18 would be sufficient on a level it would require one of 29½ or 30 to ascend this inclination and in descending the power required would be only 6½ so that the engine would have to perform its work always keeping the same velocity under resistances varying from 6½ to 29½, or as 1 to 4½, such a variation of resistance for a machine going at high velocities is alone a great disadvantage and is incompatible with economy or with the maintenance of the machinery in good repair. By reducing the gradients to 6 feet per mile the greatest power required would be only 24 which is at once a reduction of 20 per cent and the greatest variation would be from 12 to 24 or as 1 to 2.

If this great advantage may be obtained even in the present state of locomotive engines and carriages it becomes still more important when probable improvements are considered. The resistance arising from the gradients is constant and is not capable of diminution, that arising from friction would probably be much reduced.

On a railway with inclinations of 16 feet per mile the power required will be about 34 compared to 18 on a level while upon a railway with gradients of 6 ft the power will be only 24. In the first case 16 feet of this 34 is unavoidable, in the latter only 6 out of the 24 is constant so that any future improvement which should reduce the friction by one half which is very possible would on the first railway make a difference of only 9 upon 34 or 26½ per cent upon the maximum power of the engines required while upon the second railway this same improvement would be felt to the extent of 9 upon 24 or 37½ per cent.

In the first case the resistances would then vary from less than nothing to 25 and in the second between 3 to 15.

I have always had this alteration in the line in view and have alluded to it in my very early communications to the Provisional Committee before the present company was formed. I did not venture to bring it forward in the Parliamentary line and I have every reason to believe I was right. The prejudice against the introduction of inclined planes has been materially shaken in the investigations of last Session and I have no hesitation now in recommending most decidedly this alteration of the line.

It will require giving Notices and depositing plans for about 9 miles of new line and I believe that the alteration will be acceptable to Lord Holland who is the principal part affected but suppose the Directors will wish that his Lordship should be consulted before any steps are taken, there only remains to be noticed a deviation of a few yards which would improve the line in entering Bristol it will require the introduction into the Book of Reference of some houses not before included but will make no difference whatever in the extent or nature of the property required.

In enumerating these as the only deviations which I have to recommend in any new Act which may be applied for I suppose that an advantageous arrangement with the Birmingham Railway

Company will be effected. Should this not be the case it will be necessary in about a fortnight at the latest to determine upon the question of a separate entrance into London.

I am Gentlemen,
Your obt. Servt.
I. K. Brunel

The GWR Act of Parliament authorised the GWR to use part of the London & Birmingham Railway's Euston site for its terminus. Euston station was close to salubrious and newly built parts of London, but it was built at the foot of a mile-long, 1 in 68/77, rope-worked incline. The L&BR did not want the GWR at Euston and it got around the Great Western Parliamentary powers by instructing its Engineer, Robert Stephenson, to work in the most reluctant way with Brunel, finally granting the GWR a five-year lease – there was nothing in the GWR Act to prevent this. Euston as a terminus for the GWR was abandoned in December 1835 and Brunel – saved from himself – had to adopt the most operationally perfect of all London sites for a terminus – Paddington.

While trying to persuade Robert Stephenson to accept the GWR at Euston, Brunel had to write the following letter (Rail 1149/2, p15) with the utmost delicacy, tact and something close to humility.

DM 1306/8
53 Parliament Street
15 October 1835

My Dear Stephenson,
I am requested by my Directors to see you upon the subject of the best means of carrying our rails along your line from the point of junction, Kensal, to the depot, Euston. Our rails being placed at a greater width than yours – I believe – are, I think this may be done without difficulty. You may perhaps differ from me in this opinion. Have you any objection to talking the thing over with me to tell me the difficulties you foresee, if any? I will endeavour to meet them or be prepared to yield to them.

Yours truly,
I. K. Brunel

Stephenson replied to this (Rail 1149/2):

Hampstead
22 October 1835

Dear Brunel,
Since my return I have been confined to bed from severe influenza
otherwise I would have made some arrangement about meeting
you on the subject of yours of the 15th. As soon as I can move out
which I hope will be in two or three days I will take the earliest
opportunity of arranging a meeting.

Yours sincerely,
Robert Stephenson

Brunel believed he had made a verbal agreement with Robert Stephenson as to the apportionment of land at the site of Euston station to accommodate the GWR, but in writing Stephenson went back on this agreement and made no space available. In spite of this Stephenson and Brunel privately remained close friends all their lives.

PRO 1149/2

Great Western Railway

53 Parliament Street,
16 November 1835

My Dear Stephenson,
In looking over our sketch of an arrangement respecting the depot
there appears to me an omission without which the rest would be
unintelligible to anyone but ourselves. I mean the allotment of a
certain portion of the ground for the depot of the Great Western
Railway Company. I propose therefore that we should insert under
the head of Euston Square Depot:-
The space now proposed to be purchased (or purchased as the
case may be) to be divided longitudinally into two parts the
Western part to form the depot of the Great Western Railway
Company and intermediate space to form a passage for access
common to both depots.
Under the head of Camden Town Depot:-
A portion of the space belonging to the Birmingham Company
having frontage to the Canal to be set apart for the Great Western
Railway Company.
As these are consistent with what we arranged and merely
explanatory of those arrangements I think you will see no

objection to the insertion of them.
An immediate reply will oblige.

Yours truly,
I. K. Brunel

Brunel knew that obtaining the friendly cooperation of the L&BR from Queen's Park to Euston would not be easy, but when he announced his decision to have the 7-foot gauge on the GWR, the reluctance of the L&BR became a polite but nonetheless stone wall of opposition. The GWR Act of 1835 had given the company legal power to use the L&BR into Euston, but neither Brunel nor any of the GWR Directors had thought to compose a clause laying down the relationship of the two companies in sharing the line. This was a serious error of judgement. All the L&BR said that it was willing to give was a tenancy agreement for a few years. In this letter to Charles Saunders (Rail 250/82, p16), Brunel refers to 'Depots' rather than 'Stations' and expresses serious doubts about the advisability of sharing Depots with other companies:

19th Nov 1835

My Dear Sir,
I beg you will repeat to the Directors that I have seen Mr Robt Stephenson upon the subject of the best mode of arranging the Depots of the Great Western and the Birmingham and London Railways at Camden Town and Euston Square.

The result of my interview amounted however to very little as all the arrangements would depend upon whether the Great Western Railway Company are to be merely tenant for a limited term of a portion of the Birmingham Company's Depot or whether we are to purchase a portion of their land and form our own Depot apart and distinct from theirs.

Mr Robert Stephenson is of the opinion that the former is preferable and I think he would not recommend to his Directors to sell any portion of their land, particularly at Euston Square as he considers and very truly that there would be a want of room in attempting to form two distinct Depots if part of the service could be effected in common – how far having any portion in common may be consistent with the views of the Directors I could not determine and as there appeared to be no material difficulties in the way of such an arrangement to which point as Engineer I considered my attention was particularly directed we assured them in our discussion such an arrangement might be made.

Under this view of the subject it was proposed with respect to Euston Square that the space of ground purchased or about to be purchased by the Birmingham Railway Company should be divided longitudinally into two portions the western half to be devoted to the Great Western Depot and the eastern to the Birmingham – that between these two a space or passage should be left for egress common to both.

That the arrangements of the rails and crossings in the Great Western Depot should be arranged by the two Engineers conjointly as the Great Western Railway Company being the only tenants for a limited period with power to leave the Birmingham Railway Company should have some guarantee that the rails would be useful to them when given up.

That for the same reason the façade or public front of the joint Depots on the south side should form one and be determined by a joint architect appointed by the two companies.

That to prevent any competition or jealousy as to the time of starting the trains might start and ascend the inclined plane together, the one train afterwards preceding the other by the length of a train.

The arrangements were proposed on the supposition that in the Depot as upon he rest of the common line, the Birmingham Company are to construct and keep in repair all the necessary rails – the Great Western Railway Company using them only by right of the sum paid according to the agreement already made and also that the Birmingham Company will furnish the power, machinery, ropes etc necessary on that part of the line there being no Locomotive engine used on this side of the Camden Town depot.

At the Camden Town depot it was proposed that a sufficient and convenient portion of land with canal frontage should be at a part and exclusively devoted to the warehouses and Depot for goods of the Great Western – as well as Engine Sheds and repairing shops but that the yards for receiving cattle, market produce and other articles requiring large open spaces as well as the Railway Sidings and standing spaces for spare carriages should be common to both companies and subject to mutual arrangements.

These were all that appeared to be necessary to be considered by us as in any way affecting the Engineering Department and as I before stated they were acceded to on my part on the hypothesis of the Great Western Railway Company being merely tenants of the Birmingham Company and using a portion of their railway and a portion of their Depots for certain rental and with the power of leaving them at the expiration of a certain term. Were it otherwise I should certainly not advise the Directors to have anything in common however liberally Mr Robert Stephenson may be disposed to consider this subject as indeed I have always found him upon every other subject it is quite unnecessary for me to suggest that any other Engineer who might succeed him or any other individuals in a public company may have very different views and in that case the Great Western Railway Company as mere tenants would be placed under great disadvantages besides it has always appeared to me that Mr Robert Stephenson and most other persons with whom I have discussed the subject have a very limited idea of the degree of accommodation and inducements which must be offered to the public in these Depots and should the one company be disposed to afford greater accommodation than the other to their passengers they would be debarred from reaping the benefits of their improvements by the inaction of the other company.

Should beg to suggest therefore that before the Engineer details of the arrangements of the Depots and their connections with the main lines can be gone into between Mr Robt Stephenson and myself it will be necessary for the Directors to determine whether we are merely to use the Depot as we propose to use other parts of the Birmingham line or whether we are to purchase land and form our own depots – leaving the Birmingham Company entirely at the entrance of their Depots.

I am,
My Dear Sir,
Yours very truly,
I. K. Brunel

C. A. Saunders

In the next letter (Rail 1149/2, p163) Brunel is writing to one of his most devoted admirers among the GWR Directors, and maybe that is why he allows himself to be less than accurate when describing the effect of large wheels on friction in the axle bearings. The friction is constant for any given loading and state of the lubrication. A larger wheel cannot reduce the friction – or resistance to movement – but what a large wheel does is to overcome that resistance more easily, so the effect of the friction is less.

Mr Brunel's remarks to Mr Gibbs respecting increased width of rails.

The principal advantage of the increased width of the rails is to facilitate the adoption of wheels of larger diameter than are now used for the carriages generally both for passengers and goods – the object of increasing the diameter of the wheels is two-fold. First simply to reduce the friction at the axle and thereby diminish the power of traction required or what amounts to the same thing enables the same engines to draw a greater load – and secondly for the purpose of attaining very high velocities.

The diminution of friction at the axles is proportionate to the increase of the diameter of the wheel – the size of the axle tree remaining the same thus the present size of the carriage wheels being 2ft 10in, a 4ft 3in wheel would cause only 2/3rds of the resistance and allowing for some trifling increase in the diameter of the axle a 4ft 8in wheel would effect this saving so that the same engine would draw upon a level half as many more carriages with wheels of this diameter as it would with wheels of 2ft 10in. Suppose the increase only 1/3rd the advantage is very great. With smaller wheels such as are used for the trucks for carrying private vehicles the advantages would of course be much greater.

Larger wheels are also desirable for very high velocities, the number of revolutions is smaller and the velocity at the axle tree less while the effect of any small irregularity in the surface of the rails, the smallest of which will be perceptible at very high velocities, will be diminished. For all these reasons it is desirable that for the intended speed now sought for an increase in the diameter of the wheels should take place in the same manner as the present ones are larger than those formerly used.

On the 4ft 8in railways as now constructed the dimensions of the wheels is limited from the want of the bodies of the carriages or the platform of the luggage wagons necessarily extend over the wheels and consequently the whole load has to be raised 8 or 10 inches above the tops of the wheels and thereby limits their size – this is particularly felt in the luggage wagons and the trucks for carrying private vehicles.

By making the rails 7ft wide the bodies of the carriages, the platform of the luggage wagons and even carts and carriages on the truck may be kept so far within the wheels as to leave their diameter unlimited and at the same time the whole load may be kept even lower that at present and all the arrangements of the interior of the carriages may be simplified and particularly gentlemen's carriages even stage coaches, carts and wagons of all which it appears probable a very great number may be carried on the Great Western Railway may be placed on very low trucks nevertheless with wheels of the same diameter as the other carriages. These are the principal objects of the wide railway.

There are many less important indirect advantages such as the greater scope for the convenient arrangement of the interior of passenger coaches – the facility of constructing carriages to hold a greater number of people which is a great consideration as the present carriages weighing nearly 4 tons carry only 1¼ tons of passengers consequently ¾ of the power is wasted.

The greater width will give much greater steadiness and lastly it facilitates the construction of more powerful engines or in other words engines capable of greater speed.

G. H. Gibbs Esq,
11 Bedford Square,
London

4: TRACK LAYING

'I conceive I have effected an improvement'

B runel reports to the Directors (Rail 1008/35) that his track-laying system is perfection – so perfect that it has defied the laws of nature.

18 Duke Street
Westminster
22 January 1838

Great Western Railway

Gentlemen,

I am happy to be able to inform you that the trials which have been made upon a portion of permanent rails completed at Drayton have been such as to furnish a decided practical result in the experiment of the application of continuous longitudinal bearings of timber and a result from which safe conclusions may be drawn as to the advantages of the use of timber compared with the system of separate stone blocks or transverse sleepers.

The peculiarity of the plan which has been adopted consists principally in two points – first in the use of a light flat rail secured to timber and supported over its entire surface instead of a deep, heavy, rail supported only at intervals and depending on its own rigidity – secondly in the timbers which form the support of this rail being secured and held down to the ground so that the hardness and degree of resistance of the surface upon which the timbers rest may be increased by ramming to an almost unlimited extent.

The first, namely the simple application of rails upon longitudinal timbers is not new indeed as mentioned in a former report I believe it is the oldest form of railway in England – but when lately revived and tried upon several different railways it has I think failed & I believe very much from the want of some such means as that which I have adopted for obtaining a solid and equal resistance under every part of the timber and a constant close contact between the timber and the ground: as I believe this to be entirely new and to merit to be well understood as constituting an essential part of the plan I trust I shall be excused dwelling upon it for the purpose of fully explaining it.

In all the present systems of rail laying the supports whether of stone blocks or wooden sleepers simply rest upon the ground and consequently only press upon the ground with a pressure due to their own weight this is trifling compared either to the weight which rolls over them or even the stiffness of the rail which is secured to them the block or sleeper must lie closely on the ground if you attempt to pack under them beyond a certain degree you will only raise it [no one would pack more gravel into a void than was necessary to fill that void] *and for the same reason it is impossible to pack under the whole surface* [Brunel's emphasis] *of a block or sleeper one corner or one end is immediately pushed up a little more than another and from that moment the block or sleeper is hollow elsewhere.* [This is also untrue. Packing is done so that these bad effects do not happen.] *If the block yield as the weight rolls over, the rail itself resting on the supports is sufficiently stiff to raise it again and the support becomes still more hollow – such is the operation which may be observed by the eye more or less in the best laid railway and particularly with the heavy parallel rails. Where continuous longitudinal sleepers have been tried they have also been laid loose upon the ground …* [paper creased and torn here] *… their length makes it impossible that they should be well supported by the ground underneath or that they should continue so even if it was practicable to lay them well in the first instance it will be perceived that one or two lumps in the ground may leave such a timber unsupported for 20 or 30 feet and under the weight of an engine it must yield, spring and dance from the ground.*

[Brunel has given the reasons why longitudinal sleepers are useless on a railway and now goes on to describe the extreme and totally counter-productive measures he intends to go to in order to make use of this discarded method of track-laying. The item he will introduce to make this inefficient system of track-laying quite perfect is – piles. He will drive telegraph-pole-sized timbers into the ground and attach his longitudinals to them.]

In the present plan these timbers, which are much more substantial than those hitherto tried are held down at short intervals of 15 to 18 feet so that they cannot be raised. Gravel or sand is then rammed and beat under them until at every point a solid resistance is created more than sufficient to bear the greatest load that will come upon it as the load rolls over the ground cannot yield neither can the timber which is held tight to the ground spring up as the weight leaves it and if the rail be securely fixed everywhere in close contact with the timbers that is also immoveable; such was the theory of the plan and the result of the experiment has fully confirmed my expectations of its success.

The experiments have been made under several disadvantages and I am glad that it has been so as we are more likely to perceive at once and to remedy any defects which might arise otherwise have laid concealed for a time. The packing upon which it is evident everything depends was effected during a long continued wet and while no drainage at all existed looking forward to the necessity of repacking once or twice the timbers and packing were left completely exposed – the severe frost which immediately followed converted the wet sand into a mass of stone [sic] which we have in vain attempted to disturb and the continual dry frost has generally evaporated the water originally con... [triangular piece missing from edge of page] ... the packing has shrunk considerably and exposed surfaces [have] crumbled away while the ... [paper torn away] ... is still so hard within as to resist the pickaxe and has been with difficulty broken through at some points with a smith's cold chisel and hammer. Under these circumstances with engines weighing between 14 and 15 tons and from want of adjustment with more than half of this occasionally thrown upon one pair of wheels constantly running over the rails.

The timbers have stood most satisfactorily – I think generally there is less motion than I have seen in the best laid blocks – and I am convinced that with good packing no perceptible yielding would occur indeed such is now the case at several points where the packing is good. Upon the whole the result is such that it may now be safely asserted that the objections which have been urged against the use of a continuous support of timber do not exist, certainly in this mode of construction and that no new or unforeseen difficulties (exist)... [The final page of this letter is missing from the record]

Brunel's certainty about his new system of track-laying was based on a trial that took place when the track was, by his own admission, frozen to the ground.

Brunel sends off to Nicholas Wood a description of his method of laying track (DM 1306/iii). In his lengthy introduction to his description he creates a strange mixture of mock modesty, flattery, the defensive and the infallible. The introductory section develops until it resembles a roll of drums before the unveiling of the Great Secret. Brunel is convinced that he has discovered the Holy Grail of railway track-laying technology – using the oldest system of track-laying in England but with the Brunellian perfecting ingredient – piles – to hold the track to the ground. But he is labouring under misconceptions of his own, very inventive and fertile imagination. He has only a couple of miles or so of track laid on frozen ground and is running an experimental train over it with apparent success. The error of the piles is as fundamental as the error of the broad gauge to accommodate large wheels. He is fixated on what appears to be a wonderful idea that no one else has thought of – because no practical engineer would think of it.

18 Duke Street,
Westminster
12 February 1838

Dear Sir,
I have delayed sending you the accompanying drawings of the methods of laying our rails until I had satisfied myself completely by experiment of its success & particularly of the proportions & dimensions for the timber. I had no wish to give publication to it but as it must be published sooner or later I much prefer that it should appear in a work such as yours & have wished that it should appear in such a shape as should be most creditable to the work & most useful to the Public, a months constant working under continued close examination of every part makes me now determine with confidence my future plans & I send you a drawing of the timber work as it will now be laid & which hardly differs in any point or dimension from that first adopted – I propose also to make some slight improvement in the rails but the annexed cross section & the following description represent that adopted in the first 22 miles of the Great Western.
I send you one of our screws one half are made with square heads & the other half (used for the inner flank of the rail) with countersunk heads. They vary in length from 6½ to 8½ inches long according to the thickness of the wood.
I will not endeavour to describe the principle of construction but

have particularly to request that you will have the goodness to adopt entirely your own course and style.

I will endeavour to explain myself to you but you must then explain it to the public.

My railway is I believe on your authority the oldest form of railway in England, a flat, light plate resting on and secured to a beam of wood which rests upon the ground, the iron forming the hard smooth surface, the wood affording the necessary stiffness – all this is very old and has lately been revived by several engineers besides myself but I think not successfully & as I conceive from the want of some method of securing the timber to the ground & in this & perhaps in the details of construction my plan differs & is I think new – In all the systems of rails hitherto adopted at least to my knowledge whether on stone blocks, transverse sleepers or longitudinal & continuous bearers – the whole is simply laid on the ground & the degree of artificial hardness of the ground on which the support rests but particularly the closeness of contact of the block or sleeper with the ground is merely that due to the weight of the block or sleeper. Under a block you may ram tolerably hard – but this is still limited in the block lifts [sic] but the closeness of contact is still more limited by the weight under a block 2ft square it is impossible to ram equally, it must invariably be resting only on a few detached part – assuming the weight of the block and rail to be 6cwt what must be the compression where 10 or 12 times that weight is added – it must be & is with the best material considerable – what must it be with a sleeper – weighing with its rail (taking half the sleeper) at most 2cwt. What possibility is there of a surface of ground or of an equal bearing or a close contact which will not yield considerably under a change from 2cwt to 60cwt or 70cwt with the longitudinal bearers or sleepers it is worse still, from their length it is impossible to support them equally & continuously – if you ram at one place you lift the bearer & make it hollow at another & when a weight rolls over it, it springs and dances from the ground even if the timber were laid on a true & hard bed of concrete or stone – a thing very difficult to obtain and render permanently true in practise & on an embankment, however slight impossible, still if laid loosely or resting only with its own weight – it will buckle and spring under the effect of a three ton roller such as the driving wheel of an engine. It is this want of density of the surface of the ground & want of close contact that prevents solidity in the ordinary rails &

and has rendered the attempts I have seen at continuous bearers still less solid & more elastic & it is this which I propose to remedy but before I describe the mode I must beg you to understand & receive this long attack upon the system hitherto adopted by men of far greater talents & expressions than myself, merely as it is so meant, as tending to explain the particular point upon which I conceive I have effected an improvement.

[Now Brunel finally gets to the point.] *I take a long timber about 14 or 15 inches broad by 6 inches thick & fastening it down* [this refers to his intention to drive piles into the ground – see below] *securely at intervals of 14 or 15 feet I beat the ground underneath it to almost any degree of density – the timbers spring to this but I find that with the most careful beating with hard blows at the same time as the opposite side of the timber & using of sand that when the timbers are sprung 5/8th or 3/4 of an inch in the centre of the sand it is as dense as it can be made – it is almost like soft sandstone the contact is everywhere perfect & the flexure of the bearer ensures a pressure of about one ton per foot forward – and this close contact is ascertained even after considerable shrinking or sinking of the ground – but this is also so easily ascertainable there is no fear of ramming too much at one part or of lifting the whole it is beat everywhere as hard as it can be.* [The 6-inch-wide timber that has been beaten with sledgehammers 'with hard blows at the same time as the opposite side of the timber' is actually the longitudinal sleeper that will support the rail. The pine-wood surface is thus seriously dented and damaged by this treatment, so Brunel corrects this.]

Upon this irregular surface of the timber is laid a plank of hard wood, the thickness of which is regulated by the level of the timber & the surface of the hard wood is then planed perfectly true & to the required level – upon this are screwed the rails with a piece of felt – plates were introduced under the joints of the rails to prevent the ends of the rails squeezing into the wood [Brunel was concerned about dents in the wood!] *& then plates were tied across to maintain the gauge of the rail but I am disposed to think that both plates and ties are unnecessary the ends do not squeeze in & the transverse timbers appear to answer all the purposes of the ties.*

I should observe that great pains are taken to maintain perfect levels and gauge & I think I can rely upon the maximum error in the first being 1/8th inch and in the gauge still less.

Referring to the drawing I need hardly say that the piles are for the purpose of holding down – those piles vary in length from 9 to 14 feet according to the material in the cutting – on embankments from 12 to 30 feet – so as to reach original ground but in embankments above 20 to 24 feet or which have not long ceased to sink perceptibly – piles are driven but not used at present the longitudinal timbers are made 12 inches square & it is not proposed to secure them to the piles until the embankment is perfectly consolidated & in the meantime the stiffening of the timber is the only substitute but as this will take place on only 2 miles out of 22 it is an exception not affecting the general plan.

The piles are beech – the timbers American pine, the hard wood American Elm, Oak or Ash, the whole kyanised – we consume about 420 loads of pine & 40 loads of hardwood per mile – about 6 tons of bolts & 30,000 wood screws. The rails weigh 43 lbs to 44 lbs per yard & and I think them full stiff.

The ballasting is brought up to the upper surface of the timbers and in each space between the rails there is a cess pool with a cross drain at every 60ft.

The result of my careful and daily and continued experiments is that I find no movement whatsoever between the rail and the timber & when packing is [the word 'improved' here is crossed out] *good – no movement whatsoever of the timber. When the packing is imperfect (the severe frost came on before it was completed) the movement is not greater than what I have frequently observed with good blocks & requires close observation to detect.*

Upon the whole I am perfectly satisfied in the stability – the permanence of this perfect correctness it is greatly superior to anything I have ever seen with the ordinary mode.

I trust you will make your observations freely, my plans have been so strongly – I may say, bitterly – attacked by most that although I should regret it, I could not feel disappointed at your following the same course. I need hardly say that our increased width of gauge – diameter of our wheels – particularly the driving wheels of our engines – our six wheeled carriages – the sacrifices we make for curves and level are all peculiarities quite distinct from the system of laying the rails but should you wish for any information upon these parts of my plans I shall be most happy to give it to you.

I suppose you are aware of the engines now making for use by Messrs Hawthorns from plans furnished by Mr Harrison the

Engineer. I cannot but think it is a beautiful plan, well worth referring to in a work such as yours but of this you are of course the best judge.

I certainly feel proud of having been the first to adopt them.

I am, my dear Sir,
Yours very truly,
I. K. Brunel

N. Wood, Engr, Killingworth

Later in the year Brunel writes to Wood (Rail 1148/2, p 36) 'regretting' the latter's conclusions on the track:

18 Duke Street,
27 December 1838

Dear Sir,
I regret very much the determination you have come to, it would have been much more agreeable to me that you should have witnessed the experiments I have made and have satisfied yourself of the results and if you had seen occasion to have done so as I think you must to have qualified the expression of opinions formed upon very different results – rather than that I should be obliged to show that the conclusions to which you came were erroneous in so far as they were founded upon insufficient data.

I am suffering from inflammation in the eyes which prevents me writing to you myself.

I am my dear sir,
Yours very truly
I. K. Brunel

PS. I will send you the results of my experiments.

The Stephensons, Brunel and Nicholas Wood all believed that total rigidity of the track was necessary. Stephenson decided on stone blocks to carry the rails, but this was a disaster because stone bocks are more difficult to prevent from sinking into the ground than longitudinal sleepers. Brunel's track consisted of several components: a heavy longitudinal sleeper, covered by a thin strip of hard wood, planed to slope inwards, and several screws to hold the rails down. However, there were no 'fishplates' to hold together the ends of the rails. The blow received by the rail end caused a crushing down, so that the rail end began to move up and down and put a strain on the holding screw, which began to be pulled out of the wood, and as the rail began to dance up and down so the ripping out of the securing screws became worse. This then required the changing of a longitudinal sleeper, which meant first unscrewing and taking away a whole rail.

The broad gauge piles – the heart of Brunel's improved track design – were a disaster. Piles were driven 20 feet or more into the ground in a double row, one for the up line and one for the down, every 15 feet! Enormous physical effort was required to do this. Eight men were required to turn the windlass on each wooden pile-driver, to raise a half-ton, cast-iron weight. The piles were driven into the ground as far as Sonning cutting, 34 miles from Paddington, although the track was not attached to the piles west of the original Maidenhead station. Between each pile the track sank under the weight of the trains – Brunel said this would not happen – so the piling turned the Paddington-Maidenhead track into a roller-coaster, causing many derailments. Brunel abandoned the pile system two months after the opening; thus another core feature of his designs for a perfect railway was removed, leaving the 'difficult to pack' longitudinals lying 'loosely on the ground'. Meanwhile, just a few miles away there was a track system in use that was as near perfect as wit of man could invent.

Joseph Locke's track – which Brunel did not tell his Directors to look at – consisted of wooden sleepers laid transversely beneath the rails. Cast-iron 'chairs' were screwed to the sleepers and the double-headed rails were laid into the mouth of the chair and held to gauge by an oak block. Cast-iron plates were bolted across the ends of each rail, holding them firmly in line and preventing the ends from jumping up and down. Locke's track was much simpler in its construction than the fussiness of Brunel's track, it was the easiest of all to maintain, and the wooden wedges took some shock out of the blow inflicted on the rail by the rapidly moving wheels. George and Robert Stephenson, Brunel and Nicholas Wood saw this track as fit only as a temporary way to be used by contractors during construction. Brunel dismissed it because it had in the past been used only as a temporary way, and also – probably – because he thought it was too simple. Locke laid this type of track on the Grand Junction Railway but was ordered to replace it with Stephenson's primitive stone blocks. When the GJR opened only about 20 miles was still laid with the transverse sleepered track. But Locke was fully in charge of the London & Southampton and his track was used from the outset.

It became the British standard for more than 100 years.

Brunel stated in a Report read at the Shareholders' Meeting in Bristol on 15 August 1838:

> *I find that the system of piling involved considerable expense in the first construction and requires perhaps too great a perfection in the whole work and that if a part of this cost were expended in increasing the cross section of the timber and the weight of the rail a very solid and continuous rail would be formed. For this as a principle as for the width of the gauge I am prepared to contend and to stand or fall by it, believing it to be a most essential improvement where high speeds are to be obtained. I strongly urge upon you not to hesitate on these two main points which combined with what may be termed the natural advantages of the line will eventually secure to you a superiority which under other circumstances cannot be attained.*

Beyond Taunton and to the north, south and west of the great trunk route, the geography of the land did not have the 'natural advantages' and the tracks were frequently sinuously curved, so that the broad gauge was not suitable. Brunel, having denied the inconvenience of having two gauges in Britain, realised that he could not have two gauges within his own railway, so he was obliged to extend the 7-foot gauge into areas where it was, by his own admission, unsuitable.

5: RAILS

'We shall get a beautiful straight rail'

B runel's specification for a 'bridge'-shaped rail – an inverted 'U' shape – caused him and the rail manufacturers great difficulties. Rail-making techniques were primitive, and in demanding this unprecedented form of rail he caused rolling mills to become more efficient – even to the extent of giving rail-makers precise instructions as to how they could produce his rails. As with the demands arising from his designs for great ships, Brunel forced the pace of improvements in techniques. The Brunellian bridge rail was a complex shape to roll and caused huge difficulties in the first few years of production. It is curious to read Brunel, in this first letter (Rail 1149/2, p168), saying that the length of the rails was 'not important' and mentioning 12 feet as ' a good length'.

Great Western Railway
Experimental Rails
1836

It is essential 1st that the surface from A to B should be perfect. Quite smooth & flat and of a clean, true form that on the whole length of the bar this surface should be quite straight particularly free from lateral bends, any small curves vertically will be comparatively unimportant provided the bar spring straight when screwed down.

2nd. That the under surfaces should be quite parallel to the upper surface but in other respects the sides and the side flanges may be as rough as it may be convenient to make them.

As to the quality of the metal – that which is least likely to exfoliate and will give the smoothest and hardest surface at A-B will be considered the best.

The comparative thickness of the different parts shewn in the gauge are not essential or even very important but they cannot well be less to obtain the requisite strength – and beyond this is of course an object to have as little metal as possible.

The particular length of the bar is not important – 12 feet is a very good length, they should not be less than ten, eventually three or four lengths may be fixed upon and to one of each of these [sizes] each bar must be cut off with precision

After passing through the first pair of rollers the bar must be passed through a second pair, case hardened and grooved at least 5/8th inches deep to receive & finish the surface [sic]

IKB

J. Guest Esq, MP

Brunel is constantly held back by the contractors who cannot produce what he wants – in the following case (Rail 1149/5, p36) not enough of the screws that will hold the rails to the longitudinal sleepers. Factories for rails and ironwork were overwhelmed by the demands on their services – the sheer volume of material required because of the large number of railways under construction. Railway-building drove the construction of larger iron foundries and iron-working premises, more heavily equipped and with greater manpower.

18 Duke Street
9 April 1836

Sir,
I am desired by Mr Brunel to write to you about the screws which in consequence of his being confined to his bed he cannot examine them as a sample.

Mr B. says if you will pay more attention to the slots of the round heads the sides of which must be quite square and not with round corners like those sent the screw will do. The quantity you talk of delivering in April is very far short of what you originally intended and Mr B. had thought that you could at least have done double that quantity. Mr B. will be glad to know what quantity you can possibly do this month and whether you can undertake to deliver 500 gross [500 x 144 = 72,000] (of screws) per week for the next five weeks the screws to be well made in every respect if you can do this Mr Brunel can give you an order you will be pleased to bear in mind that 3,000 gross is the quantity originally calculated upon from you. Mr Brunel says that he wishes you to take every opportunity of improving the screw and that about 15 or at most 16 threads in 3 inches will be the proper number. Are the goods sent by Kenworthy delivered at Drayton you do not say in your Invoice.

I am Sir,
Your obt. servt.
J. Bennett.

Edwd Mace Esq, Liverpool

Later in the year he wrote to the GWR's rail supplier, Guest, Lewis (Rail 1149/2, p159):

18 Duke Street
28 November 1836

My Dear Sir,
I enclose you a template of the rail we now want and which I have reduced to 6 inches as you recommended – accompanying this is a short statement of our requisites as to quality of metal distinguished from the quality of the rail when made all things considered – I should say that I should not stipulate for all or by any other words define the quality of the material except that the rails should be of close equal in quality to No 2 iron and in point of workmanship to possess the qualities required in the annexed statement and to obtain which I suppose would require good metal – independent of the stipulation that it should be equal to No 2. I should wish as soon as the rollers are finished to have ten tons by way of experiment.

I am, Dear Sir,
Yours very truly,
I. K. Brunel

Subsequently Brunel had a wasted journey from London to Dowlais, high up on the South Wales moors. He wanted to talk to the manager of Guest Lewis's rail-making mill about improving its technique for producing his unique 'bridge rails'. So now he has to write this long letter (Rail 1149/4, p10), explaining how he wants his rails manufactured and treated after rolling so that a perfectly straight rail is produced. The processes were thoughtless, damaging the rail, and Brunel gives his ideas on how a perfectly straight rail could be produced. His detailed, comprehensive suggestions still leave one wondering at the primitive – and expensive – way that miles of Brunel's bridge rail were produced.

It must be understood that the iron bar is white hot while being forced into the shape of the 'bridge rail'.

Dowlais,
March 8 1838

Dear Sir,
You ought to have written to me to say that you should not be here that I might have postponed my journey if I had wished. I have received every possible assistance and attention but I wanted to have seen you as it is impossible to write all I could have said.

I have tried a number of rails and am quite satisfied that they may be made perfectly straight with very little trouble but with some attention and good tools.

As regards the tools, the rails must be laid on a <u>flat bed</u> to be sawn. They get a <u>set</u> by being supported on a few points as they are now and the bed must come up to within ¼ inch of the saw so that the rail may not overhang 4 or 5 inches as it now does and by which means the end gets bent down by the saw and it would be better that the bed should extend beyond the saw that the scrap, and if a long one, may not weigh down and bend the rail before it is cut.

The rail must then be flattened and straightened <u>entirely</u> by slapping it down on a flat plate and these plates should be cast <u>in one piece</u> and be quite flat – to slap the rail down properly it should be lifted at least 2 feet 6 inches and let fall. This is higher than a man can well lift and the weight of the rail requires three men which when they exerted themselves I found was sufficient but if not looked after the whole time they will not lift it high enough and I should therefore recommend some simple contrivance of a long pair of tongs slung near the middle by which the men something like what I have here sketched but which you will easily improve upon perhaps it would be better to sling the tongs and for a chain to be pulled up by a separate lever but this I leave to you – I want the rail lifted 2ft 6in at least and slapped down first at one end and then at the other end <u>not lifted by the ends</u> – of course the higher it falls from the better – half a dozen good slaps – then a blow or two on each edge and this repeated twice and then finish with 6 blows on the flat and the rail will be perfectly straight. I think it likely that a few blows with a heavy hammer with a swage not less than one foot long and fitting the rail thus just to get the ends quite flat might be a good thing.

It *must be then put into the grooves. [These 'grooves' must be those through which the red-hot iron ingots were drawn – or pushed – to produce the 'bridge rail' shape.] Now these grooves must be quite different things from those you have which are very badly made – they are anything but straight at some places they are too tight for the rail to go in and at other 3/16 inch too large and not deep enough – they must be made 28 feet long and have 12 inches hollow and this hollow must be given rather more towards the ends that in the middle – say about like this:*

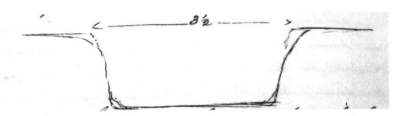

To *strike this curve you will find the centre part of 16ft in length is 100ft radius and the two ends about 85ft radius. These grooves must be cast perfectly true and the rail when pressed in must fit tight and bear hard upon the black lined parts and be free at the dotted lines:*

To *ensure these grooves being cast perfectly true and smooth they must be cast upside down and against a metal surface which must be prepared in the following manner.*

You *must cast a curved bed of this section, file it up clean and then plane up a cast bar of the section of the rail.*

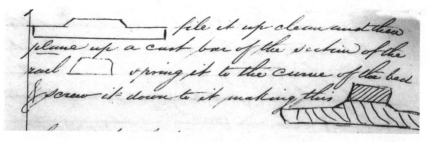

Spring it to the curve of the bed and screw it down to it making this.

This will be the bottom of your mould and a groove cast upon this will I think be a good job – if you wish to cast these three grooves in one trough as at present you must of course have three such patterns but I should recommend your casting each groove in a trough of its own. A bad casting is not then of so much importance – however this is a matter for you to decide.

If you have any difficulty in obtaining the planed bar I will get that done for you – you must have six grooves at least in order that the rails may stop in them some time.

When in the grooves that must be rolled as at present but with a roller <u>at least twice</u> the weight with a rib to run in the hollow of the rail – turned to guide it – rolling on the rail. The roughness of the present one prevents it acting. I enclose a section of the roller I should recommend the part A-B to be turned, these dimensions will give about 12½ cwt.

After the rail has been left as long as possible in the groove it must be laid on a curved bed to cool and the ends must be protected and a small dwarf wall built to keep the wind off.

These will form all the new tools and machinery required namely: a bed to carry the rail to the saw, a flattening plate, tongs to lift the rail, a swage, grooves and rollers and a cooling place.

In the manipulation there are some points required to be attended to. In the rails rolled this morning there were many flaws from sand and dust rolled in. More care must be taken to keep the iron clean. Secondly the leading end of the bar – that which the behinder [sic] lays hold of – gets very much bent much more so that the other – this end must be straightened by slapping down edgeways before it is sawn and then at least 18 inches must be cut off this end, two feet would be better. The saws must be inclined a little to give a slight bevel to the end but very slight – 1/32nd of an inch will be almost enough. No time need be lost in the filing up *the ends if they are sawn clean it is enough they must be carried without losing any time hot as possible into the grooves and rolled at least 3 times each way, the roller passing right off the rail at both ends and lastly in dragging the rail it ought if possible to go end ways from the flat plate to the grooves. If you must take it sideways you must be much more careful that it has a good, clear slide and that it gets no blows.*

With these precaution I am convinced that we shall get a beautiful straight rail and at a less expense than the present mode of hammering them straight or rather crooked.

If you adopt these means and take pains and give me a perfectly straight rail I will take 25 feet lengths without accuracy not dead lengths but anything between 24ft 6in to 25ft 6in square joints and a far less number of holes viz:- 24 in the rail of 25ft and no particular accuracy in their position and I feel that I shall thus give you much more than I ask. You will turn out a beautiful rail at a less expense than the contract rail and I shall be satisfied.

I forgot to say that with the exception of a few blows at each end with a swage I must not have the rails struck with anything.

I should wish very much to see you about all this immediately. I am now going to Town and shall be in Town all next week. If you will think it over and order the tools etc that there may be no time lost and then come up to Town to me I should feel much obliged.

I am, my Dear Sir,
Yours very truly,
I. K. Brunel

PS. I observe in the rolling some mischief caused by the notches in the rollers there ought to be no notches at all. In the lower finishing roll and those on the side which form the hollow ought not to be so coarse.

Written in the margin of the first page of this letter is: '*Lengths of the GW rails to vary from 24 to 27 feet, holes to be round & 5/8 1/32 [sic] diameter. If there is a curve of, say, 5 inch in the rail it will be accepted rather than have it struck with a hammer. Pattern to be a little altered to the template furnished.*'

Further faults needed to be corrected later in the year (Rail 1149/5, p15):

18 Duke Street
3rd December 1838

Gentlemen,
With regard to the sample of rail which you have sent me there are
two faults which must be remedied. First as regards the weight –
60lbs is really quite enough and we must not exceed it – comparing
the piece you have sent me and my original section I mean that now
adopted – there is a slight excess in height, a slight increase in
thickness of the lower flange and a slight diminution in the width
of the hollow – each very small in itself but as near as I can measure
making about 27½lbs to the yard – now as there is no difficulty in
slightly reducing the rail in height (except turning off some of the
rails, it must be done 96 inches at a-a in one roll and at B in the
other does it [sic]

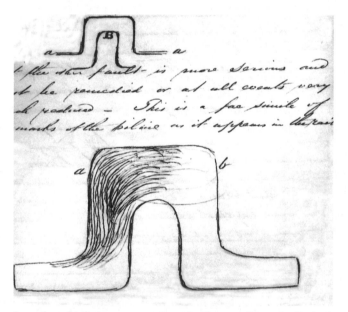

But the other fault is more serious and must be remedied or at
all events very much reduced – This is a facsimile of the piling as it
appears in the rail sample you sent me.
This is a very correct copy of the lines shown and the piling here
is as perfect as I could wish it and there is <u>no reason at all</u> why ours
should not be as good and I must therefore request that you make
it so.
As regards the holes they must be upon the parallel lines exactly

21 inches apart at each end of the rail there you have sent me it is a very sound piece and therefore these only appear when brought out by a little and – but the line A-B is very bad and such a rail I am sure would split you know best what alterations are required in your rolls but I am sure there can be no difficulty in making the top piles head down thus

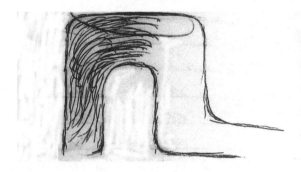

With respect to the rails with the narrow hollow I had expected to have heard from you as to some mode or system of morticing the timber. I am anxious to give the rail a full and fair trial but before I can recommend this to the Directors I wished some plan to have been designed for making the holes in the wood or what would be better for rendering very great accuracy in these holes unnecessary.

Yours very truly,
I. K. Brunel

Thos Evans Esq, Guest Lewis & Co

In the letter of 8 March 1838 he said that there was 'no particular accuracy' in the spacing of screw holes along the flange of the rail. Here (Rail 1149/5, p19) he gives instructions on how to space the holes along the base of a rail starting with 'exact', then degrading to 'about'.

18 Duke Street,
Westminster.
7 December 1838

My Dear Sir,
Since I wrote to you I have examined a piece of your iron rail and find it quite free from the defect in the piling of which I complained so much in the sample you sent me.

This is a very correct copy of the lines shewn and the piling here is as perfect as I could wish it and there is <u>no reason at all</u> why ours should not be as good and I must therefore request that you will make it so.

As regards the holes they must be upon the parallel lines exactly 21 inches apart – at each end of the rail there must be two exactly 2½ inches from the end and if you have two gauges about half the length of the rail you can easily set off the holes from each end as in the accompanying sketch [missing] and if the centre of space a-b is less than 17 inches the hole must be half-way as at C. If less than 8 inches then the last hole must be left out and a put halfway between c & f. You will easily learn to fill up the space and all I shall require will be that the two centre spaces shall not be more than 22 inches each or less than 13.

In writing to you I consider that I am communicating equally with Messrs Harford Davis & Co and have to request that you will acquaint them with all that passes.

I am, Dear Sir,
Yours truly,
I. K. Brunel

F. Evans Esq, Guest & Co.

Brunel watched all contract performances with a penetrating gaze and pounced on any backsliding. Guest & Co received this Brunellian broadside (Rail 1149/5, p71) on 8 February 1839:

18 Duke Street
7th Feby. 1839

Gentlemen,
In a conversation held this day between Mr Davis and myself, Mr
Davis whom I suppose to be your authorised agent, expressed an
opinion that objectionable or defective rails must be rejected by
some agent of the Company's either at the works or at Cardiff –
such an opinion is so totally at variance with all the terms of the
contract or the arrangements made between Mr Evans & myself
that it would be almost unnecessary to refer to it but to prevent the
possibility of any future misunderstanding I must object to receive
any rails until such a statement is corrected and I have therefore
given immediate directions that no persons employed by the
Company shall unload any rails at our wharf at Bulls Bridge until
further notice. Rails are to be delivered made in conformity with a
certain specification, if rails are delivered at our wharf which are
not in conformity with this specification of course they are not the
rails constructed for me and therefore they will not be received.

I regret that the question should have been raised as it has
compelled me to give the directions I have referred to which may
put you to temporary inconvenience but it cannot alter the simple
& almost self-evident result of a contract that if defective rails are
inadvertently or otherwise sent to us the defects must be removed
by you or the rails rejected our having landed them at the wharf
cannot render us liable to receive & pay for that which we have
not contracted for and which you ought not to have sent.

I am, Gentlemen,
Yours very truly,
I. K. Brunel

Messrs Guest Lewis & Co
Messrs Harford Davis & Co

Brunel's concern and care for his railway permeated into every crevice of
the operation. There has been another collision between trains due to a
lack of signal/point interlocking and the employment of men working 12
hours a day or night to operate by hand the various signal and point
levers. In this letter (Rail 1149/5, p67) Brunel answers a passenger's
complaint, and in a following one he alerts Charles Saunders to a lack of
civility among the staff dealing with the public.

18 Duke Street,
February 7 1839

Dear Sir,
I am very much obliged to you for your note the faults you speak
of are unfortunately my department and although I have not
exactly the power of entirely correcting them it is my business to
render them as few as possible and by using every means reduce
the chance of such accidents –
You have been most unfortunate in being twice inconvenienced
by them the more so as I believe you have been tolerably free of
such casualties.
The policeman whose business it was to watch the switch in the
case of the last accident has been dismissed.

I am, Dear Sir,
Your most obedient servant,
I. K. Brunel

Mr William Venables

Meanwhile problems persist with Guest Lewis & Co (Rail 1149/5, p78):

18 Duke Street
25th Feby. 1839

Gentlemen,
A considerable quantity of rails have now arrived at the
Company's wharf at Bull's Bridge and I am sorry to say that a very
large proportion – upwards of one half – require straightening or
are otherwise defective a cargo lately arrived from Messrs
Harford's appears to have exactly the same defects and in about
the same proportion as those from Messrs Guest –
These defective rails are laid aside and unless I receive written
directions from you to adopt means to straighten them at your
charge they cannot be included in the certified payment.
I much fear that there will be considerable difficulty in
straightening them cold and I hope directions have been sent to the
works to use much greater care in the original straightening.
I can safely assert, from having myself superintended the making
of several rails to ascertain the fact – that a very little attention to
the first operation of straightening while the rail is hot ensures

without any expense a perfection which can never be attained afterwards and which it has been expressly stipulated should be attained.

I am, Gentlemen,
Your obt. servt.,
I. K. Brunel

Messrs Guest Lewis & Co
& Harford Davis & Co

6: LOCOMOTIVES AND CARRIAGES

'We go regularly now at 30 to 35 miles per hour'

The story of Brunel's original carriage designs is as peculiar as the story of his locomotive specifications. Both are illustrations of the problems he made for himself by becoming fixated on a single bright idea. The first carriages were, mechanically, very poor and the best of them carried fewer people than a standard gauge carriage.

In Mr Francis Whishaw's *The Railways of Great Britain*, published in 1842, he described the best of these carriages as '"Posting Carriages" which hold eighteen persons fitted up in a style of elegance not met with in any other railway conveyance in the Kingdom (save only the royal railway carriage). It is furnished with cushioned seats all around except at the doorways and a table extending down the middle so that for a party it is a most excellent contrivance ... in the middle of each side there is a glass door 2ft 4in wide and 6 feet high... On each side of the door there are two lights and above these there are three smaller lights [along the length of the roof – this was what became known as the "clerestory" roof].'

The width of Brunel's original carriage was 7ft 6in from the roof eaves to the level of the seating, but then the walls had to come inwards to avoid the 4-foot-diameter wheels, which were outside the body, so the floor was only 6 feet wide (see *History of the Great Western Railway*, E. T. MacDermot, Volume 1, p431). Because of this strange arrangement the seating had to be arranged along the sides and carriage ends, leaving a space for the central doors. Thus they could carry only 18 people – less than a 1st Class carriage on the London & Birmingham Railway. The bodies were 18ft 6in long, carried on two axles placed only 10 feet apart. This was too short a wheelbase for the 'high speed' Brunel envisaged and the carriages would have 'hunted' from side to side at 30mph, making the occupants glad of their luxurious upholstery. They were also without ventilation and thus very stuffy. They were only of any use for party travel – a family, for instance – and by 1849 only three were left in service, the final example being scrapped in 1856.

All the original Brunellian carriages were hopelessly impractical – and, running over the dreadful system of track-laying Brunel had dreamed up, they were constantly derailing and could not be used at high velocities (Daniel Gooch to the Gauge Commissioners, 1846). Their worst faults were being only four-wheeled, and with the two axles being far too close together – only 6ft 6in to 7 feet apart under a body more than 18 feet long (MacDermot, Volume 1, p433)! How Brunel could have allowed this is a greater mystery than his specifications for locomotives.

And yet, while designing and ordering these monstrosities to be built, Brunel, as early as August 1837 – nearly a year before the railway was opened to Maidenhead – turned out a design for a perfectly proportioned six-wheeled carriage, *but* these had their bodies *over* the 4-foot wheels – a design he had stated to be 'inconvenient'. In the early days of his infatuation with large wheels, Brunel had stated that he intended to have larger than 4-foot wheels, but that could not be, once he was obliged to bite the bullet and admit that the standard gauge people had the right idea about carriage bodies. His new design had straight-sided walls and transverse seating and, with their perfectly spaced three axles, would have run beautifully smoothly on the standard gauge as much as on the broad gauge. The 1st Class version could seat 24 and the 2nd Class 72 passengers. The 4-foot wheels came through the floor and were covered under cowlings beneath the seats. By raising the carriage bodies over the wheels he had removed his stated reason for the broad gauge. He could have had his large wheels on the 4ft 8in gauge, which would have reduced somewhat the seating capacity but he would not have made his railway incommunicado from the rest of the country's railways. The GWR began to change the gauge of its railway in 1872 and adopted the standard gauge 3ft 6in wheel in 1875. All that then remained was to abandon the last remnant of the Broad Gauge, which took place in May 1892.

In the following letter (Rail 1149/2, p222) Brunel and Saunders are planning the coaching fleet, for four classes of passenger. Since the 3rd Class travelled on the GWR sitting on transverse planks in what appeared to be coal wagons, one wonders if the 4th Class passengers were carried standing up on flat-bed carriage trucks! But no – in fact, there never was a 4th Class. Brunel was a great believer in class and privilege, but even so he never called those who travelled on his railway 'customers' – they were 'passengers'. He envisaged a very luxurious and strongly hierarchical railway with levels of comfort extending from what we would call a 'super 1st Class' accommodation – but which he intended to called 1st Class – to the 3rd Class. He is slightly confused in this letter to his Directors as to how the class system in railway carriages will work: his '1st' would in fact be 'super 1st', his '2nd' is '1st', his '3rd' is '2nd', and his '4th' is '3rd' – but this is only in the planning stage and in the course of the letter he changes the system.

18 Duke Street,
Westminster.
1 June 1837

Gentlemen,

Having considered with Mr Saunders the number of carriages likely to be required during the first six months of the working of the railway when opened to Maidenhead I think it is necessary that immediate steps should be taken to ensure the completion of 55 coaches of all classes and I should propose to divide them in the following proportions and different classes.

It is assumed that there may frequently be 3,500 passengers or journeys to perform in the day and that occasionally there may be 6,000 – and that these may consist of 4 classes and in the proportion

1st – 1,000
2nd – 1,500
3rd – 1,500
4th – 2,000

The first I suppose to be persons travelling for pleasure or desirous of obtaining any comfort and willing to pay an increased charge and the carriages for their accommodation would be superior to that are usually termed mail coaches first class and might be called private trains or some other distinguishing name – the other three classes being called first, second and third as on the other railways. The number of each of these coaches to accommodate the passengers as classed above would be

Private 10
1st Class 15
2nd ditto 15
3rd ditto 15
Total 55

And probably about 15 or 20 platforms [flat-bed trucks] might be for private carriages and even stage coaches. I think may very likely use them. For 1st and 2nd class drawings are in progress and I am prepared if it be considered desirable to advertise at once for tenders for their construction and in order to facilitate this also to prevent the risk of inconvenience from the introduction at any time of too many new arrangements I have made them nearly similar to the [London &] Birmingham carriages except their being more roomy and comfortable and having large wheels although not too large as I should ultimately recommend. In the details of the buffers and the connections of the carriages I have introduced some alterations which I consider very material improvements.

With respect to the 3rd class and platform luggage wagons I am not quite prepared to propose any immediate steps.

I am, Gentlemen,
Your obedient servant,
I. K. Brunel

The Directors of the Great Western Railway

As far as locomotives were concerned, Brunel had told Gibbs that an advantage of the broad gauge was that larger, more powerful locomotives would run on it. However, his specification for broad gauge locomotives would produce smaller engines than those on the standard gauge. In his diary (19 October 1827) he had said how he wished to be recognised – and his specifications for locomotives certainly brought him to the astonished notice of locomotive builders. His various stipulations were actually contradictory one to the other and made an impossible puzzle to solve. He wrote to the manufacturers with a lofty superiority, radiating supreme confidence in the superior knowledge he thought he possessed on this subject, while in fact talking rubbish. He had told his Directors that, looking at the 4ft 8in gauge railways and locomotives, he felt they were not big enough for the job they had to do – then, in a very superior tone of voice, ordered engines that were smaller, lighter and less powerful than those he had condemned.

The infamous Brunellian specification for locomotives is to be found as the endpapers of Rail 1149/2, p191, and tattered and mended, it looks as old as it actually is – 1836.

18 Duke Street,
Westminster.
Undated

Gentlemen,
Specification.

I am authorized on the part of the Great Western Railway Company to apply to you amongst several other Manufacturers to know whether you will undertake & generally upon what terms but more particularly within what period to supply one or two Locomotive Engines. The particular form and construction of the engines will be left to your own judgement, the object of the Company being to induce Manufacturers to turn their attention to the **improvement** *[my emphasis] of Locomotive Engines and to afford them an opportunity of introducing such improvements as may suggest themselves when unchecked by detailed and particular specification of the parts, it being intended that the result of the trials of the various engines thus finished should lead to more extended orders to those manufacturers who shall have made the Engines best adapted to the objects of the Company. These objects can be particularly defined but most principally related to the speed – to the related economy of the first construction – of the subsequent repairs and of the consumption of fuel – generally to the performance of the greatest quantity of work at the greatest speed at the least expense and in the most convenient and advantageous manner.*

The comparative importance of those objects and the best means of attaining them will be left for you to determine, but the following are a few conditions which <u>must</u> *be complied with.*

A velocity of 30 miles an hour to be considered the standard or minimum velocity – and this attained without requiring the piston to travel at a greater rate than 280 feet per minute.

The Engine to be of such dimensions and form as to maintain without difficulty with a pressure of steam in the boiler not exceeding 50lbs the square inch a force of traction equal to 800lbs upon a level at 30mph.

The weight of the Engine exclusive of the tender but in other respects supplied with water and fuel not to exceed 10½ tons and if above 8 tons to be carried on six wheels. The width clear between the rails will be 7 ft, the height of the chimney as usual. All materials and workmanship to be of the best description and except when modifications may be necessary to comply with the conditions above stated or for the purpose of improvement to be similar to the same parts of the best engines now used on the Liverpool & Manchester Railway.

Drawings of the proposed Engines to be submitted to me as the Engineer of the Company before Execution and if during *execution any material alteration is proposed it will be necessary that I should have the opportunity on the part of the Company of objecting to it if I should consider it an experiment not worth the making. I beg to request an early reply to this communication and to repeat that the object of the Company is by a **liberal order limited by as few conditions as possible**, the time of delivery being the most important to afford Manufacturers an opportunity of making those experiments which the specific nature of the Orders generally given may have hitherto prevented.*

The 1st March 1837 is the period by which we hope you would be enabled to complete the order.

I. K. Brunel

Messrs Murray & Co, Engineers, Leeds
Messrs Stephenson & Co, Newcastle
Messrs Sharp Roberts & Co, Manchester
Messrs. Fonerton & Co, Liverpool
Messrs Mather Dixon & Co, Liverpool
Messrs Jessop & Co, Butterley Ironworks
Messrs Tayleur & Co, Vulcan Foundry, Warrington
Messrs Maudslay & Co, Lambeth

The only fast, main-line railway then operating in Britain was the 30-mile Liverpool & Manchester. In 1835-36 new engines for the L&MR were constructed by local firms, including the Vulcan Foundry at Newton-le-Willows. The Vulcan Works had been established by Robert Stephenson in 1830, in partnership with Charles Tayleur, to build locomotives for the Liverpool & Manchester Railway and railways on the western side of Britain. This removed the expense incurred by Stephenson when he had to transport locomotives overland from his east coast works at Forth Street, Newcastle. Mather Dixon of Liverpool, the Haigh Foundry of Wigan, Sharp Roberts of Manchester, and R. W. Hawthorn of Newcastle also provided the L&MR with locomotives.

Brunel was concerned to keep the speed of the piston low. He was not entirely alone in this. In 1836 the Locomotive Superintendent of the L&MR, John Melling, became worried that the piston speeds of his engines were increasing as the demand for line speed increased. This became something of a – short-lived – craze, with the Vulcan Foundry, Mather Dixon, R. W. Hawthorn and even Robert Stephenson's Newcastle works building short-stroke engines, some with a 12-inch stroke driving on a 5-foot wheel – that is, a lever 6 inches long to turn a 60-inch wheel. The short stroke slows the piston but it also reduces the power of leverage exerted by the piston through the connecting rod to the crankshaft, so the engine is less powerful. Any advantage from a reduction of friction in carriage axle bearings due to larger wheels was probably cancelled out by the weakness of a short-stroke engine. Brunel did not approve of short-stroke engines and preferred large-diameter wheels to slow the piston speed – or gearing, with the asssociated power loss.

The short-stroke idea very quickly died the death among the locomotive manufacturers of the North, and short-stroke engines were rebuilt with the more usual 18-inch stroke. In 1834 Robert Stephenson's works brought out the first British goods engine with six wheels, all coupled, and inside cylinders. The cylinders were 16in x 20in and the driving wheels were of 4ft 6in diameter. The following year Stephenson brought out his 'Patentee' locomotive. It had six wheels arranged as a pair of driving wheels placed between leading and trailing carrying wheels (a 2-2-2 wheel arrangement). It had inside cylinders 12 inches in diameter with an 18-inch stroke driving on 5ft 6in wheels – a leverage ratio of 1 to 7. With the addition of the Stephenson Link valve gear in 1843, these two types became the basic British goods and passenger locomotive designs, modified and enlarged over the years, but basically the 1834/5 design. These engines could have had 7-foot axles placed under them, but Brunel set out his specification and the conventional engines of the period did not conform to it.

Brunel was as much mistaken over his locomotive specifications as over the need for a broad gauge. He had a blind belief in his 'decided opinions'. On 4 July 1837 the Grand Junction Railway – a Joseph Locke production – opened to the public with engines having 13in x 18in cylinders driving 5ft 6in wheels. The boilers held steam at 50lb per square inch, and if steam arrived in the cylinders at 40psi, which is a reasonable assumption, that produced a tractive force at the rim of the driving wheels of 1,840lb. Brunel never altered his June 1836 specification for locomotives, but soon their design was taken out of his hands.

Brunel demanded an engine weighing only 10½ tons – in fact, he even contemplated using four-wheeled engines, as his specification shows. He was still convinced in August 1838 that all locomotives were unnecessarily heavy, the usual weight at that time being 14½ to 18¾ tons. Of the 10½ tons, not all would be loaded on the driving wheels. The light weight he demanded obliged designers to save weight, so they produced boilers that were too small, with only a small amount of heating surface and a fire grate that was also small, so the supply of steam was correspondingly small. Cylinders were small to keep down weight and driving wheels large to keep piston speed within his specification.

The Vulcan Works designed engines with 10-foot wheels. These were made as plate iron discs, heavy and effectively a sail for the wind to press against. Brunel raised no objection. The Haigh Foundry and T. E. Harrison, a designer with the firm of R. W. Hawthorn, designed an engine that drove through gears. Harrison's engine came closest to Brunel's specification on weight and piston speed by having the boiler and the cylinders/driving wheels on separate carriages – an idea picked up again decades later to produce the ultra-powerful Beyer-Garratt type.

It was very unfortunate that Brunel did not send his specification and invitation to build locomotives to the Rennie Brothers. Did Brunel have a prejudice against them? His comment in his diary for 6 May 1828 could be a clue that he did not greatly admire them. George and John Rennie, sons of Sir John Rennie, had an engineering works in Holland Street, Blackfriars, London, maybe 2 miles from Brunel's office in Duke Street. In 1838 they designed and built engines of the 2-2-2 wheel arrangement for Joseph Locke's London & Southampton Railway (L&SR), and 0-4-2s for William Cubitt's London & Croydon Railway. Both types worked perfectly from the outset. The L&SR engines were conventional standard gauge machines with 13in x 18in cylinders driving 5ft 6in wheels, and normally reached 40mph between stops, and with light loads as much as 50. At 30mph their piston speed was 458 feet per second. They weighed only 11 tons, without their tenders and without water in the boiler. Instead of trekking to Liverpool – in the days before there was a railway – Brunel could have gone a couple of miles to the Rennie Brothers. But he did not.

While contending with his massive project and its problems, Brunel has always to deal with his domestic problems, keeping his office and staff in order (Rail 1149/2, p91):

Great Western Railway
18 Duke Street
4th July 1836

Sir,
Mr Hammond has forwarded to me a copy of his letter to you of 30th ult and your reply the latter is characterised by a degree of temper approaching to insolence – peculiarly improper after the

moderate and kind letter addressed to you by Mr Hammond.
I shall not require you services after the quarter which ended on
30th ult.

I am sir,
Your obedient servant,
I. K. Brunel

Mr Milnes

Below is a letter written by John Hammond to his Assistant Robert
Archibald. Hammond makes a cheerful dig at Mr Brunel.

Great Western Railway Office,
Maidenhead.
14 July 1837

My Dear Sir,
By all that's good you must get on faster, you must crowd in the
men everywhere and work night and day. I begin to feel queer
about our completion. I will be with you tomorrow and in the
meantime reflect how the earthwork can be forwarded.

Either today or tomorrow there will be at Kew Bridge 20 sets of
wheels and axles for you. I hope you got a good supply from
Paddn. Do you want rails, chairs or castings for wagons.

For the love of fame and our great master's name push on the
work.

Yours truly,
J. Hammond

Seen at paddington. in author's collection.

The Mather Dixon engineering company was founded in 1826 in
Liverpool to build stationary engines, but soon became involved with
locomotives. The firm went out of business in 1843, and it is possible that
it lost money building locomotives for the GWR to Brunel's impractical
specifications. The following letter (Rail 1149/2, p92) concerns the costs
of three Mather Dixon locomotives, *Premier*, *Ariel* and *Ajax*. Brunel, as
ever, does not want to pay. *Ajax* came to the GWR with a pair of 10-foot-
diameter driving wheels made of solid wrought-iron plate – as were the
leading and trailing carrying wheels. Brunel's specification caused

Mather Dixon to use this vast diameter, but Brunel says 'I never told you to make a solid plate wheel', which was of course true. These wheels were very heavy and to reduce weight elsewhere Mather Dixon skimped on the strength of other components, particularly the boiler and the valve gear. Brunel criticises the performance and reliability of the engines as if he had no responsibility in the matter. He mentions letters received, but none of this very important correspondence – the other side of the argument – has been preserved.

Great Western Railway
22 July 1836

Gentlemen,
I have to acknowledge the receipt of your reply to my letter of 25th June and am glad to find that you will undertake the manufacture of a locomotive engine. I am anxious to know, however, whether I may expect its completion within the period I mention in my letter, namely by March 1837 or what will be the earliest time you can fix. You will easily perceive how absolutely necessary it is that the time should be positively determined that I may make my arrangements accordingly. With respect to your observations regarding the peculiar construction required, I think you will find upon consideration that there is no great difficulty in complying with the conditions I have laid down.

First. With regard to the speed you will observe that a six feet wheel and a 12 inch stroke or a seven feet wheel and a 14 inch stroke gives the required proportion without the intervention of gearing – with it of course there is no difficulty and I am by no means prepared to say that even an eight feet wheel on gearing might not either of them be advantageously employed if judiciously applied.

With respect to the draught of furnace being diminished I think you will find you are mistaken – this draught will depend on the quantity of steam discharged and the pressure at which it escapes – but not upon the velocity of the piston except in so far as that velocity governs the quantity. In any given engine therefore it may certainly be the case that if the velocity of the piston be reduced to 280ft per second the draught will be seriously diminished but that will be owing to the quantity of steam discharged into the chimney being diminished. If by a differently proportioned cylinder the same quantity of steam be used and discharged which would be the case in our engines the same draught will be caused with the difference that by having the piston to travel at a less velocity we could afford to send the steam off at a higher pressure and consequently rather increase the draught. The dimensions of the boiler therefore will not of necessity be increased but I think it very likely that a larger boiler requiring a less violent fire would be advantageous on general principles. I think you will find that the increased length of the axles and diameter of the driving wheels and a trifling increase in size of cylinder will be the only sources of increased weight in the engines and at the power or force of traction I have named I think I have allowed nearly two tons excess over the weight of the engines now in use to cover these causes of increase.

I have no objection however to increase this limit to 12 tons but I do not believe that you will find it necessary and weight will be of course an objection to an engine although not so serious a one upon the Gt Western Railway as upon others – as the levels are very favourable none exceeding 5ft per mile a circumstance which may influence you in your arrangement of the engine as it causes great equality in the strain upon the engine. The width of the rails is a point I have well considered and I see no reason at present to alter my opinion. I shall feel however much obliged to you for any arrangements, particularly objections to that or any other arrangement which I have proposed.

I am, Gentlemen,
Your obt. servt.
I. K. Brunel

Mather Dixon & Co, Liverpool

To Tayleur & Co Brunel wrote (Rail 1149/2, p85):

Great Western Railway
Litchfield
August 8th 1836

Gentlemen,
After the conversation which I had on Saturday last with Mr Loom at your manufactory I write now to confirm the order which I then gave for two locomotive engines of the class firstly described in

your letter of 23rd ult namely 14 inch cylinders with 16 inch stroke and 8ft driving wheels free [sic] of traction 800lbs on a level at a speed of 30 miles per hours at the price, date of delivery and other conditions referred to in the same letter and also of two engines with the same lengths of stroke and diameter of driving wheels but of such reduced dimensions of cylinder and capacity of boiler as may be sufficient to maintain a force of traction of 500lbs at the same speed and which I understood Mr Loom to say he expected would weigh about 10 or 10½ tons and that he would endeavour to finish them at the same time or as quickly after the others as possible. I shall feel obliged by your informing me of the price of these last two including as I presume the other price does the cost of tender – and the necessary connections.

I shall also feel obliged by your letting me know as soon as you have determined upon the arrangements of the Engines and prepared the drawings.

I am, Gentlemen,
Yours Obedient Servt.
I. K. Brunel

Messrs Tayleur & Co

...and to Mather Dixon & Co (Rail 1149/2, p89):

18 Duke Street
August 31 1836
Great Western Railway

Gentlemen,
In reply to your enquiries whether I should entertain any strong objection or preference to either of the different modes of constructing a locomotive engine namely a multiplying motion [geared drive] or large diameter driving wheels or a very short stroke I should certainly prefer either of the first two to the last. As regards the adoption of a multiplying motion – I am by no means satisfied that it may not be very advantageously employed and although quite aware of the objections generally entertained against it I should be very glad to see the experiment tried and if judiciously constructed and of excellent workmanship I think a satisfactory result might fairly be anticipated. I consider driving

wheels of the diameter you mention as the alternative.

The price you mention of course includes the tender. When you have determined upon the plan of construction and prepared a general drawing I shall feel obliged by your informing me. I have nothing to add but that you will have the goodness to consider the order for one Engine to be delivered on the First of May 1837 confirmed and I should have been glad to have given the order for two which I supposed you could have done with almost the same sped as one.

I am, Gentlemen,
Your obedient servant,
I. K. Brunel.
...

Brunel, being *the* great individualist, does not realise the value of standardisation – the interchangeability of parts (Rail 1149/2, p102):

Bristol
6 September 1836
Great Western Railway

My Dear Sir,
With respect to the buffers it is immaterial to me how they are placed between the engine and the tender as I expect from the great variety in the construction that every engine must always be worked with its own particular tender which as it may be made at a later period may at the other end be adapted to the carriages as they may ultimately be determined on – At the front of the engine I shall instantly adopt as I expect to do with all the carriages high buffers in the [...] 3ft 9in will be a very good height for this – can you adapt this to your present planning?

I certainly thought that I had written to confirm the Order for the Engines which I gave verbally not being at home at present I cannot refer to the particular letter in which I thought I had done this – I am glad to find, however that you have proceeded with the plans and on my return I will write again upon the subject.

I am very much pleased though not surprised to hear that you find the difficulties attending my peculiar construction appear to diminish as you proceed: if this should gradually induce you to make a few more engines while you are about these two I should probably be able to extend the order.

I am, my dear sir,
Yours truly,
I. K. Brunel

J. Grantham Esq. Mather Dixon, Liverpool.

The Haigh Foundry Co produced two engines for Brunel with the singularly unattractive – un-Brunellian – names *Snake* and *Viper*. They had 6ft 4in driving wheels and a piston stroke of 18 inches, but to reduce the piston speed to Brunel's 280 feet per second the piston rods drove through gears to the wheels, at the ratio of 3 to 2. These engines were useless and were very considerably rebuilt. The boilers were reused on new frames, the gearing was removed and smaller-diameter cylinders were fitted, driving directly onto the crankshaft of the driving wheel. In the conventional form the engines had a long life, retiring in 1868-69. Brunel wrote to the Haigh company as follows (Rail 1149/2, p103):

Bristol
September 6th 1836

Gentlemen,
Although I had not mentioned the tender in my circular I considered that in consequence of the great variety in the construction likely to result from the nature of the specification it would be absolutely necessary that every engine had its particular tender and I also considered that the price you mentioned must have included the tender however with the explanation given in your favour of the 3rd inst I have to request that you will proceed with the work.

You have not informed me whether I am to consider the order as extended to more than one engine which I should wish to have done.

I shall be anxious to see the particular proportion and dimensions which you propose giving to the gearing as upon that will depend its success allow me to suggest at the outset great width of face and large diameter such as under ordinary circumstances might be thought excessive.

I am, Gentlemen,
Yours very truly,

I. K. Brunel

Haigh Iron Foundry Co

Later that month he wrote to Sharp Roberts & Co (Rail 1149/2, p117). In leaving the designer 'entirely free to adopt your own plans', Brunel is specifying the parameters but absolving himself of responsibility for the result.

18 Duke Street
26 September 1836

Gentlemen,
I have received your drawing of the engine you propose for our railway. With respect to the general arrangement of the engine I should have preferred larger wheels but having no decided objection to these with their present dimensions I prefer leaving you entirely free to adopt your own plans in this respect – there are a few points however upon which I should wish to be satisfied and which are not particularly shewn in your drawings. I allude to the steam passages both as regards their form and dimensions and both the supply and waste pipes and I should feel obliged by your sending me the drawing of them as quickly as possible. In the meantime however you can I presume proceed with other parts of the engine. As you may consider the order given subject to the period and place of delivery being somewhat more definitely fixed. We shall want the engine at the London end in ten months (the average of the times you mention).

I observe you propose to make only one engine – is this all that you can undertake?

I am, Gentlemen,
Your obt. servt.
I. K. Brunel

Sharp Roberts & Co, Manchester

Likewise he wrote to Tayleur & Co (Rail 1149/2, p122 and p133):

18 Duke Street
October 11th 1836

Gentlemen,
I only received yesterday your letter of the 6th the drawing arrived
the day before. I should very much prefer the arrangement of the
engine if you can make the passages of the valves and thence into
the cylinder as much as 1/9th the area of the piston at present they
are not quite 1/11th. I should also wish the diameter of all the
steam pipes to be very much enlarged. I would take the whole
apparatus from the mouth of the steam pipes in the boiler to the
valve box just as drawn and increase the dimensions by about one
half which would rather more than double the area. This can be
done without any material alteration of form except in the throttle
valve which cannot well be brought lower on account of the tubes
but this may be differently arranged perhaps in the manner I have
sketched in pencil [there is no sketch in the records] *the part of the*
pipe A branching out double was to enter on each side of he valve
– instead of above. I should moreover wish the shoulder of the
entrance into the slide valve box rounded in the manner I have
sketched in pencil at B.

You may perhaps consider these very large dimensions to the
steam passages useless but at the same time you will admit that
they cannot prejudice the action of your engine and I shall feel
obliged therefore by your adopting these alterations and shall
moreover fully trust to your skill in carrying out my views in the
points practically into effect although you may not yourself
consider them important.

If you can, by lengthening the slide or by any other arrangement
lessen the quantity of steam wasted between the slide and the
piston I think it would be worth doing it is now upwards of 1/20th
of the whole quantity used and when the dimensions are increased
it will be more than 1/16th which becomes considerable.

I shall send the drawings back by tonight's mail addressed to the
Vulcan Foundry.

I am, Gentlemen,
Your obt. Servt.,
I. K. Brunel

Messrs Tayleur & Co

Bristol
20 October 1836

Gentlemen,
Your letter of the 14th has been forwarded to me here. I should
wish very much to have an opportunity of meeting you as you
suggest and talking over the different points upon which I wrote
to you but it is impossible for me to come to the north at the present
moment & I am afraid not for the next month or six weeks. If
therefore you have anything to say with respect to any part of the
engines which ought to be immediately proceeded with so as not
to delay their completion by the period already fixed I shall feel
obliged by your writing – the consideration of other parts not so
immediately wanted may perhaps be postponed till the beginning
of December when I will come down.

With regard to the latter part of your letter I have not the means
here of referring to previous correspondence but I feel convinced
that I have written some time ago to confirm the order (upon the
terms stated by you) of two large engines and two smaller ones
with a power of traction of 500 lbs – the two first to be delivered
at a stated period the two next at the same time if possible or as
soon after as you can. On my return to Town I will refer to this
letter and send you a copy of it in case it should have miscarried.
In the meantime I hope you will proceed as rapidly as possible and
I shall be very glad to enter into the question of a further order as
soon as we have settled some of the principal features of these first
engines.

I am, Gentlemen,
Yours very truly,
I. K. Brunel

Messrs Tayleur & Co
Vulcan Foundry
Warrington

Brunel writes to Sharp Roberts again in October and November (Rail
1149/2, p141 and p143):

Exeter
26 October 1836

Gentlemen
I have examined the drawings you have sent me and the section of

your locomotive engine. I am very glad to find that you attach importance to the perfect freedom of the passage of steam – you will probably consider that it is quite unnecessary to carry this subject still further than you have done but as I am very anxious upon this point as even if carried to excess no positive injury can result. I shall feel much more satisfied if you will increase the diameter of the steam passages to five inches in the double part and 6½ inches at the single part and the passages of the throttle valve should have at least when full open an area of 30 to 35 square inches. I should wish also that the waste steam passage should be 6 inches diameter although I am aware that the through valve tube is not so large and that the nozzles as at present make contact very much but I am now about to make some experiments which if successful will enable me to leave a much freer exit for the steam and to use a larger chimney and I should wish therefore that the means be provided for making the waste steam pipe 6 inches.

With these alterations I have to request that you will immediately commence the construction of two engines to be delivered complete in London the one on 1st August and the second on 1st October 1837.

I am, Gentlemen,
Your obt. Servt.
I. K. Brunel

Messrs Sharp Roberts & Co, Manchester

18 Duke Street
Westminster
12 November 1836

Gentlemen,
I had expected in the course of this month to have paid you a visit at Manchester and to have ascertained how far you had advanced with the making of our engines and also to have entered into some arrangements with you for a further supply at the successive period alluded to in your letter of the 13th but having received no answer to my letter of 26 Oct I presume the engines then ordered are in process and I am now merely desirous to understand from you that such is the case and to know whether you will accept an order for two more to be delivered one by the middle of November 1837,

the other the first week in January 1838 at the price of £1,350 (you say from £1,350 to £1,450 in your letter of 22 Sept) with respect to the definite period which I have fixed for the deliveries and referring to your letter of the 13 ultimo in which you say that from the unsettled state of the workmen you cannot bind yourselves to a positive time but will use every exertion & pressure this to imply that of course you will not allow orders for other parties received subsequent to ours to interfere in any way and that unless prevented by some internal and unavoidable act such as those alluded to you will deliver the engines at the period fixed upon. If you are disposed to make any offer for the delivery of a larger number before the 1st January 1838 or of others after that I shall be glad to hear – in all cases and particularly as regards the present order of two engines or that for two more which I offer I assume that we have the priority over any orders from other parties not actually confirmed at the present date.

I am, Gentlemen,
Your obt. Servt.
I. K. Brunel

Messrs Sharpe Roberts & Co, Manchester

Brunel writes to locomotive manufacturers to discuss 'very important points' within locomotives that had been built to his stated specification and that have rendered them practically useless. And without seeing how they will work he is asking to increase the order – the important thing appears to be not whether they work well, but whether they can deliver them as soon as possible. Thus to Mather Dixon (Rail 1149/2, p153) he writes:

18 Duke Street
12 November 1836

My Dear Sir,
When you were in Town I spoke to you I think upon two points connected with our locomotive engines both very important but upon which nothing definitive was decided. I hope you have now had time to make up your mind to enable you to come to a decision, first as regards the price of your engines, secondly as to the number of periods of delivery of a further order beyond the two

which you have in hand for us to be delivered July and August next. I am prepared on the part of the company to increase our order to six or eight engines if we can agree upon these two points – as regards the first there is but one desideratum, as regards the latter the earliest possible delivery date and consequently a priority over all other orders received at the time or subsequently is one especial condition – probably you will agree with me that we shall arrange all this much better when I come to Liverpool which I shall do the first week in December and if you will reserve this right of priority till then I should prefer postponing the business – but at the same time as I think your proposed construction of engines will answer some of the principal objects I have in view I wish to secure an uninterrupted supply to the extent I have mentioned with the least possible delay and therefore if necessary to prevent the supply being interfered with by other orders I will enter upon the subject at once by correspondence an early reply will oblige.

Yours very truly,
I. K. Brunel

PS. I observed in your drawing of a carriage frame a section of an axle constructed with a hollow tube – as this is a mode of construction which I have always proposed to adopt I shall be glad to know if that was what you intended and what you think of it and whether it has been fairly tried.

J. Grantham, Mather Dixon & Co

Brunel is very attracted to Thomas Melling's idea of building an engine with the boiler on one rolling chassis and the cylinders and driving wheels forming another vehicle; the imaginativeness, daring and novelty of it recommends it to him (Melling was Locomotive Superintendent of the Liverpool & Manchester Railway). Another part of the following letter (Rail 1149/2, p202) shows Brunel's absolute opposition to 'headhunting'; he considers that offering an inducement – or, as he says, 'seducing' – an employee to leave an employer is positively immoral. He was to be involved by a third party – much to his alarm and disgust – in a 'headhunting' incident in 1839, during the building of his SS *Great Britain*. The wording of letters he wrote on that occasion are similar to this one.

18 Duke Street
17 April 1837

Sir,

I am glad to hear by your letter of the 15th that you have formed the plan you mentioned of separating the boiler from the engine I shall certainly have some engines made on that plan. With respect to your former letter which I received after I had written to you enquiring about your patents – any answer to it might be construed into an inducement to you to leave your present situation and I cannot do this – and although you may think it hard that you should not endeavour to better condition yet so long as you are a servant of a Company I can have no communication with you which would not be sanctioned by them.

I hope you won't think that I am acting harshly towards you or that I do not appreciate a great deal of useful information which I have obtained from you but I must not act so as to be open to the imputation however unfounded of seducing a person from the employment of the Liverpool & Manchester Railway Company and cannot therefore give you any advice how to act – you must form your own opinion and act upon it.

I am Sir,
Yours very truly,
I. K. Brunel

Mr Thomas Melling
Engine shed, Liverpool railway station.

The distance between the inside edges of the rails on Brunel's broad gauge railway was 7ft 0¼in. In the early days of planning and of ordering engines and carriages, he told locomotive carriage and wagon suppliers that the gauge was 7 feet, as in this letter to Mather Dixon (Rail 1149/2, p205). However, 7 feet from wheel flange to wheel flange across the axle would have made a tight fit on the rail and it seems likely that he was obliged to ease the rails out by that quarter of an inch to give some clearance in running.

18 Duke Street
Westminster
April 21st 1837

Gentlemen,

Are you disposed to turn your attention to the manufacture of wheels and axles for our carriages and if so will you at your earliest convenience let me have a good, detailed, drawing of the parts as you would propose to make them and the price the periods and place at which you could finish and deliver ten or fifteen sets that is twenty or thirty pair of wheels and axles – it would be desirable to have a few in the month of June and the rest in the following month or in the beginning of August at the latest – the following are the principal dimensions and conditions which I think necessary but I shall be happy to receive any observations upon them from you.

Gauge of Rails 7ft
Wheels 4ft 6in diameter wrought iron spoke, the nave to be fitted on to the axle with a very slight taper – warmed and shrank on tight with a small key to prevent twisting.
Axles of best scrap iron 3¾in diameter between the wheels, 4¼in at the nave and an outside bearing of 5in long and 2¾in diameter.

The other dimensions and your mode of construction I leave to you to suggest merely requesting that the dimensions of the parts be written on the drawing and that the estimated weight of the axle tree and other principal parts may be also written on the drawing or mentioned in the tender to prevent mistakes.

I have made a similar application to two other manufacturers who are making engines for us – but in the event of either or both of them not furnishing their proposition I shall be glad to know what larger quantity you can supply within the same period as the above.

I am, gentlemen,
Yours very truly,
I. K. Brunel

Messrs Mather Dixon

Brunel has to turn from ordering wheels and dealing with locomotive problems to dealing with the problem of a tough and possibly bad-tempered military man. Major James, of Salford, alleges (Rail 1149/2, p204) that he is offended by the sight of a decorative, Brunellian feature – the straight top of the Bath-stone parapet wall of Saltford Tunnel – which he can see from his house. Another reason, then, to purchase the old boy's house, which was in the way of the railway.

18 Duke Street,
Westminster.
April 21st 1837

Sir,

Mr Frere has forwarded to me your letter of 17th you are quite right in supposing that in the construction of the different works of this railway the Directors of the Company as well as myself will feel pleasure in attending on minor points to the specific wishes of those whose adjoining property would be in any way injured or annoyed when it does not affect the efficiency of the general plan of the rail road. In the present instance the parapet wall which you fear will be a dessight [sic] from your house forms an essential part of the ornamental front of the tunnel entrance which is designed to be in the same style as the other works in the neighbourhood and is part therefore of the general plan and an iron railing over a Gothic archway would be very inconsistent with the general plan. I will endeavour however to obviate as far as possible your objections by some other means.

I am Sir,
Yours very truly,
I. K. Brunel

Major James

Simultaneously with Melling's idea for a 'divided' engine, Mr T. E. Harrison, working for R. W. Hawthorn in Newcastle, also patented designs for such a machine. Brunel eagerly seized upon Harrison's patent and, indeed, became firm friends with the designer. He thought that Harrison had invented a new generation of really super-fast steam engines. The idea of a 'divided' engine could be said to be the pioneer of the system later used with great success in Southern Africa, and in Britain – the Garratt. As we shall see, Brunel refused to have one named after him – the glory of being the first engineer to use them would be sufficient honour for him – but he suggested that one be named after Harrison, and the entire class – for many were to be built – were to be known as 'Harrisons'. Brunel was very excited by the complex and unconventional engine. What a wonderful way to open his unique, 7-foot-gauge railway, with these startlingly new locomotives. Without waiting for trials he commissioned Hawthorns to build three locomotives to Harrison's design and, because they were totally new in concept, he admits the difficulty of estimating their cost and 'trusts to the respectability of your house' to be charged the right price.

T. E. Harrison's patent locomotive, *Thunderer*, arrived, dismantled, by canal at West Drayton in January 1838. The GWR engine shed was then at West Drayton, on a flat piece of ground on the up side of the line immediately west of the main road. Daniel Gooch took one look at the locomotive and was appalled. *Thunderer* had its boiler on a six-wheeled chassis with a tender coupled to the rear of it. The engine itself was on a separate four-wheeled carriage in front of the boiler. The four wheels were 6 feet in diameter, each pair coupled together. The two cylinders were 16in x 20in, mounted nearest to the boiler. The pistons drove connecting rods attached, one on each side, to a cog wheel, which in turn engaged a larger cog fixed around the leading axle. The ratio of the gearing was 2.7 to 1, making the driving wheels effectively just over 16 feet in diameter.

On 12 May GWR Director Mr Gibbs rode on the footplate and, driven by John Hammond, the Resident Engineer for the London Division, was taken up and down between Slough and West Drayton, a distance of 4 miles. According to Gibbs, the engine, running without any load behind it, achieved 60mph, in spite of the rails not being properly screwed down to the longitudinal sleepers. (*Birth of the Great Western*, Professor Jack Simmons, p37.) With only a weak hand brake applying wooden brake blocks to the tender's wheels, and with no means of reversing the engine whilst it was in motion, it does not seem possible that they accelerated to 60mph and then came safwly to a stand in four miles.

Brunel wrote to Hawthorn's as follows (Rail 1149/2, p253):

18 Duke Street
1 July 1837

Gentlemen,
Mr Harrison has left with me your letter of 20th ult addressed to him on the subject of the manufacture of some locomotive engines on the plan of his own patent. I have arranged with Mr Harrison the principal dimensions and he will undertake the finishing the necessary drawings and giving you directions as to the work. On the part of the Great Western Railway Company I accept your offer of making three engines one to be completed ready for delivery by the 2nd October and the other two in the course of the following ten days – with respect to the price I admit that with an

*entirely new machine it is difficult for you previously to estimate the cost with any precision and upon this point I am willing to trust to the respectability of your house it being understood that only a fair manufacturer's profit will be put upon the real cost price and that the expense of new patterns really required shall be divided amongst the three engines and if other engines are subsequently made a proportionate allowance shall be made upon them as well as for any new tools which may have been necessary in fact that patterns and tools shall not be charged as is occasionally done for pieces of machinery which are not only new **but are not likely to be required again*** [my emphasis].

I shall be most anxious that these engines should be amongst the earliest to run upon our line as well as that the workmanship and execution should be in every respect the best possible as the success of the experiment will depend much upon this and if it be successful <u>*great*</u> <u>*numbers*</u> *of similar engines will certainly be immediately required.*

I am, Gentlemen,
Your obt. servt.
I. K. Brunel

Messrs Hawthorn

Early the following year Brunel writes to Hawthorn's (Rail 1149/5, p18), refusing to pay that company's charges until it agrees to pay for all the damage done to one of the Harrison engines when its tender tank fell off the chassis while the engine was in motion.

18 Duke Street
7th December 1838

Gentlemen,
I assure you that I have not overlooked or neglected the subject of your letters of the 14th and 24 ultimo applying for a payment on account for the engines made by you – but I have been placed in a difficult position – in the first place the sums charged for these engines is so much greater than anything I had reason to expect and I must say also much greater than I think ought to be charged for them and the examination of the details of the account confirms me in this opinion besides this we have but one engine in

working condition and the accident which still renders the other useless – did in my opinion solely arise from a very careless piece of workmanship for which as a manufacturer is answerable for anything you alone must be answerable.

If the Company has to bear the expense of such an accident there is an end to all responsibility on the part of a maker the inconvenience and indirect expenses which invariably consequent upon such incidents are already sufficiently serious to the Company but the repairs of the actual damage to the engine cannot & must not fall upon any but you – if this point is agreed upon I can recommend a payment of £1,000 on account next Thursday and in the meantime I will send you details of the amount of costs with some remarks for your consideration.

I inclose Mr Gooch's Report in reply to your letter of the 14th ult, and in addition I must say that the fastenings were altogether insufficient and therefore it would not have been necessary to inquire into the question of any previous damage but none such had taken place from any unusual causes.

I am, Gentlemen,
Your obt. Servt.
I. K. Brunel.

Messrs Hawthorn & Co

In 1837 a letter (Rail 250/82, p86) was sent by Henry Booth, Company Secretary of the Liverpool & Manchester Railway, to the GWR Directors complaining that the GWR had been poaching his engine drivers and suggesting that all railways form a combination to pay the same wages all around the country. This was not sensible economics, since living conditions were different around the country, and, as Brunel points out, it would be a bad policy because it would give the men the idea that they too ought to form a combination to increase wages.

18 Duke Street,
Westminster
Sept 19th 1837

My Dear Saunders,
I am sure the Directors and you know me sufficiently to have been able to reply confidently to the letter which you have received that

neither I nor anyone acting by my directions could have been guilty of tempting men from the employment of other companies.

Our Superintendent of Engines, Mr Gooch, who has been in the North to ascertain the state of progress of our engines and to insure that proper enginemen should be ready to work them happened fortunately to return yesterday and I have had an opportunity of learning from him exactly what has been done.

Of six men that he has engaged from the neighbourhood of Liverpool and Manchester and Birmingham one only is in the employment of either of the companies and this man (John Liver I believe) had given notice of leaving long before Mr Gooch was even in my service and he came to Mr Gooch recommended by an Officer of the Liverpool and Manchester Railway.

No temptation or inducement of any sort has been held out to men in the employment of this company or the Grand Junction but on the contrary it has been plainly stated to men who have offered themselves that such proceedings would not be sanctioned connected as the enginemen on their Lines are with the manufacturers who are making our engines it is highly probable that the circumstances of good men being wanted to accompany their engines has been a subject of conversation amongst the men and that they may have been asked even to make inquiries and it is a natural consequence that the men should avail themselves of the supposed demand for their services either as an excuse if they wanted to leave or in hopes of adding to their own self-importance if they remained. This is the natural consequence of our wanting men of a class who must of course come from the neighbourhood of these railways and in some way or other and at some time have been connected with them but I repeat that neither I nor any Agent of mine to my knowledge has directly or indirectly induced any man to leave his employment in their service to enter ours.

With respect to the amount of wages to be given I have been guided by the London & Birmingham and believe it will be found necessary to give higher wages here than in the north but upon this point I will be prepared on Thursday. As Mr Booth refers to the advisability of agreeing to give the same wages on all railways I think his proposition amounts to this. I will just observe that I think it would be very improper to set such an example to the men as combination we could hardly complain if in their turn they were to 'agree' also as to a minimum and one company that might think *it necessary to secure more careful men would be precluded from doing so.*

I am Sir,
Yours very truly,
I. K. Brunel

In the next letter (Rail 1149/3, p55) Brunel refers to the Birmingham, Bristol & Thames Junction Railway (BB&TJR), which gained its Act in June 1836 for a railway from Willesden on the London & Birmingham Railway south to Kensington. The line would cross on the level at right-angles the GWR's 'Paddington Extension', the Act for which would not be obtained until July 1837. Brunel did not expect a railway company's officers to behave in an ungentlemanly way, but the 'Birmingham Company' was rude and obstructive to the GWR even before the start of construction of the Paddington Extension. Three months after the incorporation of the Paddington Extension Railway the atmosphere between Brunel and the secretary of the BB&TJR, Mr Hoskins, is acrid.

21 September 1837

My Dear Signor Angello [Mr Lamb]
I heard last night on my arrival in Town of the proposal for a conference today – but neither the Directors nor I had had the slightest notion of the subject – now as I shall hardly have time to talk over the subject with them and as they have by this time probably [...] our long correspondence, I fear they may be somewhat unprepared – however – nous verrons [we shall see] it would have been better to have let them know.

Your quotation of the fable reminds me of the practice imputed to a certain old gentleman – who had better remain nameless – who could quote the Bible to suit his purposes. Anything may be perverted. I should say that the character of the Wolf and the Lamb were used not merely symbolically of the stronger and the weaker parties in the bustle of this world but also of two parties, one of whom has the means of harassing the other. We are the Lamb, very willing to be left alone, wishing to annoy nobody. You brought an Act, we could have prevented you easily, we did not but only required non-interference from you. We could have hindered you, if not stopped you, we did not, but on the contrary have in a quite inoffensive style suffered some annoyance and never by a single act annoyed or hindered you. It is then like the Wolf that you have shown your teeth – snarled at us – would find one little thing after another as grounds of complaint. All we say is leave us alone and I think you will find us to continue as Lambs. I fancy I can see the Wolf screwing up his lips and giving a slight snarl. On this point, perhaps on turning over the leaf we may come to some other fable reversing the picture and shewing some instance of the effect of indignation of the stronger [should he have said 'weaker'?] *party when too much roasted. Come what may I shall only desire to assure you to preserve the acquaintance of a gentleman of whom under sometimes very unpleasant circumstances I have not a single word to say in complaint I only hope then individually you may be able to express yourself equally satisfied with my conduct.*

Believe me,
Yours Truly,
I. K. Brunel

W. Hoskin Esq, Thames Junction Railway Office, Austin Friars

Returning to the subject of the Harrison engines, Brunel wrote thus (Rail 1148/2) to their designer:

18 Duke Street
Feby 6th 1838

My Dear Sir,
I congratulate you upon the success which has attended the trial of your engine. I am puzzled as to the name – I am much obliged to you for the offer of naming it after me but it is quite inadmissible I do take considerable credit to myself for having at once adopted what I believe will prove a most important change in the construction and I shall be very much gratified if hereafter when the success becomes equally evident to all my name – my 'early 'patronage' as you call it is – is remembered but I have no pretence to anything beyond this and my name [on the engine] might mislead –
I should prefer a distinct class of names which if possible should in some way have reference to their peculiar character and at the same time if possible which would admit of the addition of your name in speaking of them – I should propose that the first should bear your name simply but that I think as we have others making,

& which will I hope could follow, it would be a pity to fix your name until we determine which is the best of the three and in the meantime it will be called 'Harrison's engine'.

You ought to have sent me some details – does the gearing make much noise – how does the boiler work? I am very sorry that you have no reversing motion as it will prevent my venturing upon a greater speed as I otherwise should – at all events until I have ten miles clear run will not be until before the opening of the whole [line] – I trust you have applied good brakes and then there will be plenty of steam.

I imagine there must be some screen to protect the engineman or he will be cut to pieces by the wind – have you arranged anything – and lastly let me call your attention to the appearance – we have here a splendid engine of Stephensons it would be a beautiful [sic] ornament in the most elegant drawing room and we have another of Quaker-like simplicity carried even to shabbyness but very probably as good an engine but the difference in the care bestowed by the engineman, the favour in which it is held by others and even oneself not to mention the public is striking – a plain young lady, however amiable, is apt to be neglected – now your engine is capable of being made handsome and it ought to be so.

Yours very truly,
I. K. Brunel

T. E. Harrison Esq

Daniel Gooch (1816-89) was recruited to the GWR as Locomotive Superintendent by Brunel in July 1837. A Northumbrian, he had started his life in engineering at an iron foundry in Tredegar, South Wales. Late in 1833 he moved to the Vulcan Foundry at Newton-le-Willows, then two years later he transferred to Stephenson's Newcastle factory, working in the drawing office of the most advanced locomotive works in the world. He would have seen the designing and perhaps had a share in the design of locomotives destined for Moscow and New Orleans. These were broad gauge engines, 6 feet for Russia and 5ft 6in for New Orleans. Gooch became a dedicated supporter of a gauge wider than 4ft 8in because of the extra space between the frames of such an engine, in which could be accommodated larger bearing surfaces and more easily accessible machinery. He was undoubtedly the best locomotive engineer in Britain when he took up his post on the GWR on 18 August 1837, and remained supreme in design for many years. He was the first locomotive engineer to design locomotives as a standardised kit of parts, thus reducing manufacturing and maintenance costs. He had years of locomotive design and construction experience, while Brunel had no locomotive experience at all, yet Gooch was subordinate to Brunel.

The locomotive fleet of the GWR on the opening of service, 4 July 1838 consisted of 20 engines. Daniel Gooch wrote in his 'Diaries'.

'I was not much pleased with the design of the engines ordered. They had very small boilers and very large wheels. Those made by the Vulcan Company had wheels 8ft diameter and three of them only had 12 inch diameter cylinders – two of Mather Dixon's had 10ft wheels and 14-inch diameter cylinders with very small boilers. Those made by Hawthorn were on a patent plan of Tom Harrison's having the engine and boiler on separate carriages and coupled with ball and socket steam pipes. These were immense affairs, the boilers were large........in one the cylinders coupled direct to the driving wheels which were ten feet diameter and the other had a spur and pinion gearing 3 to 1 with a six foot wheel making the wheel equal to 18ft diameter. The same plan of gearing was used in the two engines built by the Haigh Foundry. Their wheels were 6ft diameter and the gearing was 3 to 2 but the cylinders were small. I felt very uneasy about the working of these machines feeling sure they would have enough to do to drive themselves along the road.'

The locomotives listed below – with the exception of *North Star* – were so inefficient and so prone to failure, so frequently derailing and becoming damaged that the GWR gave up issuing a timetable very soon after open to Maidenhead and ran on an *ad hoc* service until December 1840 when enough of the Gooch designed 'Star' and 'Firefly' class became available.

	Arrived	Scrapped
Robert Stephenson		
North Star	11.1837	1.1871
Vulcan Foundry		
Vulcan	11.1837	4.1868 after rebuilding
Aeolus	11.1837	4.1867 after rebuilding
Bacchus	12.1837	6.1842
Apollo	1.1838	8.1868 after rebuilding

Neptune	3.1838	6.1840
Venus	9.1838	7.1870 after rebuilding

Mather Dixon

Vulcan	11.1837	4.1868 after rebuilding
Aeolus	11.1837	4.1867 after rebuilding
Bacchus	12.1837	6.1842
Apollo	1.1838	8.1868 after rebuilding
Neptune	3.1838	6.1840
Venus	9.1838	7.1870 after rebuilding

Sharp Roberts

Lion	5.1838	6.1847
Atlas	6.1838	6.1872 after rebuilding
Eagle	11.1838	12.1871 after rebuilding

Haigh Foundry

Snake	9.1838	11.1869 after rebuilding
Viper	8.1838	1.1868 after rebuilding

R. W. Hawthorn

Thunderer	3.1838	12.1839
Hurricane	10.1838	12.1839

(*The Locomotives of the Great Western Railway. Part Two. Broad Gauge.* Railway Correspondence & Travel Society)

In an August 1838 Report to his Directors, Brunel denied all responsibility for the poor to useless performance of these engines — and yet not only had he made the crippling specification he had also demanded to scrutinise the drawings for the engines and make changes as he saw fit before the work of construction took place.

In December 1838 Gooch was told to report on the condition and performance of all the engines. Very reluctantly he had to criticise Brunel's specifications and the resulting engines. This earned him a furious letter letter Brunel (nowhere to be found, unfortunately) but Brunel soon forgave him his Report. In January 1839, Gooch was made a 'Chief' – co-equal with Brunel – reporting direct the Board. But that did not prevent Brunel for several years after, lecturing Gooch, telling him –

I should guess – that which he already knows and demanding explanations of daily events in the train operating saga.

Of these the best was the *North Star*. This had been a 5ft 6in gauge engine bound for New Orleans. It was well designed and made in the Newcastle works of Robert Stephenson. It was not in any way influenced by the ideas of I. K Brunel and would have worked just as well on 4ft 8in gauge. *North Star* weighed 18 tons 4 cwt. The boiler had a diameter of 4ft. Its 167 fire tubes and the water surface of the firebox provided a total 724sq ft of heating surface with a relatively large, 13.6sq ft, firegrate to burn the coke. The boiler was designed to pressurise steam to 50 pounds per square inch and this was fed to relatively large diameter cylinders, 16in with a 16in stroke – which was rather short for the driving wheels 7ft diameter. A 16inch stroke entails an 8inch long crank on the driving axle to turn the 84-inch wheels. *North Star* had a decent amount of heating surface and firegrate and larger diameter pistons than usual and it was a successful engine in spite of the short stroke. The engine was given 16 x 18inch cylinders in 1854.

All the other 19 engines had been designed under the influence of Brunel's specifications – although none of them conformed to all the stipulations – had they done so they would never have hauled a train at all. As it was none of them were successful in their original form but several were improved by rebuilding to a more conventional design and these remained at work for many years. Six came from the Vulcan works in two batches. The first three were the best. These weighed 18¼ tons – 7¾ tons more than specification. Their boilers were 3ft 6in diameter with 147 fire tubes and these and the water surface of their fireboxes provided only 584sq ft – and that with a mere 9sq ft of firegrate to provide the heat to the water. Steam was raised to 50 psi to feed 14x16in cylinders whose pistons had to drive 8ft diameter wheels.

The next three from Vulcan were even smaller – as specifically requested by Brunel – with cylinders only 12 inches diameter by 16 inch stroke, an 3ft 3in diameter boiler and firebox giving 510 sq.ft. heating surface and a mere 8ft square firegrate. The engines from Mather Dixon came in various forms but all were smaller than the Vulcan Foundry engines. *Premier, Ariel and Ajax* had a mere 476sq ft heating. Premier had 14½ x 14½in cylinders driving 7ft diameter wheels Ariel had 14in cylinders while *Ajax* had 14 x20 inch to drive a *ten foot* diameter wheel – slow piston speed – the wheel being made a solid disc of iron. The three Sharp Roberts engines had 455sq ft of heating and the Haigh Foundry engines 51sq ft – but they drove 6ft 4in wheels through a geared up drive 3 : 2. *Thunderer* and *Hurricane* were patent engines designed by T.E

Harrison and came from the works of R.W Hawthorn. They had their boilers on a separate carriage from the cylinders and driving wheels but in spite of this had only 625 sq.ft heating. *Thunderer* had four driving wheels, 6ft 4in. diameter but these were driven through a gearing in the ratio of 27 to 10. *Hurricane* had a direct drive to 10ft diameter wheels. Brunel had occasion to 'fly' along his route at great speed on one or other of these, but they were tolerably useless on trains. *Thunderer* was quickly scrapped – but its boiler was used to drive a stationary engine. *Hurricane* was also scrapped and its boiler was used to power a goods engine called *Bacchus*, built in 1849.

The locomotives built for Joseph Locke's London & Southampton Railway in early 1838 had 13in diameter cylinders with an 18in stroke, driving a single pair of 5ft 6in wheels. The firegrate had an area of 9.3sq ft and the total heating surface within the boiler was 539sq ft. The engine's built to Brunel's specification were not much bigger than those on the standard gauge.

The GWR Directors were thoroughly disgusted at the state of Brunel's track and the engines they went to ride on the London & Birmingham, to make comparisons. The primitive method of track construction gave as rocky a ride as Brunel's track. They returned, consoled, to Paddington that theirs was not the only rough railway.

Meanwhile, just a few miles away, on the London & Southampton Railway, the Rennie Brothers' engines had been running, since the opening in May 1838, in a regular time-tabled way over the 30 miles from Nine Elms to Woking. The service had commenced a week earlier than originally planned in order to carry thousands of race goers to Woking for Epsom during Derby Week. Joseph Locke was the Engineer. His track, which shortly became the standard British track for the next 100 years, was faultless and the Rennie engines worked perfectly, covering the 30 miles at an average speed of 23mph inclusive of 7 stops.

The success of the L&SR, track and locomotives, from the first day of its week-early opening, was well documented in the newspapers and periodicals but Brunel did not recommend his Directors to ride on that line.

Brunel continued to micro-manage all civil and mechanical engineering matters on the Great Western – and there was also the large problems of constructing the PS *Great Western* and her engine but for that at least he accepted the assistance of experts – and in the midst of all his vast worries he found time to write to those few whom he greatly admired and whose friendship he valued. On 29 March 1838 news came to him that his Resident Engineer at the Monkwearmouth Dock project, Michael Lane, had been injured. The nature of the injuries is not revealed. Michael Lane had been a Foreman Bricklayer in the Thames Tunnel when Isambard was one of the three Resident Engineers employed by his father, Marc. Isambard developed a great respect and admiration for Lane's character and craftsmanship. After the death of Brunel, Lane replaced Brunel as Chief Engineer of the Great Western Railway.

I read these letters to Lane when I was working on unsorted archives at the old GWR Record Office at Portchester Road, London. Whether they ever reached the National Archive at Kew, I do not know.

18 Duke Street
29 March 1838

My Dear Lane,
The account of your accident distresses me very much – I must insist upon your having the best advice that can be procured without regard to expense – I hardly know who to wish to, to request them to see that you have everything you want. Do not trouble yourself about the works. I will think of somebody between this and tomorrow.

Yours very truly,
I. K. Brunel

Two days after writing that Brunel was aboard his brand new ship, the paddle steamer *Great Western*, en voyage for Bristol. Approaching Canvey Island a fire broke out in the engine room. Brunel attempted to go down a wooden ladder to the engine room but the ladder was burnt, the rungs gave way and he fell 18 feet to the engine room floor, injuring himself severely. In spite of being in considerable pain and great weakness he kept up his instructions to assistants on the GWR and messages of condolence to Lane at Monkwearmouth. Brunel's handwriting is the worst I have ever seen, and the weary, painful scrawl is not helped by the fact that he had a quill with a very blunt end.

18 Duke Street
2 April 1838

My Dear Lane,

You must wait some days before I can send you more directions as I am also laid up in bed from an accident and I am at present in a small public house on a little island near the mouth of the Thames where I was put on [by] those from the steam boat where the accident happened. [The letter continues illegibly.]

Yours very truly,
I. K. Brunel

When Brunel writes again to Lane he has been so ill that he has forgotten that he wrote to him on the 2nd.

18 Duke Street
13 April 1838

My Dear Lane,
In answer to your enquiries I am getting on very well – though very sore and weak from bruises. I have not a broken bone about me – and but for excessive weakness this is the first attempt at writing I being very black and blue and very sore. I should be quite well I hope in a week to be able to attend to business again. I wish I could hope you would get on as well.
I was brought home on Saturday.

Yours very truly,
I. K. Brunel

In addition to his injuries, Brunel was worried about the construction of the first section of the GWR from Paddington to the east bank of the Thames and also the success of his great experiment, the paddle steamer *Great Western*, then the largest ship in the world. She had made her maiden voyage from the mouth of the Avon to New York on 8 April 1838, taking 15 days on passage, and set out for home on 7 May.

He now writes to his dear friend Thomas Guppy (DM 1306/vii):

11 May 1838

My Dear Guppy
Thank you very much for your inquiries – I was much grieved to receive by your letter a confirmation of the report which had reached me through a friend in Paris.
I am not particularly well in body or mind – I don't get away – I am still lame in the left foot and my back is weak. I don't write

this letter without leaning back to rest and in consequence I suppose of the state of my stomach I am nervous anxious & unhappy in fact blue devilish –

An unfortunate number of things crowding upon me requiring attention & thought – all in arrears & I am quite incapable of getting through them – everything seeming to go wrong – we talk of the 30th for opening & now everybody believes it but me – I suppose I want a dose of salts –

Yours very sincerely,

I. K. Brunel

19 May 1838

My Dear Guppy

Thank you very much for your letter – I wish it had been yourself instead I should like a good skeming [sic] chat such as we have had sometimes.

What is the truth in these conflicting accounts of the GW steam ship – by this time probably you know the best information I am most anxious – 15 days at all events seems the maximum and under the circumstances it is as you say an admirable voyage – beyond all expectation good – but again why are they not back? – If she has arrived today I suppose Claxton will have sent me parcel there being no post. [The PS Great Western dropped anchor off the mouth of the Avon on 22 May after a passage of 14 days from New York.]

The GWR goes on well – but what with the circumstance of my not having seen much of it and what with my nervousness I am very frightened I can hardly say of what I am particularly anxious Hammond and the others have worked most zealously and have all my instructions but still one's own eye is the only one after all – and I dread the trial of each part of the line as it comes into operation – the engines are running today from Maidenhead to Hanwell and we had trips from Paddington up to the crossing of the Thames Junction. On Tuesday we intend running with some Directors from Hanwell to Maidenhead in hope to be open the 3rd [of June] – we still talk of 30th [of May].

I thank you very much for your advice. I wish I could follow it – and still more do I thank you for your kind offer of assistance and so sincere do I believe it that I should accept it but that on consideration time is too short the press too immediate for any remedy now – it would require more thought of method to avail myself of the assistance of a person new to those about me than to struggle on as it is – I need hardly say that the subject of a former conversation has frequently forced itself upon me but I have not allowed myself to think over it until I find myself better fitted for cool consideration –

Certainly the kindness and consideration of all around me, our Directors especially, is almost enough to relieve my mind from anxiety and that is saying much indeed but it's uphill work still to keep my spirits up – you will find this a desperate long scrawl and rather over much about self but it's a recreation – next to a pleasant chat – after many a dozen dull letters I have had to write with still a fearful heap of arrears by my side.

Yours sincerely
I. K. Brunel

Only four days before the opening of the GWR to Maidenhead, Brunel was still weak and easily tired after his fall on 31 March. He writes again to Thomas Guppy with reference to the offer Guppy made to be an Assistant.

1 June 1838

My Dear Guppy
If I don't find you I shall leave this at [...] –
I want very much to see you to ask whether there was any new obstacle (except one that I shall refer to) to an arrangement I once proposed and then felt afraid of – relating to you and I working together –
There is one great and new difficulty – I am not the man I was and apart from all gloomy considerations as far as I can drive these away – I question whether I should be able to work as I have done – This however of course makes me more anxious – now supposing this not to be an impossible objection to you – are you disposed to think of the thing – would it on your own part (if we did upon talking it over agree on the thing) be absolutely successful – to delay the thing for any long time because during the next months I must by some arrangement get my business forwards for it is in tremendous arrears – Let me hear from you then I may make up my mind and be relieved one way or the other – it is fair to tell you before you even think of it that first I must lay by a good deal at

first – that all my business is in tremendous arrears and in confusion then much method and much hard work will be required even to put things in order.

Yours truly,
I. K. Brunel

In the early morning of 4 June 1838 Brunel was at Paddington for the opening of the line to the Maidenhead station. He was ashen-faced and walking painfully with the aid of a stick. However, only seven days later, as the next letter, to Harrison, shows (Rail 1149/4, p109), he was completely recovered from his injuries and is his hyperactive, rumbustiously confident old self. In this 'hyper' mood, when writing the letter 'd' at the end of a word the upright of the letter is curled and coiled over the rest of the word like the tail of a scorpion. However, his mental agitation in the letter is considerable, as the opening lines show. He is referring to the start of a campaign by the shareholders and some of the Company's Directors to have him removed. The track was bad, the trains ran sedately and everyone was disappointed – because Brunel had promised so much for his new system of track-laying. By 20 June Mr Gibbs was writing in his diary: 'Shares have fallen to 16 and reports of all kinds have been set on foot by the advocates of the old system. Brunel's character and reputation demand our best attention at this time to the re-packing of the line, the changes which have been suggested in the [carriage] springs etc.' (*Birth of the Great Western*, Professor Jack Simmons, p39)

London terminus
13 June 1838

My Dear Sir,
With respect to the additional wheels to the engine with a tender tank. I think it the best provided it is all securely attached to the engine frames but this as well as the alternative necessary for the pumps you really must take in hand at least through Messrs Hawthorn as neither I or anybody about me have time to attend to it which must be the case if made in London and let me beg of you to expedite the work if you have any wish that your plan should have a fair trial on our line and that in spite of all my exertions anybody should not be prejudiced against them pray get it to work. A few weeks ago our Directors were willing to wait

before we ordered more engines and looked forward to having many of yours now I am pressed every day to order at once for the next two years supply. This is very annoying to me but must be still more so to you and yet I have no answer to give but cannot run the engine to do any work even if we had Maudslay's gearing neither the tank nor the pumps would allow us. And these you must take in hand immediately. As to our using a tender I don't exactly see how as we have no tender to spare and are short of them as it is.

Pray let me hear that you are getting on with them.

Yours very truly,
I. K. Brunel

T. E. Harrison Esq, Sunderland

In another letter to Guppy (DM 1306/vii), he writes:

12 July 1838

My Dear Guppy
A splendid storm is brewing and although we have no umbrella or shelter and must weather it out one is curious to know beforehand whether it will be snow hail or rain or all three – and thunder and lightning to boot – am certain [...] is going on to do neither more nor less than to condemn all my plans adopted in the GWR and to dispense with the necessity of giving me any further trouble –

I need hardly say that Liverpool is the gun whence all this shot principally comes – our friend Parsons – Sharp and some others of their class are most active – now I want to learn all I can of what they have to say – then as to the engineering opinions – will you pick up what you can of the arguments made opinions given – and names as much as possible – I understand this is no joke – but a serious attack our Directors certainly look upon it much nay almost as 'une affaire finie'.

I am by no means disposed to treat it lightly though a good attack always warms my blood and raises my spirits –

Yours sincerely
I. K. Brunel

Below his signature Brunel writes: 'There are two letters here one from truly a lady's hand and one note in a clerk's hand – what shall be done?'

The next letter (DM 1306/vii) refers to the half-yearly meeting of the shareholders, to take place on 15 August. This developed into the 'splendid storm' Brunel has just mentioned, as the arguments for and against Brunel's railway were aired.

31 July 1838

My Dear Guppy
When I received yours this morning I immediately determined to join the party but I am nailed for Thursday and Friday – I fully hope however to be at Liverpool on Saturday morning and shall try hard to persuade you to cross again –
  Now the points are – do the carriages run smoother and with less noise – it is a continuous bearing and exactly what is its construction – and what is the packing –
  Does it not jump or creep under the wheel [there is a simple sketch here of a half-circle resting on a horizontal line]? *(If it's not held down I'm sure it must.)*
  The Hanwell embankment has been particularly quiet – it was a false alarm – no foundation whatever –
  We had a smash on Sunday night – a return engine and train (no passengers) ran into some earth wagons – the engine (North Star) jumped off 6ft from the line _hard_ _against_ *the other line into which we lifted her – in spite of long axles the crank axle is not strained* _in the_ _slightest_ *and the others only very slightly – but for the feed pipes being broken she could have worked home.*

Yours very truly
I. K. Brunel

Returning to the matter of the 'Harrison' engines, a year earlier Brunel had written:

18 Duke Street,
Westminster
July 31 1837

My Dear Sir,
It would be most desirable that you should procure enginemen one for each engine who will be identified with the new plans and take an interest in their success. I shall feel very much obliged to you therefore to make what arrangements you find necessary for that

purpose.

The wages I propose to give are 36/- a week when they first come on trial and 40/- as soon as they prove themselves competent to the work with premiums and rewards for good repairs and performance of their engines which may amount to 5/- or 6/- more.

Since I saw you I have been travelling on the Grand Junction and on the London & Birmingham railways – the annoyance of ashes is most distressing and <u>must</u> *be got over – the first step towards this will certainly be much larger chimneys with less violent draft [sic].*

Pray turn your attention to it.

Yours very truly,
I. K. Brunel

T. E. Harrison Esq

As we have seen, Harrison's engines proved to be a great disappointment to Brunel – and a lot of trouble for Gooch (Rail 1149/2):

18 Duke Street,
Westminster.
September 3rd 1838

My Dear Sir,
Your engine here so far from being in work does not, I am sorry to say, appear much nearer completion than it was – we have seen nothing of the gearing wheels yet.

There does not seem to me to be any arrangement for the coke – what are you going to do about this – something of course must be done. I am very anxious to see you as the engines sadly want a master – some-one who is responsible or interested for their success.

Yours very truly,
I. K. Brunel

In reply to your enquiries the road is running really very fairly. We go regularly now at 30 to 35 miles per hour I think the line smoother than any other I have been on [he had not sampled the London & Southampton] *our traffic is very large and our trains heavy. We took down 400 Rifles and brought back 400 Grenadiers, arms and all – could not be much under 90 tons last week at about 32 miles an hour and you could stand up in a carriage without holding the whole way.*

Yours very truly,
I. K. Brunel

T. E Harrison Esq, Newcastle.

Brunel had become Engineer to the Monkwearmouth Dock, Sunderland, early in 1832, but once he became Engineer for the Great Western the following year, having responsibility for such a far-away place became an increasingly onerous duty. He therefore appointed his great friend from Thames Tunnel days, Michael Lane, as his Resident Engineer. Even so, the Dock responsibility became an ever greater worry as the worries of the Great Western – both railway and ship – developed. He also wanted to have the great talents of Michael Lane at his command on the GWR. Here Brunel writes to Tom Harrison asking for help (Rail 1148/2):

18 Duke Street
September 19th 1838

My Dear Sir,
It would be a great relief to me to see the Sunderland Docks in the hands of some other person provided it could be done without prejudice to the Company and with the prospect of the work being fairly handled
When I shall have left them – both of these objects will be attained by your having the goodness to attend to the work and I shall really feel very much obliged to you for doing so. It will be more satisfactory to the Directors to have advice within reach and I have found that distance gives rise to many disagreeable circumstances which have induced me for some time to wish to resign the Works.
I have written to Lane to put himself in communication with you freely on any point – and he will remain as long as may be absolutely necessary but I should very much wish him to return.
I was about to write to the Directors on the subject of the care requisite in working the gates particularly large ones and in which I rather think they have run serious risks already. Will you turn your attention to it and speak to Lane.
I am very much obliged to you for your earlier letter.

Yours very truly,
I. K. Brunel

T. E. Harrison Esq

Harrison's *Thunderer* was delivered to the GWR at West Drayton in January 1838, and *Hurricane* in October, as described below (Rail 1148/2). Both were taken out of service in December 1839.

October 25th 1838

My Dear Sir,
You will be glad to hear that we are not likely to have any difficulty in raising the steam of the 'Hurricane' and I presume therefore with the 'Thunderer' whose boiler we used. I applied my nozzle to the blast pipe and we ran steadily at 45 miles an hour with a light train certainly as the steam was blowing off plentifully the whole way – there is still room for some improvement with blast pipes and I think it will do famously.

The engine wanted power however and I have not yet ascertained the cause – with that train (two 6-wheel and two 4-wheel and a truck) we ought to have gone more than 45 mph. The 'Thunderer' will be out in a few days.

Yours very faithfully,
I. K. Brunel

T. E. Harrison Esq

Following the great success of the transatlantic wooden paddle steamer PS *Great Western*, Brunel and Guppy were working on designs for the engines and hull of what was to be the largest ship in the world – an iron-hulled paddle steamer to add to the fleet of the Great Western Steamship Company. It was to be called the *Great Britain*. Early in October the *Rainbow*, a small iron steamship propelled by a very primitive Archimedean screw propeller, arrived in Bristol. Guppy informed Brunel, who at once realised the possibilities of a screw propeller – although not one shaped like a horizontal earth auger. Brunel was at once seized with the possibilities of this form of propulsion.

9 October 1838

My Dear Guppy,
I will certainly try and find somebody to go by the Rainbow and have no doubt that Lean manage it – the valves of the Wilberforce are not so easily examined as any person competent to examine them must be a manufacturer and therefore most likely prejudiced.

I am – I confess – even if I saw them working perfectly well I should strongly recommend an old firm – we know how they work and we have the benefit of all past experience in them – there is but little room for improvement and supposing the new ones to work perfectly the gain can be but small while in our case any risk is serious.

I send you a paper once given to me by Mr Gibbs – you will learn nothing from it – others may and I have therefore written to Mr Gibbs for the name of the author and permission to use it – tell them it is private – to show to anybody you like. [sic]
Clifton Bridge shall progress.
Yours truly

Meanwhile problems persist with the 'Harrison' engines (Rail 1148/2):

18 Duke Street,
Westminster.
12 November 1838

Dear Sir,
I have ordered the wheels to be got ready to be sent down to Newcastle but I do not understand how any part of the damaged one can be used again.

The spokes being cast into the nave and if not used again why send them down I do not understand either the object of dispensing with the flinches particularly just after the occurrence of an accident in which the utility of flinches to the driving wheels was so evident – but for them the engine would have left the line entirely and much mischief might have been the consequence. The insides of the tires do not appear to have been recessed to receive the bent ends of the spokes and consequently that would, I think, very soon have got loose.

As regards the cost of the new wheels they must be ordered immediately whoever is to pay for them to prevent delay with Messrs Losh if they don't receive the order immediately from

Messrs Hawthorn they may consider it as received from the Company but if ever there was a case where the repairs of the damage from an accident clearly falls upon the manufacturers this is the case and I certainly consider Messrs Hawthorn responsible for all the consequences. The accident has arisen solely and entirely from the dropping of the tank and after examining the mode in which it had been attached immediately after the accident I found the fastenings had been so slight so defective in materials and altogether so shamefully unworkmanlike that I am only astonished that the tank has stopped on that long.

I have written to Messrs Hawthorn to this effect.

I have had the Thunderer out several times but as yet she does not do so well as the Hurricane – no want of steam however.

Yours very truly,

I. K. Brunel

T. E. Harrison Esq, Sunderland

Mather Dixon of Liverpool agreed to build six locomotives to Brunel's specification. After all the urgings to hasten to build, Brunel now starts to complain about prices (Rail 1149/5, pp10, 35, 40 and 47):

18 Duke Street
20th November 1838

Gentlemen,

Your account for three locomotives engines and two tenders lately forwarded to the Directors of this Company has been referred to me. I can hardly express my astonishment I feel at the amount of charge for these engines and I am even more surprised at the discrepancy between this charge and the limit originally fixed. I trust there has been some mistake.

In your letter of December 10th 1836 you stated that you find it very difficult to make any accurate calculation but as a safe limit you fix £1,850 and so late as March 16th 1838 you confirm this by stating that as you expect the four last engines will be more expensive than the first two, you charge the two first at the maximum but promise that if upon the whole six any reduction can be made the Company shall receive the benefit of it. I think upon a little consideration you will feel that it would be quite contrary to the terms upon which the engines were ordered to make any charge beyond the £1,850 as regards the amount itself although I hold it unnecessary to go into it I must say that it is incomprehensible to me, it is far beyond anything we have paid or been charged for engines of greater power and more effective and I should think more costly in their construction.

I shall be anxious to hear from you immediately on the subject.

I am, Gentlemen,
Yours very faithfully,
I. K. Brunel

Messrs Mather Dixon & Co

Paddington
26 December 1838

Dear Sir,
I wrote to you from Bristol some time ago not having received any reply the letter I presume must have miscarried in some way – the purport of it was to the effect that I did not know of any circumstances such as you referred to of changes & alterations ordered by me which could account for the increased charge made by you for the engines and wishing to have what you referred to and what were the specific alterations and the expenses attending them.

You are aware I suppose that there are no men here to put together the last Engines sent by you and that they lie here in pieces – something must immediately be done in them.

I am My Dear Sir,
Yours very truly,
I. K. Brunel

J. Grantham Esq, Mather Dixon & Co

18 Duke Street
January 1st 1839

Dear Sir,
I have this morning received yours of 29th. I am most anxious I can assure you to bring this matter relating to the cost of the last engines to a satisfactory conclusion but I think this is very unlikely

while we differ upon some of the preliminaries which whether they affect the question much or little are point upon which I feel bound in justice to myself to clear up before we proceed any further.

As to original construction of the engine proposed by you and described in your letter of yesterday I agree also as to the subsequent proposal on your part to increase the stroke of the cylinder and my reply consenting provided the wheel was increased but the 10ft wheel was not then thought of because the increase of stroke referred to by you in your letter of July 8th 1837 was only to 16 inches and in my reply of the 27th July 1837 to your letter referring to a drawing which by some mistake I had not received I remarked that I was very anxious to see the drawing as I observed by your letter that you had gone **boldly to 10ft instead of 9ft as we had talked of.** The subject of the 10ft wheel was then discussed and no particular objections that I can recollect were urged on either side I think you had not then arrived at the conclusion that inside framing would be necessary indeed the 10ft wheel was never mentioned by me till after I had received this letter of yours of the 26th July.

You must not therefore allow such an impression to operate in your mind – If you can refer to our correspondence you will find it exactly as I have stated, my view of the matter is this that in the course of manufacture of the engine changes were proposed by one party and the other and adopted and consequently so far upon my responsibility which I have no desire whatever to shake off which involved larger wheels and outside frames upon these two points therefore might arise a question whether the change having been made with my knowledge and sanction the Company should bear the whole or part of the increased cost if that is the view you are prepared to take of it I will enter upon the matter and give the Directors my opinion of what it is fair for them to do but if the 10ft wheel and the consequences which you say arises from its adoption are to be considered by you as **ordered by me** I must refer you simply to our correspondence – whence the contrary would appear and leave you to address the Board direct upon the subject as I decline most decidedly to sign the accounts in their present state.

I am, Dear Sir,
Yours truly,
I. K. Brunel

J. Grantham Esq, Mather Dixon & Co

18 Duke Street
12 January 1839

My Dear Sir,
You will have received advice from the City Office of a further
payment of £2,000 on account which has been made to you and
which closes the account for various articles supplied by you
independent of the Locomotives and leaves a small balance only
upon the two first engines or to any payment on account of other
engines which may be delivered by you there is a point to be
determined and which it is more important to your credit and to
our interest that it should be determined satisfactorily than even
the price of the engines and that is their efficiency. The two first
engines the 'Premier' and the 'Ariel' never worked well they are
neither creditable to you or to us they never acquire speed and are
not to be depended upon and their deficiency appears to arise from
radical defect in their construction & which have [sic] frequently
been complained of by me.
The valve gear and the construction of the boiler by which the
depth of water over the firebox is too limited appear the most
defective parts. I had hoped that these defects which were
discovered at the outset and of which your Superintendent
Kearsley has always been fully aware would have been remedied
on the other engines but from a close examination of these which
I have made since I wrote to you I am sorry to find that exactly the
same objections exist and that consequently the same result may
be expected under these circumstances after having suffered so
much inconvenience from the repeated failures of the two first we
must be more cautious in receiving others and I must caution you
that we cannot in any way accept them or render the Company
responsible for them until I have been satisfied that they do and
can continue to perform efficiently the work for which they are
intended.
I confess to you that I do not think this can be attained without
a complete alteration of the valve gear and at least the addition of
a large dome over the firebox which might perhaps enable us to
work the boiler much better without priming* and the same
alterations are required to the two first**. Mr Gooch has been
directed to afford every assistance which our small establishment
enables him to give without interfering with our own work to your
men it being clearly understood that it is merely assistance and that

it shall in no way affect the question of our right to refuse the engines if they should not be effective engines but I sincerely hope that there may never be any occasion to exercise such a right and as the most likely course to prevent such necessity and to save you unnecessary expense I strongly advise you to come to Town and satisfy yourself what is best to be done to the engines and to have it done at your own manufactory.

I am, My Dear Sir,
Yours very truly,
I. K. Brunel

J. Grantham Esq, Messrs Mather Dixon & Co

The locomotive *Ajax* was built by Mather Dixon and was delivered on 12 December 1838. It had 10-foot-diameter, solid-plate driving wheels driven by 14in x 20in cylinders. Here (Rail 1008/35, folio 20) Brunel is very pleased with its work after four months on the line – it was scrapped 14 months after Brunel wrote this letter.

18 Duke Street,
Westminster.
23 April 1839

Gentlemen,
Within the last 10 days I have had several opportunities of examining the working of the Ajax – all the gearing of the engine appears to me to work very smoothly indicating sufficient strength and good workmanship. There is no priming & plentyfull [sic] supply of steam with a train consisting of three railway carriages three loaded carriage trucks & a horse box – and average speed of 30 miles per hour was maintained exclusive of stoppages and it

---

* 'Priming' occurs when fiercely foaming boiling water gets into the steam pipe to the engine's cylinders. Water in an enclosed cylinder will inevitably cause destruction. A tall dome enables the steam-collecting pipe to be placed far enough above the water level to prevent carry-over of water.

** Brunel has not referred to *Ajax* but he must be thinking of that engine when suggesting these improvements because he then refers to 'the two first', ie *Premier* and *Ariel*.

appears to me that when the engine was better known &
understood by the engineer that the performance would be
improved as in that experiment there was an excess of steam but
the engine appeared throttled – During the high gales of last week
this engine has been much more delayed than the others but the
comparison has been made only with the two Stars, the Atlas &
Lion engines of greater power – and which have been longer
running – to what extent this delay is to be attributed to want of
power or to increased resistance from the surfaces exposed I am
not yet prepared to say but from the performance of the engine in
fair weather I think that in power and speed it will be about on a
par with the Vulcan – large engine while the workmanship is very
superior and the consumption of coke singularly small.

There are some trifling alterations required in unimportant parts
of the engine but which can be better done when it is thrown off
work for a day or two, at present it is necessarily in constant use.

I am, Gentlemen,
Your obedient servant,
I. K. Brunel

Brunel considered himself to be the highest authority on the GWR –
saving only the over-arching authority of the Board of Directors. Even
after Gooch had been made 'Chief Engineer', Brunel still exerted
authority over him (Rail 1149/5, p191):

18 Duke Street,
Westminster.
18 July 1839

My Dear Sir,
I want to know what engines ran with the different trains on
Sunday last and what engines were in working condition my
enquiry has reference to the Aeolus having taken the 9 o'clock train
which is always a heavy one. I am going by the 8 o'clock train this
evening and should wish to find your answer left with Reeve for
me when I come.

Yours very truly,
I. K. Brunel

D. Gooch Esq

The *Evening Star* was the third of Gooch's 'Star' class engine to be built at the works of Robert Stephenson & Co for the GWR. It arrived at West Drayton engine shed in July 1839 and ceased work in June 1871 (RCTS: *Locomotives of the GWR*, Part 2). Brunel wrote to the GWR Directors as follows (Rail 1008/35 folio 48):

18 Duke Street,
Westminster
5th Sept 1839

Great Western Railway

Gentlemen,
In consequence of the unfavourable results of the working of the
Evening Star engine last received from Messrs Stephenson I have
examined the steam passages which in Mr Gooch's opinion were
of insufficient dimensions and were probably the cause or one of
the causes of the defective working of the engine.
The dimensions of these passages, the eduction from the
cylinders, are very different from those in the North Star and in my
opinion the contraction is sufficient to cause a considerable loss of
power and to prevent the engine ever being so effective as the
North Star and I consider that the terms of the contract are not
complied with and consequently I cannot recommend that the
engine should be received until such alterations be made as shall
remedy the defects referred to.
I am sorry to say that I believe the next engine now on its way
[Dog Star, which arrived in September 1839] *is exactly similar and*
consequently that the same objections will exist to its being received.

I am, Gentlemen,
Your Obedient Servant,
I. K. Brunel

The Directors of The Great Western Railway

To Gooch he wrote (Rail 1149/5, p314):

18 Duke Street
11 January 1840

My Dear Sir
The Dog Star driving wheel is gone – it is barely capable of moving and quite unfit for use with a train and the North Star is going –
Have you and [...] any new ones – or what do you propose to do – you must provide for them <u>*immediately*</u> *– We are today as badly off for engines as we have ever been.*

The new tender alarms me very much it is much too weak and is twisting – at first I supposed it bad workmanship but on examining it I observed a radical defect in the construction – the whole weight is upon the inside frame without any transverse support to the underframe except at the two ends.

The necessary consequence is thus [a sketch is included] and horizontally this.

This must be remedied immediately I was not at all aware of their construction I mean I had not looked into it or I should certainly objected to it. You should try and let me know better where to write to you.

Yours very truly,
I. K. Brunel

D. Gooch Esq

Brunel is walking through Stothert's works in Bath where a locomotive is being built for the GWR. He sees a great crack in one of the locomotive's cylinders and orders it smashed before his eyes (Rail 1149/6, p127):

Bristol
Sept. 24 1840

Gentlemen,
Passing through your shops on Wednesday last I happened quite accidentally to observe that one of the cylinders then fixed in the new engine had a large flaw or defect in it and upon enquiring of a workman who stated himself to be the Foreman of the job I was told that it was proposed to patch it – indeed such must have been the intention or the cylinder would not have been in place.

The flaw was so large that it could not escape attention of the most careless observer it was such as to render the cylinder perfectly useless. I do not believe that a workman would have *thought of using it in the most contemptible worst managed shop in England except with an avowedly fraudulent intention and yet I find such a thing in an engine in which you profess to put the perfection of workmanship and materials and upon the success of which (as being your **second** and which I consider a much fairer criterion than a first) so much of the character of your House depends – you cannot yourselves deny that I have no alternative but to suppose either your Foreman or those called Foremen are utterly neglectful of their duties that they actually do not inspect the work and never saw the cylinder or that they could succeed in defrauding the Company and concealing such work. In either case your workmen are spoilt, they have learnt that they may scamp their work and it will be some time before this most mischievous effect is remedied.*

All confidence on my part is completely destroyed – more than this I must believe that the workmen who found they might proceed to fix such a piece of work will as a matter of course do many worse things in those parts less exposed to view.

I have felt with the Directors every desire to encourage your establishment but I shall neglect my duty to the Company if I did not now advise them to withdraw the order last given or at least to attach such conditions to it as will secure them, as far as is possible, against loss by the consequence of bad workmanship. I stated to your Foreman that I should require the defective cylinder to be broken in my presence as a security against its being used again. My object is principally for your advantage to shew the men that such work will not be allowed.

I am, Gentleman,
Your obt. Servt.,
I. K. Brunel

In the next letter, to the GWR Directors (Rail 1149/7, p49), Brunel pleads for Driver James Hurst. Hurst came from the Liverpool & Manchester Railway where he had allowed a young Daniel Gooch to ride on his engine, and was invited by Gooch to accompany the locomotive *Premier* by sea from Liverpool to London and to be the GWR's first engine driver. Hurst got into several scrapes with other members of staff but Gooch always got him off the charge and Hurst felt untouchable. In this instance the regular guard for his train was missing and Jim wouldn't go without him. In those days, when the only brakes on a passenger train were the tender handbrake and the guard's handbrake, it was essential to have a guard who knew the route intimately so that he could be of assistance to the driver in stopping the train at stations, according to the gradient. Moreover, on the Cheltenham line there were the two Sapperton Tunnels to go through, where the gradient changes from steeply up to even more steeply down for many miles. The replacement guard was not considered experienced enough by Driver Hurst and he refused to go with him.

18 Duke Street
18th June 1842

Gentlemen,

I have the satisfaction of submitting to you the names of sixteen enginemen who have conducted themselves well in every respect during the last 12 months and upon whom no fines have been inflicted by you during the whole period – indeed, with one exception there has not even been a complaint and in this case the man was reprimanded.

In addition to the sixteen to whom according to the Rule Book laid down by you the premiums of £10 becomes due I have strongly to urge upon your favourable consideration the case of James Hurst.

This man is an excellent servant to the company, useful and trustworthy in a very high degree but somewhat tough in his character – he holds a responsible situation as the Head Engineman in the Cheltenham branch and as such has conducted himself well – last year he earned and received the premium of £10, he had almost done so this year when on 29th December he was fined 10/- for refusing to take the train from Swindon [to Cheltenham] if Burton the sub-Inspector was sent in charge instead of a regular guard – I really believe the man considered Burton inefficient & I think if under the peculiar circumstances of the case he were strongly admonished but the premium allowed that a good servant would be encouraged and no bad precedent established as there are few men who have the same claims as Jas. Hurst.

I am, Gentlemen,
Your obt. Servt.
I. K. Brunel

To the Directors of the Great Western Railway

7: CIVIL ENGINEERING

'I fear we are every day in greater difficulties'

Hugh McIntosh (1768-1840) is believed to have started his working life as a navvy, digging canals. In 1803-07 his men excavated the ground to make the East India Dock in London, and so efficiently that he was awarded seven more contracts during the development of London's docklands. By 1830 Hugh had his son David, seven years older than Brunel, as his partner and they were running a highly efficient national civil engineering business, highly respected by the engineers of the day. By the time Hugh and David McIntosh contracted to work for Brunel, in 1836, they were constructing major railway projects, viaducts and earthworks from the south to the north of England with a value of not less than £1,175,150.

In 1836 Brunel was a novice in civil engineering but this did not affect his attitude towards the McIntoshes. Beneath the overt courtesy was a class consciousness – even the greatest, the most efficient contractor with many great achievements to his credit was a mere servant, an employee, under the direction of an ambitious young man out to achieve glory for himself. That I have arrived at such an opinion is the result of years of 'living' with I. K. Brunel – I do not get this feeling when reading Robert Stephenson or Joseph Locke. The firm of Hugh & David McIntosh worked with all the great engineers over a period of 40 years without having to take an argument to law – until they came up against Brunel.

The father and son partnership took on five contracts with Brunel during 1836-37. Contract 9L consisted of building the line from Acton to the Hanwell Viaduct and was taken up by Hugh McIntosh alone. David McIntosh took on Contract 3L, earthworks from the western end of the Hanwell Viaduct to Southall. In the eyes of the law they were acting as separate individuals with entirely separate contracts. Mr Stevens, the GWR Solicitor, warned Brunel against his peculiar course but nothing would dissuade him from continuing. On 26 May 1840 Hugh McIntosh asked for his surety bond to be returned, but Brunel said that his Directors had minuted that no moneys were to be released. In 1842 McIntosh sued the GWR for the money Brunel was withholding and the case was dragged over stone wall after stone wall until 1865, when the

Vice Chancellor of England, Sir John Stuart, found in favour of McIntosh; indeed, Sir John said that if the GWR did not pay up instantly it would be committing a fraud on the McIntosh estate. The GWR was ordered to pay £125,000 – Brunel's legacy to the Company he loved – a great loss that made the Company's financial situation very considerably worse when, a few months later, the British banking system collapsed, leaving the GWR all but bankrupt.

It is interesting to see the 'Covered Way' mentioned in this letter to Hugh McIntosh (Rail 1149/2, p192). This would have been a roofed-over cutting somewhere near Acton to appease the delicate sensibilities of a landowner, but Brunel managed to charm the latter otherwise and the 'cut and cover' tunnel was not made.

18 Duke Street
18 March 1837

Sir,
In reply to your inquiry I send you a list of the Bridges which as far as I can at present determine will be required on Contract 9L.

Bridge over Road No 27 Hanwell
Mr Turner's Accommodation in field No 35
Mr Wood's ditto No 34
Parish road ditto No 37
Ditto Skew ditto No 38
Mr Woods ditto near East end of field No 47
Covered Way
Bridge for road No 2A

Mr Archibald [John Hammond's assistant] *has the various drawings for these bridges and the Covered Way and if it will be any accommodation to you will have the tracings or copies made for you.*

With respect to the cross sections of the cuttings and embankments I have directed that the slopes of the former should be one and a half to one and carried only six inches below the line of the rails – in gravel – in other respects I have no observation to make upon the sections as now executing.

I take this opportunity of reminding you that we are bound to fence Mr Wood's property before proceeding with any of the work and to request that this may be immediately attended to unless Mr Wood gives you written indemnity.

I am, Sir,
Your obt. Servt.
I. K. Brunel.

H. McIntosh Esq.

He wrote the following (Rail 1149/5, p5) to David McIntosh:

18 Duke Street
5 March 1838

Dear Sir,
Since writing the enclosure I have received the confirmation of a
report which had reached me of one of your bridges (Woods East)
being nearly 18 inches out of line with three other bridges close by
there is no alternative the error is far too great to be remedied by
anything short of rebuilding and not an hour must be lost if every
expedition be used I will assist by allowing the wing walls to
remain and by preparing a design to enable you to do this – but
this is entirely conditional upon every means being adopted to
expedite the work on one side it will be merely adding brickwork
which can be done at once.

Yours very truly,
I. K. Brunel

PS. I leave Town this evening and shall be glad to have a few lines
from you to satisfy me that you will do your best.
IKB

David McIntosh Esq

Brunel became personally involved in arguments with Morton Peto's and
David McIntosh's Foremen – maybe with others too, if the letters were
to come to light. He would go to the works and attempt to give orders to
the Foreman who – perhaps because of Brunel's approach, but certainly
because the Foreman was not Brunel's employee – would offer some
resistance. This would be 'quite inadmissible' in Brunel's view and a feud
would develop between, say, a Foreman of Carpenters and the Engineer
of the Great Western Railway. Brunel would become indignant and
would write to the contractor criticising his choice of Foreman; at least
once, Brunel ordered Morton Peto to sack one of his Foremen.

18 Duke Street
17 March 1838

Dear Sir,
I believe the enclosed to be a true and unexaggerated account of
what took place. Watson's obstinacy or desire to embroil has for
some time been a source of great annoyance and it seems it dictates
more than ever as the work is so near to completion I have no wish
to inconvenience you by requiring a change of men but you must
endeavour to insure a change of conduct.
   I was at Southall late on Saturday and not finding Watson I
stopped your men from renewing the plates at the west end of the
embankment as I wish you to carry some ballast over the canal
bridge and I shall feel obliged by your giving directions that this
may be commenced on Monday morning and pushed on there is
but a short distance to ballast and it should not be the work of a
few days.

I am, Dear Sir,
Yours very truly,
I. K. Brunel

Mr D. McIntosh

Brunel abused frustrated contractors, men in demand, men with full
order books, who did not need to work for him. Once abused they steered
clear in future. William McKenzie did no work for Brunel and Thomas
Brassey only one small job. Second-rate contractors, men just starting
out, men with half empty order books, they took the risk of signing up
with Brunel. And it was a risk. A Brunellian contract made him the sole
arbitrator in any dispute that might arise within the contract.
   Employing second-rate contractors retarded the construction of the
railway and caused Brunel and the GWR Company a lot of misery. If he
had treated first-class contractors with more respect he would have
attracted tenders from even more of the first-class companies and thus
got the work done faster. It took months to find a contractor for Box
Tunnel.
   William Ranger was one of the several small or second-rate contractors
who took on most of the construction of the Paddington-Bristol route for
Brunel. The 'Acorn Bridge' referred to in the following letter (Rail
1149/2, p227) is a twin-arch bridge a mile or two west of Shrivenham,

which carried the railway over the Wilts & Berks Canal and the Swindon-Oxford road.
The Acorn bridge is the brick, twin arch over the A420 west of Shrivenham. When built the easternmost arch spanned the Wilts & Berks canal.

18 Duke Street
3rd June 1837

Dear Sir,
It was with great astonishment and regret that I observed when last at the Acorn Bridge that nothing was being done towards the long delayed erection of the steam engine. I cannot for one moment suppose that anybody would pretend to get the excavation for this bridge without some means of pumping and I see no preparations for any other means than that of an engine and there appears as regards this some cause of delay which is not communicated to me and unless I have immediately a clear and satisfactory explanation of all the present circumstances of your future plans and unless I can be satisfied that these plans are not only efficient but will immediately be carried into execution I shall wait no longer but without delay take all those steps which I consider necessary to regain a portion of the time which has been negligently wasted and proceed with the work in such a manner as I may find necessary. I regret being driven to this decision but the monumental dilatoriness of your proceedings and latterly by the apparent abandonment of all attempts to proceed leaves me no alternative. I shall feel obliged by an immediate reply.

I am, Dear Sir,
Yours very truly,
I. K. Brunel

Wm Ranger, Esq

Three days later (Rail 1149/2, p231)...

18 Duke Street
Tuesday June 6th 1837

Dear Sir,
I returned from Bristol this morning and found your reply to my
letter of 3rd.
I shall be glad to find that the arrangements which you propose
and which ought to have been made some months ago are carried
into effect immediately and I trust that the forbearance I have
shewn up to the present time will not lead you to suppose that I
shall refrain from acting most decidedly if you do not proceed
vigorously in future – as to the other part of your letter I shall not
remark on it further [Brunel then goes on the remark on it in some
detail] *than to say that even if you had mailed a day or a week for*
instructions as to the depth to which the foundations were to be
carried it would be ridiculous to allude to it after the weeks and
months during which the work has stood still without any cause
but I can easily shew you or remind you that not an hours delay
has been caused [sic].
You further observe that you 'regret that you are not permitted
to explain personally to me'. This is quite unintelligible – you have
not yet asked to see me **once** *that I have not made an appointment*
my porters book you your own notes will shew that I have seen
you oftener than any other contractor on the line I have been and
always shall be desirous of communicating personally with you
whenever you wish it and I shall be happy to see you any day this
week at almost any time you may appoint.

I am, My Dear Sir,
Yours very truly,
I. K. Brunel

Wm. Ranger Esq

Ranger was a poor manager of his business and his backers had small
capital means. Brunel had to attempt to keep Ranger at work by
recommending the GWR Directors to lend him money against the
collateral of his working equipment, but eventually Brunel was forced to
dismiss Ranger, and Hugh and David McIntosh took over his work.
Ranger sued the GWR for non-payment and lost because he had, as the
learned judge pointed out to him, signed a contract giving Brunel
absolute power over him. Ranger's creditors forced him to appeal and
appeal again, but he finally gave up the unequal struggle in 1859.

However, back in 1837 Ranger was making every effort to cooperate.

Brunel wrote the following to William Singer Jaques, a member of the GWR's Bristol Committee of Management (Rail 250/82, p89):

Oct. 30th 1837

My Dear Sir,

Ranger was with me on Saturday evening. Mr Saunders fortunately was present. He [Ranger] seemed to have no idea of flinching from any increased exertion – he seemed fully aware of his situation and of the power of the Company to 'send him to prison' as he expressed it on the seventh day – but in a very manly and straightforward manner expressed his determination to do everything which could be done. He indeed placed me in some difficulty by asking me to state what I should do if I took the work into the Company's hands to retrieve lost time and if I would tell him he would do everything or if I would name any Superintendent whom I thought likely to be able to carry on the work he would at once engage him and pay them handsomely.

*I am not much in the habit of paying attention to 'promises' or being influenced by fair language but I assure you both Saunders and myself felt that he **spoke the language** at all events of an honest sensible man determined to do his best.*

I have directed Mr Frere to watch closely and report exactly all that is done, to assist Mr Ranger with any suggestions or advice he may ask for and we must I suppose endeavour to judge of his conduct and efforts during this week what probability there is of any real substantial improvement.

I am, my dear Sir,
Yours very truly,
I. K. Brunel

W. S. Jaques Esq

A few weeks later Brunel wrote to Thomas Osler, Secretary to the Bristol Committee of the GWR, regarding the Ranger situation (Rail 250/82 p.95.):

Bath
Nov 27th 1837

Dear Sir,

On Saturday next expires the month which was allowed to Mr Ranger in order to afford him a fair opportunity of proving his willingness and his means of expediting the works. Before that day arrives I propose to make a report to the Directors on the subject but I think it would be desirable that the steps which have been agreed upon to improve the securities for the money advanced to Ranger should be completed before the Directors can come to any decision as to future progress of the works as should any difficulty occur the prevent the completion of these securities between the present time and Saturday next the policy of incurring further risks might become questionable. I find however Mr Ranger will himself give every assurance in forwarding the business and enabling me to comply strictly with the instructions received from the solicitors as to the possession of the stock and plant and also that I shall be able to report that the works are proceeding more satisfactorily.

The near approach of 30th Nov and the necessity of my being in Town to examine several plans before they are deposited [these were plans to accompany Bills for GWR route deviations and other matters to be deposited in Parliament ready for the 1838 Session] *will prevent my attending to Committee tomorrow.*

I am Sir,
Yours very truly,
I. K. Brunel

Thos. Osler Esq

Contract No 1B was for the line from just outside Bristol Temple Meads station, from the Canal Feeder, eastwards to the edge of Keynsham, involving a 100-foot-span stone arch over the Avon, three tunnels, earthworks, bridges, arched retaining walls and masonry. No 2B was the continuation through to the east side of Keynsham. These two mighty contracts were let to William Ranger, who was also heavily involved in Sonning Cutting and simply did not have the wherewithal, neither financial nor personal, to carry out the work. Brunel had estimated the cost of construction of contract 1B at what was surely a very unrealistic price of £52,600, and £58,500 for 2B. Ranger's price for both contracts was the cheapest offered – £63,000 for No 1 and £54,585 for No 2. David McIntosh also tendered for both contracts: £101,700 for 1B – which, given the size of the works, seems realistic but, at double Brunel's estimate, never likely to succeed – and £60,500 for 2B. The way matters turned out, Brunel got the cheapest, but not the best.

Ranger was given notice to commence work in March 1836, and Brunel and the Directors hoped to open the line from Bristol to Bath in April 1838. David McIntosh was awarded contract No 3B from the east side of Keynsham through – and under – Saltford village, up to and including the big stone arch carrying the Bristol-Bath road over the line near Newton St Loe. Brunel's estimate for this work was £66,000 and McIntosh tendered for £60,290. Mr Oldham, who had contracts in the London Division, bid £52,725 for 3B, but Brunel thought this was unrealistically low. Next eastwards was the Twerton contract, 4B. This went to the man who owned the village of Twerton, which was to be partly demolished – Charles Wilkins.

Ranger was subsequently thrown out of 1B and 2B. The heavy tunnelling and the Avon bridge were completed by labour directly employed by the GWR, directed by Brunel and his Resident Engineer, George Frere. The rest of Ranger's Bristol work was taken over by David McIntosh.

Frere reported thus (Rail 250/82, p95) to Thomas Osler:

Bath
28th Nov 1837

My Dear Sir,
The works on Contracts No 1B and No 2B have been proceeding during the past week at the same point as have been stated in my two former letters with the exception of the wing walls of the Avon bridge the building of which was suspended on Friday last by the Contractor's Superintendent on his own responsibility as I have since been given to understand by the Contractor.

The cutting west of No 2 Tunnel which I informed you in my last was resumed is now carried on in the same way previous to the suspension and some good blue pennant stone has been got out of it.

In No 2B Contract the numbers of men employed on No 2 cutting have been slightly increased, the masonry proceeds as slowly as before.

I cannot conclude this without stating with respect to the spirit in which the exertions of the Contractor are made that nothing appears done on either of the Contracts until the necessity is pointed out and then though it may be done with perfect willingness it appears done as if in obedience to orders rather than from an anxiety to profit by the suggestion and as I cannot be expected to foresee everything that may be required even if I could feel justified in interfering with the proper province of Mr Ranger I fear much less progress is made than might fairly be expected.

I am, My Dear Sir,
Yours truly,
George Frere.

Thos. Osler Esq

The following summer Brunel was having problems at Box, as also related to Osler (Rail 250/82, p115):

18 Duke Street,
Westminster
June 18th 1838

Dear Sir,
In reply to your note of 14th I fear that I am paying the usual penalty of a bad reputation – this is more saddled upon me than I ever deserved – with regard to the Box contracts I think nothing is wanting for me. I sent my revisions some time ago on Thursday last. Mr Burge came to Town I met him between 6 and 7 in the morning and he went down to Bristol again that evening with everything again settled as far as I was concerned so that I lost no time. The drawings I believe are at Bristol but to prevent delay I have sent another copy to Mr Frere.

With respect to Mr Ranger's proceedings I fear we are every day in greater difficulties notwithstanding the stoppage at Reading and the hopelessness of his case he has by some means scraped together a few hundred paid the balance of the wages due to the men and resumed work with unusual spirit and promises next week to do wonders whether he can stand another week or not I have not means of knowing. I should be wrong to advise any course which should prevent his struggling through his difficulties if there is a chance of his doing so but conceiving this to be impossible the less we pay him the better and that you ought therefore to be careful and not to pay him more than is just sufficient to pay the men's wages and decidedly we ought not to be paying his brother and

Brickwell while they are living comfortably as Frere suggests in his letter to me this morning they care not how the work proceeds or stands still men in such a situation as the whole body seem to be can only think of present existence the future is quite beyond their calculation stopping their pay would decide the point if they are merely living upon the company as I suspect there will be a crisis – if they are really endeavouring to carry on the works £10 cannot be vital.

Yours etc,
I. K. Brunel

Thos. Osler Esq

The bridge over the Thames at Maidenhead consists of two spans of brick, with a mid-river pier conveniently placed on a central island. Each of these arches spans 128 feet of water with a rise, from the springing of the arch to the crown, of 24ft 6in. When Brunel designed the bridge, it was revolutionary and very daring to construct such large spans in brick – arches of this size had always been made in stone. The bridge is approached from both ends by tall viaducts consisting of four semi-circular flood water arches. The bridge was widened during 1891/92 to take two extra tracks: two new bridges, conforming very closely but not precisely to Brunel's original plan, were built one on each side of the 1838 bridge. Thus the Brunellian bridge is encased in newer brickwork except that, from the towpath under the bridge, one can see the shape of the original, although even those bricks may not be the originals.

The work commenced on the foundations early in June 1836 under the contractor James Bedborough.

Maidenhead bridge was the cause of several rumours. In the summer of 1836 the rumour arrived at the Thames Commissioners that construction work on the bridge was blocking the waterway and towing paths. Without going to see for themselves, the Commissioners' man, William Payne, was instructed to write a letter of complaint to Brunel. Brunel was justifiably incensed. He wrote to Payne (Rail 1149/2, p64):

18 Duke Street,
Westminster
29 August 1836

Sir,

I have taken all due steps to ensure the security of the Navigation during the construction of the bridge – and at considerable expense and in a much more complete manner than I believe you yourselves would have provided had you been executing the work. I have designed the largest arch of any bridge above Southwark for the express purpose of including the whole of the present Navigation channel and the wide towing path under one arch. I have done what I suspect I will be severely criticised for, namely a 2-arch bridge, for the purpose of throwing the only pier required on an existing island. I believe this will be the only instance on the entire river of a bridge being built without in the slightest degree altering still less injuring the navigation. After doing all this – far more than we could have been compelled to do – unasked – it is rather vexatious to be interfered with in the manner we have been.

I hope you will put all right and restore the good feeling you feel disposed to cultivate. I have explained what I intend and cannot be responsible for the statements others may choose to make. The bridge has been designed peculiarly with regard to the navigation and without consideration of expense on the part of the railway. If the Commissioners are discounted and troublesome there is still time for me to save £10,000 and still build a bridge as they can find no fault with – but it would be by no means as convenient as the one at present intended.

I remain,
Your obt. servt.
I. K. Brunel

Bedborough ran out of money without completing the foundations and gave up the contract on 17 March 1837. During his tenure as contractor Brunel wrote to him as follows (Rail 1149/2, p170):

18 Duke Street
6 December 1836

Sir,
In calling your attention to the means to be adopted to expedite the work of Contract 5L [earthworks and bridges from the bridge over the Iver road to the bridge over the Maidenhead turnpike] *it*

was clearly for the purpose of having it completed in six weeks less time than required by the specification counting from the date of the Notice [the formal notice, issued by Brunel, to commence work] *and if you will turn your attention seriously to this the Directors are prepared as I have said before to act liberally towards you in offering a premium proportionate to the time saved but I shall recommend any such premiums to be in cash to be paid at the satisfactory completion of the work and not as you suggest by assisting you with the loan of rails or otherwise during the progress of the work. Let me in conclusion beg you to occupy yourself in making arrangements to follow these views rather than in endeavouring to discover grounds of complaint against your present position. You seem totally to forget the many points upon which I have endeavoured to accommodate you and lighten your work and you must bear in mind that if I find you constantly raising difficulties and endeavouring to take advantage of them I must proceed to enforce simply the terms of the contract.*
Hoping to hear from you soon.

I am, Dear Sir,
Your obt. servt.
I. K. Brunel

James Bedborough Esq

On the same day he wrote again (Rail 1149/2, p171)

18 Duke Street,
6 December 1836

Sir,
The progress in the work of the coffer dam of the Maidenhead bridge is not merely slow but most unsatisfactory to me. There does not appear any probability that in their present state they can, particularly the western coffer dam, be sufficiently watertight for the safe and proper construction of the foundations and I shall be obliged to call on you to drive another row of piles or take such steps as may be necessary to render the coffer dams fit for purpose as required by the contract. I cannot but remind you that this defect as it appears to me arises in a great measure from your not having spooned out the gravel before driving the piles as advised

to do by my Assistant.

I am, Dear Sir,
Yours very truly,
I. K. Brunel

James Bedborough Esq

Provided that he was not actually ill or seriously injured, the only day in the year that Brunel made a holiday for himself was Christmas Day. Brunel received a letter from James Bedborough on Christmas Eve and replies to it on Boxing Day (Rail 1149/2, p178). Brunel is short of contractors, Bedborough is struggling to complete Contract 5L, and Brunel, only too well aware of this, asks him to build the embankments further west. Bedborough prefers not to get any deeper into trouble – not for love or money. There is no other contractor Brunel can ask. The distinct impression is that contractors are wary of working for him.

18 Duke Street
26 December 1836

Dear Sir
I shall submit your letter of 24th to the Directors on Tuesday next. My great object is to secure the early execution of the works so as to receive the permanent rails and I have no objection to allow time for completion of the planting of fences or such other accessory works as may be necessarily delayed by the season.

As you do not wish to form the embankments from the Maidenhead turnpike up to the Thames even at a moderate increase on the schedule of prices of 5L I propose to take the whole of this embankment commencing from the Taplow road into our own hands and to commence immediately. This will somewhat reduce the quantity of rails etc required for your work and as I shall only deduct the schedule price which you think low for the embankment east of the Turnpike road you will thereby be proportionately relieved.

Being anxious to afford you every assistance I will at the same time if you request it execute the earthwork back to Road 72 Burnham which would it appears to me reduce very much your requisite stock of rails and wagons and materially facilitate your work.

This however I should only be disposed to undertake as a very great accommodation to you in consideration of my being perfectly satisfied with your increased progress and improved quality of work upon the rest of the contract. I should wish to hear from you upon this point immediately.

I am Sir,
Yours very truly,
I. K. Brunel

James Bedborough Esq

Thomas Chadwick took over the Maidenhead bridge works at the end of May 1837 and his men worked with tremendous speed. By February 1838 the bridge seemed to Mr Chadwick to be ready to stand without any support.

The brick arches were indeed daringly 'flat', the work of a great mathematical mind – and many people confidently predicted that the arches would fall once the centring was removed. During its construction the lines of bricks that would form the arch were laid on and supported by wooden centring, which acted as a former for the shape of the arches. Disobeying Brunel's strictest orders, the contractor eased the centring away from the bricks. The cement was not completely set hard in the eastern arch and as a result the lowest three courses of bricks, for about 12 feet on each side of the crown of the arch, separated, one course from the other, each by one and a half inches. The critics were delighted and, in the popular rumour that circulated, the half-inch became a gap a man could get his arm into.

I have seen nothing written to Chadwick from Brunel – one would have thought him incandescent with rage at being disobeyed on such a vital matter. The damage was repaired at the contractor's expense, but that work did not commence until late June. On 8 October 1838 the centrings were eased slightly on Brunel's instructions but this easing would not be visible to passers-by and the story grew noisily that Brunel was frightened to remove the wooden support for the arches. Brunel is said by Rolt to have acted out of 'an impish sense of humour' but he was acting not for fun but for practical engineering reasons. In any bridge there is settling, and he was being careful – the centring was there to intercept the slight lowering of the bridge that was natural and was bound to happen. At the time hundreds of people were waiting to see the bridge collapse.

As Brunel explains to the Directors of the Great Western Railway (Rail 250/82, p116):

18 Duke St
June 19th 1838

Gentlemen,
I have examined carefully the present state of the Maidenhead bridge and have procured all the measurements necessary to determine the exact amount of settlement of all the different parts of the structure up to the present moment and every means were taken from the commencement to obtain measurements from time to time as work proceeded. I have means of determining exactly and with the greatest certainty the extent to which each part has yielded to or withstood the forces to which it had been subjected.
The bridges consist of two large arches of equal span the observations were directed principally to the following points as those on which the perfection of the whole depends.
1st. The sinking of the foundations
2nd. Lateral motion in the abutments from the thrusts of the arches.
3rd. The compression of materials forming the arches and which causes the settlement of the arches.
4th. Alteration of form in the arches which might arise from the original form and dimensions of the arch being incorrect or from any excessive or unforeseen movement in the first 3 points or from inequality in the 3rd only – namely the compression from defective materials.
It should be observed that in large stone or brick bridges the movement in the foundations and abutments and the sinking of the arches is very considerable and is always foreseen and provided for to a certain extent. Frequently, however, I may say generally, in our larger arches the movement has much exceeded all previous calculation but still without destroying the stability of the structure.
The arches of the Waterloo bridge continued sinking till very lately and probably still do. Gloucester bridge, London bridge and others have all moved perceptibly to the eye. I mention these circumstances merely to show that it was no peculiar anxiety arising from the extent of these arches which induced me to take these measurements from the commencement.

The result of all these observations has been most satisfactory as regards the foundations. Not the slightest movement has taken place in any one of three foundations, they have not sunk any perceptible quantity. No lateral movement whatever has taken place.

The compression of the arch has been a trifling seven inches which was originally allowed for. The total movement including the yielding of the centring, the compression of the piers and all the other yielding has been from 8½ to 9½ inches and deducting these and taking the arch by itself between the haunches there has not been 5 inches. All this is much below those of several of our most celebrated stone bridge and besides this the material shows no symptom of unequal or excessive pressure. In the first striking of the centring it is not unusual in stone bridges to see large spalls fly off from the crushing of the material. There is less appearance of any such effect in the Maidenhead bridge than is frequently seen in ordinary bridges and much less than in any stone bridges I have before referred to.

As regards the first three points of observation and which determine the correctness of the calculations of quantity and nature of materials used nothing can be more satisfactory and if any scientific man ever did entertain a doubt as to the facility of constructing brick aches of such spans when the foundations were good these observations would at once satisfy him.

Upon the fourth point namely the alteration of form of the arch I am not so satisfied that the original form of and proportions and loading of the arch was correct and good – however – I am glad to say it is proved most evidently by the western arch but also by the eastern arch although a defective settlement in this last which I shall now observe upon.

Great care is requisite in striking the centres of large arches because the total amount of compression of material has been considerable and requiring time as well as pressure according to its state of density if the centring is suddenly removed the softer parts yield quicker than the hard and an alteration of form immediately takes place and an unequal pressure is at once created which increases the original evil – if the centres can be lowered gradually all the parts obtain their maximum pressure or nearly so before any material alteration of form can take place.

I had intended and had commenced performing this operation with unusual care on account of the attention that has been called

151

to the bridge and also because in my case which I had witnessed the engineers regretted that more time had not been given. It was with great difficulty that I prevented the contractor from striking the centrings even before the full thickness of the arch was completed. I did prevent him and I attended myself and eased the centring a few inches by excessive small movement and then directed the whole to be left until further orders. The remaining thickness of the arch having been added and being of course still green. Notwithstanding my decided orders the contractor of his own accord, within a few days struck the centring till both arches were free and, as far as I could learn, by no means equally. The Western arch followed with perfect regularity maintaining its form, the Eastern arch compressed more at one point and altered its forms to a trifling extent by actual measurement but most perceptibly to an eye accustomed to the work – one haunch at about 20ft from the centre having sunk nearly 1½ inches more than the other haunch.

Whether the original cause of this inequality in the material was in bad cement or the effect of frost I have not been able to determine I feel quite confident from a close examination that no such inequality would have been discovered nor the alteration of form taken place had proper precautions have been taken in lowering the centrings the materials and workmanship being highly creditable to the contractor and there is no appearance of any excessive pressure.

The contractor is now anxious to remove the centring as he feels confident that no further movement will take place and proposes to remove and alter the external surfaces of the distorted parts and prevent its being apparent to the eye. To this I have objected – I cannot say that I think the work is unsafe or that the bridge would not stand very well in its present state but the defect has been caused entirely by the fault of the contractor and while the centrings are still in place he has the means of restoring the defective portion and rendering the Eastern arch as perfect as the Western now is and such as he contracted to make it.

I propose therefore to direct Mr Chadwick to tighten-up the centres of both arches and to remove and replace so much of the Eastern arch as upon close examination I may consider defective but it would be more convenient to us that he should postpone this operation for a time until we complete so much of the embankment to the west as will enable Mr Oldham [the contractor for the *earthworks to the west of the bridge] to meet it within the required time and then we can remove entirely our temporary road which would interfere with works at the bridge.*

I am, Gentlemen,
Your obt. Servt.
I. K. Brunel

Another myth that has survived to this day is more puzzling. E. T. MacDermot, the official historian of the GWR, states that 'one night in the autumn of 1839 a violent storm blew them [the centrings] down' (*History of the Great Western Railway*, Volume 1, p49). This did not happen. Brunel wrote to the GWR Directors stating that the scaffolding was still in place.

The 13 miles of route between Chippenham and Bath were the most difficult to build of the entire line. There is barely a mile where the track comes within 10 feet of the natural surface of the ground. There is a tall viaduct leading west from Chippenham station followed by a 2-mile-long, truly massively wide – at the base – embankment, which leads into a steadily deepening cutting through limestone, past Corsham town, all on a 1 in 660 rising gradient.

Box Hill, a mile or so west of Corsham, was the great obstacle to the completion of the Great Western Railway. At the eastern portal of Box Tunnel, 99⅙ miles from Paddington, the gradient changes to 1 in 100 falling, and 3,212 yards later the rails emerge into daylight at the 102 milepost in a deep cutting, where the gradient changes to 1 in 660 falling. Then, 1½ miles later, the line enters the 198-yard Middle Hill Tunnel.

Trial shafts were sunk to get some idea of the nature of the ground in Box Hill on the line of the railway, then six permanent and two temporary shafts almost 30 feet in diameter and as deep as required – from 70 to 300 feet – were sunk in line across Box Hill down to the level of the proposed railway. From the bottom of these the men dug east and west to create the tunnel. Messrs Lewis & Brewer and Paxton & Orton were given the contracts; it seems as if Brunel had to take any second-rate contractor that offered to do the work because, from his evidence in the following letter (Rail 250/82, p64), Paxton & Orton 'were not men of capital'. Neither, indeed, were Lewis & Brewer, two locals running Bath-stone quarries under Box Hill.

The work began early in 1836 when the contract was advertised for sinking seven shafts – Nos 2 to 8 – down to intended rail level so that, from the bottom of these shafts, tunnelling could begin. Brunel's estimate of the cost of sinking these shafts was £11,800. Three offers were received: £10,262 from Harris & Venn, £21,330 from Copeland & Burgess, and £14,000 from Paxton & Orton. The latter's offer was accepted in September 1836. Some time later Lewis & Brewer were awarded the contract to sink No 1 shaft at the eastern end (Rail 1149/44, p90).

Paxton & Orton ran out of money during March 1837 and the vital shafts could not be completed until Brunel had worked out an unusual scheme to help them – with GWR money. Box Tunnel, even as an idea, brought unjustified ridicule on Brunel and the entire Great Western Railway project. If Paxton & Orton were to fail, the value of GWR shares would be seriously diminished. Brunel actually paid the contractors small sums out of his own pocket to help them keep going. He wanted to be repaid, but in the end what mattered more to him was not money but the completion his Great Western Railway – 'the Finest Work in England'.

Shortly after the Paxton & Orton failed Brunel reported to one of the GWR Bristol Directors, William Tothill:

18 Duke Street,
Westminster
April 12th 1837

My Dear Sir,
I think I understood that there was to be a meeting of the [Bristol] Committee tomorrow in which case I should be obliged by your bringing the subject of the Box contract before them as I must have their instructions immediately how to proceed.

I have seen the two contractors when the Notice was served upon them and endeavoured to ascertain if there was any chance of effecting any arrangement which should prevent the public breaking up of their contract.

A separation appeared the only course and they individually authorised me to effect such arrangement and agreed to abide by my terms. I ascertained that Paxton was willing to withdraw for a consideration to be secured to him by Orton out of the proceeds of the contract work. Orton would thus be left to continue the work and I have little doubt would continue and complete it satisfactorily but neither of them individually have any capital and their supporters now withdraw all supply we must therefore provide the fund the consequence is that the Company would in reality be paying off Paxton and making Orton a present of whatever profit over and above what he could make – the question is, is the mere advantage of being able to state that the Contractor has not failed at Box but is to continue the work and being able to contradict their report which will probably be circulated of the failure of a Contractor, is this sufficient to induce you with your eyes open to be giving assistance to parties and enabling them to continue what proves evidently to be a profitable contract and which without your assistance they must throw up – and which, I believe we should be able to complete for less than the contract sum – It would be a very liberal act whether the advantage to be gained in preventing unpleasant although incorrect reports is sufficient to justify such liberality, the Directors alone must judge and determine.

I should observe that I think the profit would cover the payments amply so that we should not eventually pay more than the contract sum but I think we may if they fail to do it for less.

It is right that you should know what of course would not for an instant influence my opinion, that I have at various times assisted the Contractors with small sums amounting I believe to about £200 I had almost forgotten the circumstances but should your decision be to assist the parties and this be eventually repaid to me, I should feel annoyed that you had not been informed of it.

The sum that Paxton proposed was £1,000 for the two contracts the Great Western and the Bridge, this I think too much. I have no doubt he would take £600. Orton I have no doubt calculates upon £2,000 and which I believe the Company may also save if they throw up the contract.

I shall feel obliged by an immediate reply and by a copy of this letter being sent to me as I have not time to have it copied now.

I am, my dear Sir,
Yours very truly,
I. K. Brunel

William Tothill, Esq

In August 1837 the shafts were well on the way to completion and Brunel was advertising in various newspapers for a contractor to undertake the excavation of the tunnel. The *Bristol Journal* for August 1837 carried such an advert. However, contractors did not come forward for this mammoth task. The risks of tendering a fixed price and time to dig a tunnel 3,212 yards long are obvious and by now Brunel's very harsh contract terms were well known among the contractors. The four greatest contractors of the day, William McKenzie, Hugh & David McIntosh, Grissell & Peto and Thomas Brassey, kept well away. The result of this was a full six months delay to the GWR construction project. Not until February 1838 did George Burge, of Herne Bay,come forward. He was a new man in contracting and relatively unknown until he completed the enlargement of St Katherine's Dock, London, in 1828. He agreed to excavate the tunnel in 30 months and to do so at a specified number of yards per week. If this rate of progress was not maintained Brunel would be entitled to impose a financial penalty. Burge was taking on a huge risk because no one knew exactly what kinds of rock, quicksands or water courses existed within the great hill.

The hill was formed by beds of rock and clay, originally horizontal, becoming raised and tilted, the east end being the lowest. Digging the tunnel must have been the most miserable way of earning a living. From the east the tunnellers hacked through the Great Oolite or Bath-stone, then hundreds of yards of thick clay called fuller's earth. The effect of water on this was to turn it into something resembling glue. The men had somehow to dig into it, then force the wet, slimy clay off their spades into a bucket for raising to the surface. Even picking up their feet was a huge effort because their boots were caught in the sucking mud so that the soles were gradually torn off. This fact was recorded as the experience of a tunnel navvy by the Quaker woman, Ann Tregelles, who was one of the few people who tried to help these poor men. After the inclined strata of fuller's earth the excavators encountered the Lesser Oolite limestone, then another terrible band of thick, heavy, mud – Blue Marl.

There were 18 tunnelling faces. Men and materials were raised and lowered down the shafts by platforms, or in barrels suspended from a rope wound around a large wooden drum, the latter being turned by a horse walking round and round – rather miserably, I should think. The drum had a central pivot turning in a large stone embedded in the ground and the horse walked around on a stone pavement. The site of these horse-drums including the large pivot stone can still be discerned beside the present walls surrounding the shafts.

Water was always the great enemy, flooding in as underground streams were broken into and overpowering the primitive pumps. It was freezing cold, there was water under foot and dripping down, and the dark was illuminated only by candles – a ton a week were made in Box village and burned in the tunnel – while the cold damp atmosphere was regularly punctuated by deafening gunpowder explosions, with consequent increases in air pressure on ear drums and leaving in the icy air acrid fumes that never dispersed. The rock was sodden wet and more or less impenetrable by pick-axe. I had an opportunity to try my hand at this in the underground caverns of the existing quarry. The men cut deep holes into the tunnelling face with hammers and sharp chisels, placed the explosive powder, lit the fuse and hoped that they would reach a place of safety before the charge exploded.

Thomas Gale, who was born in Box village and who worked on the tunnel in 1837-41, wrote a memoir in 1884, *A Brief Account of the Making and Working of the Great Box Tunnel*, which is now in the collection of Bristol University Library. His memoir records 'Mr George Burge with his hundred-odd horses working night and day drawing the earth up out of the tunnel and otherwise engaged at the different works of the tunnel and at least forty boys to drive the horses and twelve hundred men working day and night.' The bricks for lining the tunnel were made on the Corsham side of Chippenham by Mr Hunt, who had 100 horses and carts bringing the bricks to the tunnel for three years. Timber for scaffolding and for the centrings on which the tunnel arch was built had to come from Bath. The mortar for the bricks was made from lime and sand; the lime came by horse and cart from Tanners Lane kiln and there was a lime kiln at the tunnel, burning the limestone that was dug out, while sand was carted from pits 2 miles away. There were hundreds of horses, carts, men and boys employed to bring the materials together, and it is not difficult to imagine the state of the earth roads leading to the site with this amount of activity. As the shifts changed all these men had to pass each other, heading for bed or for work. There were no police, and the contractors' Foremen tried to keep order, but it was impossible to prevent drunkenness and fighting by men who were working so hard and so miserably in the bowels of Box Hill.

Brunel's Resident Engineer for Box Tunnel was William Glennie (1797-1856). A Scot, he carried out his duties entirely to Brunel's satisfaction, and from Box Tunnel he became Resident for the construction of the great central pillar of the Royal Albert Bridge at Saltash. Glennie's most important job was to keep the tunnel centre-line heading in precisely the right direction, both in line and in depth. The floor of the excavation had to fall from east to west at the rate of 53 feet in the mile – a gradient in railway terms of 1 in 100 – and on a compass bearing of 260 degrees – as near as I can calculate. He had to have the tunnel at the right width and height and to measure the completed work of the contractor. He watched proceedings and reported to Brunel if things were not done properly, and he carried to the contractors Brunel's instructions and admonitions. Glennie therefore spent a good few minutes of every day being lowered down and raised up the various shafts, by day and probably also by night. The working was so dangerous for everyone that even Glennie was badly hurt in the tunnel.

By 31 August 1839 1,350 yards had been excavated, 1,200 of which were entirely complete. That left 1,862 yards to complete by August 1840, but this was impossible. Not only were there unknown perils within the hill – which broke out now and then upon the workers – but there were very wet winters, especially that of 1839-40, which increased the water within the tunnel. Brunel made no allowance for these things, but held Burge to his contract and withheld payment when weekly deadlines were missed, making Burge's task, without ready cash, even more difficult. Three extra shafts were sunk to provide six additional tunnelling faces and more and more men were brought into until 4,000 men, at the very least, had been crowded into the tunnel. Brunel even had to resort to paying bonuses to Burge and his Foremen to get them to drive the men hard. The hole was fully cut through the hill during June 1841. The first train – an up train from Bristol – went through on the 30th, on a single track.

After all the terrible, appalling labour – which caused the death on site of more than 100 men and maimed at least as many more, who crawled away to the villages of their birth to die – the GWR did not have a celebratory train or banquet at the opening of the tunnel that, together with other heavy works between there and Bristol, enabled the route to be opened throughout.

Thomas Gale recalled that on the opening day the villagers of Box gave themselves over to a day of rejoicing. A silver band played all day in Box and three hogsheads of beer (162 gallons) were donated by George Burge. Well over 100 flags were hung out in the village and on the west tunnel portal and the cutting sides. Gale does not mention any contribution from the Great Western Railway or Brunel. In the evening, Gale recalls, 'we had an entertainment at the Queen's Head [Box] for the principal men of the tunnel.'

The Board of Trade Inspector reported in 1841 that the tunnel was 3,193 yards long. The Great Western Railway's 'General Appendix to the Rule Book 1936' gives a length of 3,212 yards, or 1⅞ mile.

As already mentioned there is a famous assertion that the bright disc of the rising sun can be seen – from the west end – filling the eastern opening of the tunnel on Brunel's birthday, 9 April. The bright disc of the rising sun will never track across the eastern portal of the tunnel on 9

April, but the top quarter of the bright disc of the sun does coincide with the eastern aperture of the tunnel around 6.30am (depending on the annual variations in the tilting of the earth) on 6 April, and the bottom '4 o'clock' sector of the sun would just catch the top '11 o'clock' segment of the tunnel aperture on the 7th. On Brunel's birthday the sun rises about 2 degrees to the east of the eastern portal (see *New Civil Engineer*, 4 April 1985, p 31).

The same thing happens on 6/7 September. If Brunel had wanted to aim the bore of the tunnel, like a huge gun barrel, at the rising sun on his birthday he would have been obliged to align it slightly more towards the north-east. To do this would have required a deviation of the railway from Chippenham station, going more towards the north-west then swinging back to the south-west, which course would have taken the line through the house and grounds of Corsham Court, home of Paul Methuen, Member of Parliament for Wiltshire – which, of course, could not be done.

As the problems with progress began to emerge in the autumn of 1838, Brunel, staying perhaps at the Queen's Head on the London-Bath road in Box village, wrote to Lewis & Brewer (Rail 1149/4, p184):

4 September 1838
Box Tunnel

Gentlemen,
I have so repeatedly and earnestly expressed my opinion of the necessity under the present circumstances and particularly after the great delay which has taken place of your sinking to the lower oolite for the purpose of getting rid of the water in Shaft No 7 that I had expected great exertions would have been used to attain this object. I need not say how much I am disappointed and surprised at your neglect to attend to this – I am compelled to believe that you have either deceived me as to your intention of prosecuting this necessary work or that delay arises from the greatest apathy and negligence and a total disregard of my orders and your own real interest. It is now 2 months since the water was pumped out of the shaft and you promised that immediate steps should be taken to proceed as rapidly as possible with the sinking – since then although every hour is of the greatest importance nothing has been done or so little that it is not worth mentioning – after several proposed changes of plan I was again assured that from Monday morning last every exertion should be made and the work

proceeded with day and night. When I visited the works on Tuesday morning the progress made and indeed the whole mode of proceeding appeared to me ridiculous and this afternoon being now the 3rd day about 18 inches has been done instead of 8 or 10 feet which might easily have been effected. It is not my business to control all the details of your work or to ascertain that your men are properly employed but I will observe that the manner in which hours are wasted at their meals in the night and on every occasion which can afford excuse for delay is disgraceful and would not be tolerated in the most ordinary work where no expedition was required – as persuasion and entreaty produces no effect whatever and as the case is urgent I can no longer delay taking most decisive measures. Unless the whole shaft is sunk 12 feet or at the rate of 4 feet per day between the present time and Saturday night I shall on Monday morning proceed with that part of the work at your expense and I have directed that men may be ready for that purpose and I shall also feel it my duty to request the Directors to levy the penalties due upon this contract and to continue to do so until the work is placed in a satisfactory state, I regret exceedingly that such a course should be necessary but the total neglect shown to my repeated cautions and the utter want of energy displayed leave no alternative.

I am, Gentlemen,
Yours obt. Servt.
I. K. Brunel

Messrs Lewis & Brewer

It seems very likely, from the wording of these letters (Rail 1149/4, pp188-89 and 193), that the interview between Brunel and Burge was a painful one for the latter.

18 Duke Street,
11 September 1838

Dear Sir,
After our interview on Saturday last it is hardly necessary that I should reply to your letter of the tenth but I will impress upon you very strongly the necessity of your endeavouring with the works in a more satisfactory manner and to assure you that I am as anxious

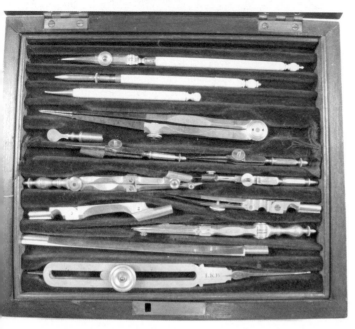

...unel's superbly made drawing pens, his initials can be seen on the lowest one in the picture. He housed ...em in a superb mahogany box to carry them on his travels around the country in his 'britzska' horse ...awn caravan – the 'Flying Hearse'. *With permission of the University of Bristol Library Special* ...ollections

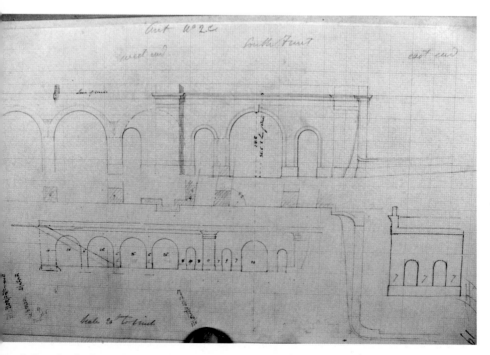

...unel's first idea for the necessary viaduct to carry the railway westwards from the station over the High ...reet. The distance of the rails from the ground is marked as 50 feet but in his second design he marks this ...36ft 6in. This is the design which was actually built.

...ith permission of the University of Bristol Library Special Collections

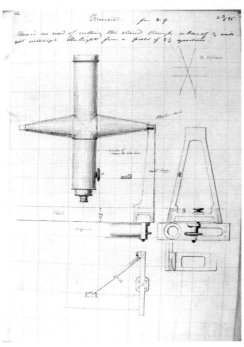

Brunel was a gifted instrument maker and hs gifts were well developed by his apprenticeship to the greatest clock maker of his time, Louis Breguet. He Brunel is designing what appears to be a surveyor's theodolite. The drawing shows the telescopic part o the instrument in a vertical position, with one pivot mounted on an 'A' frame of cast iron. To the right i a side elevation of that the 'A' frame. At the head of the page Brunel has written:

There is no need of cutting the stand through a bar of ½inch

Not interrupt the light from a field of 2¼ aperture

At the pivot he has commented: Steel axis

And just below the cross tube he wrote: Centre of screw A to be here

'Screw A' is shown lower down, near the eyepiece.

The drawing is dated 3 February 1835

With permission of the University of Bristol Librar Special Collections

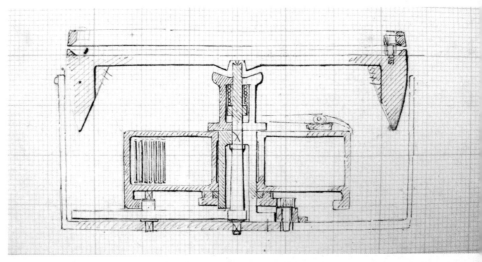

This is Brunel's 'Spinning Level' design for a 'gyroscope'. A gyroscope was used from 1817, at the Ecole Polytechnique in Paris, to demonstrate the phenomenon of the stability of a spinning weight. As a teenage Brunel was studying in Paris to pass the entrance examination for a place in the Polytechnique. He did no pass the exam but it was at this time that he became aware of the usefulness of a gyroscope for maintainin stability in some other piece of equipment. A ship's compass, for instance. His drawing here is dated 17 April 1835, four months before the GWR obtained its Act of Parliament. When the Act was obtained Brunel suggested building a trans-Atlantic steamship. This drawing implies that, as early at April 1835, he was contemplating the extension of his London–Bristol railway to New York.
With permission of the University of Bristol Library Special Collections

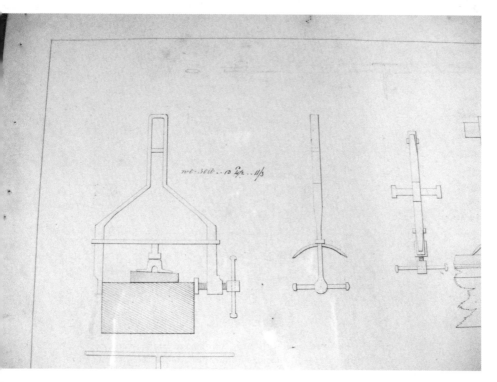

A cross section showing the longitudinal timber which lay on the ground, and on that the tapered hardwood plank on which the rail was laid. The inwards inclination of the rail head thus produced co-incided with the coned profile of the wheels of the locomotive and train. This arrangement was necessary to enable each pair of wheels – connected to each other by a rigid axle – to roll around curves where the outer wheel on the curve would travel a greater distance than the wheel on the rail of the inner curve. The clamping tool is holding the rail precisely in position to enable the drilling tool to drill the screw holes accurately. The screws would penetrate to the longitudinal. *With permission of University of Bristol Special Collections*

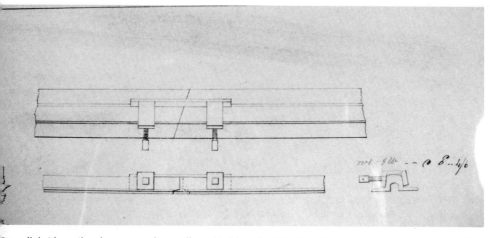

Brunel's bridge rail ends were cut diagonally and held perfectly flush horizontally and vertically by this 9lbs weight clamp costing 4 shillings and 6 pence to make. With the rail ends tightly clamped together the drill could do its work through the bottom flange into the timber. *With permission of University of Bristol Special Collections*

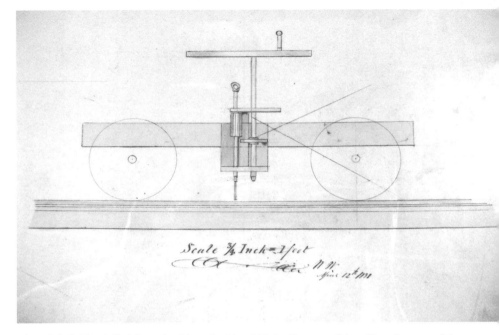

The rail drill. This drilled the web of the rail with a drill the diameter of the widest diameter of the screw, then a thinner drill would be fitted to drill the hole into the wood for the screw to bite into.
With permission of University of Bristol Special Collections

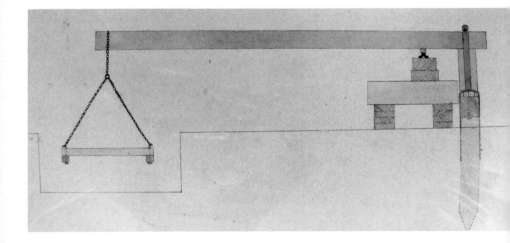

Brunel had great difficulty to obtain from the manufacturers rails rolled to the shape and dimensions he required. When that had been achieved, rails became bent whilst still hot out of the rolling mill. Nothing loth, the manufacturer would send them on their journey to London. The rails were loaded into a ship perhaps at Cardiff, unloaded into lighters in London docks, transferred from the lighters to canal barges on the Regent's Canal at Limehouse and carried to the Bull's Bridge wharf at the junction of the Regent's Canal with the Grand Junction where they were to be unloaded. By the time they got there even more rails were bent and sometimes Brunel would refuse to have them unloaded. To straighten rails he had this press constructed, a long lever with a platform to accommodate a heavy weight. He also used a smaller, lighter, version of his pile driver to hammer them straight.
With permission of University of Bristol Special Collections

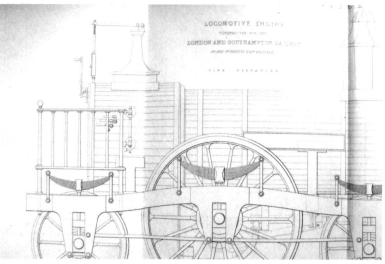

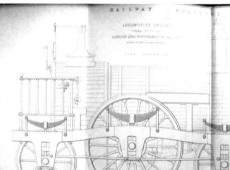

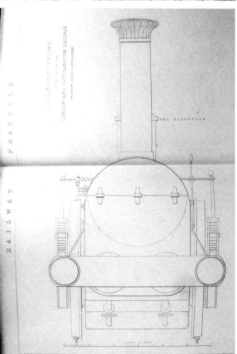

Brunel's specification for locomotives was so peculiar as to be beyond comprehension. As peculiar is the fact that he sent out invitations to build engines to these specifications only to engineering works in Liverpool and Newcastle. This entailed greatly increased costs in transporting the engines to London but also involved him in lengthy and wearisome journeys from London to Liverpool. In London there was the engineering company of the Rennie Brothers; they received no invitation to build. Did Brunel have an antipathy to John and George Rennie. I think so. If Brunel had asked George Rennie to design and construct some locomotives for the GWR - without of course hampering Rennie with ridiculous specifications – Brunel would have had a fleet of very useful, relatively trouble free, engines. These drawings show the simple, practical locomotive George Rennie designed for the London & Southampton Railway, opened from Nine Elms to Woking Common, 23 miles, on 21 May 1838 – three weeks early – so as to take Londoners to Epsom to watch 'the Derby'. On the opening day John Herepath, editor of the *Railway Magazine*, wrote:

'Although there are seven stopping places between London and Woking the engines perform their journey of 23 miles within the hour. Among the engines, those made by Rennie & Co have been particularly remarkable in the simplicity and excellence of their construction and the ease and rapidity with which they perform their journey, often at the rate of between 40 and 50mph.' With 7ft-gauge axles underneath them, the Rennie engines would have been as successful on the GWR and saved the Company a lot of money.

Courtesy the Institution of Mechanical Engineers

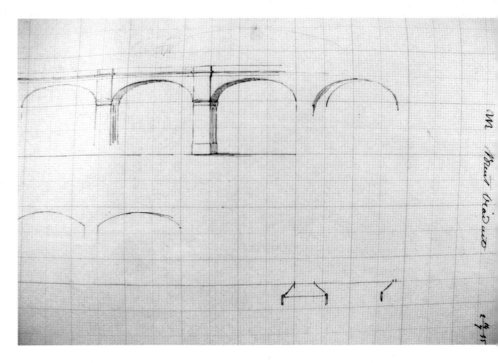

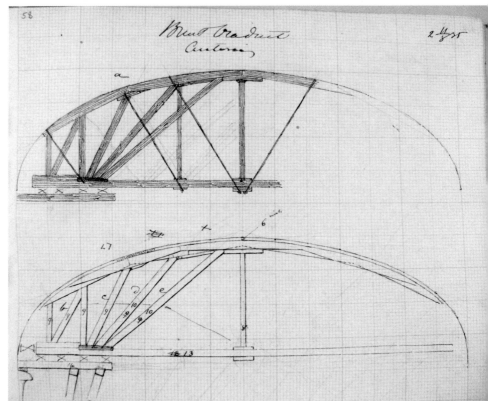

Brunel's original design for the Hanwell viaduct, with rectangular piers rising to the arches. 16 July 1835. *With permission of the University of Bristol Library Special Collections*

The final shape of the piers was a great advance on the straight-up, rectangular cross-section original design. The final design was to taper all four sides of the piers to form a 'pylon' in the ancient Egyptian style and complete the Egyptian motif by having the pier capping stones with this downwards curving shape. Marc Brunel's diaries show that he played a very large part in the design of the Brent (Hanwell) viaduct. Maybe this idea came from him. *Author. 1999*

The left-hand arch is an 'Accommodation road' arch built in 1838. Its height over the outside rail is very little different from the height of the standard-gauge arch on the right. Brunel had a broad-gauge track and more or less standard loading gauge. My photograph was taken at Iver with the safety precautions provided by Network Rail. *Author*

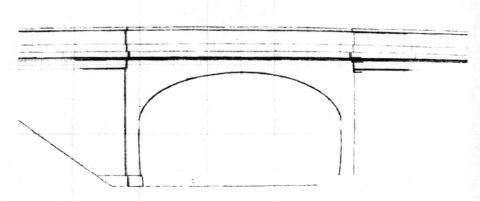

Brunel made this drawing of an 'Accommodation Bridge' – to carry a farm track or ordinary road over the line – on Christmas Day 1835.
With permission of the University of Bristol Library Special Collections

Brunel's beautiful letter to his wife was written on two pieces of paper, folded. This shows the first and penultimate pages. The final page, with his goodbye, is lost. That page was seen by L.T.C. Rolt and he published that ending in his 1957 biography of Brunel.
With permission of the University of Bristol Library Special Collections

This is the middle section of the letter page 2 on the left, page 3, right. See also page 187.
With permission of the University of Bristol Library Special Collections

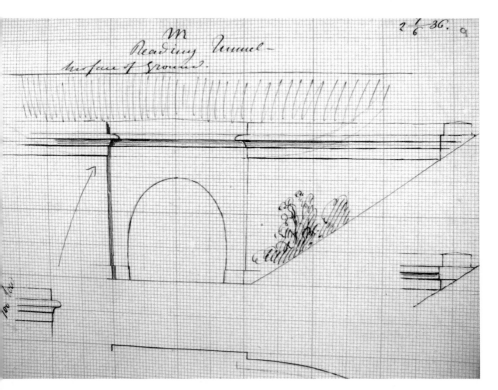

...lough station as it would appear from the trackside. This was drawn on Christmas Day 1839.
...t is unusual to find a drawing or a letter by Brunel dated 25 December.
With permission of the University of Bristol Library Special Collections

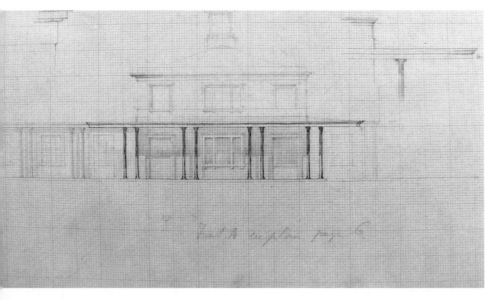

The restrained architecture of the London Division is well demonstrated in Brunel's treatment of the tunnel
face at Sonning – Reading Tunnel. 7 June 1836.
With permission of the University of Bristol Library Special Collections

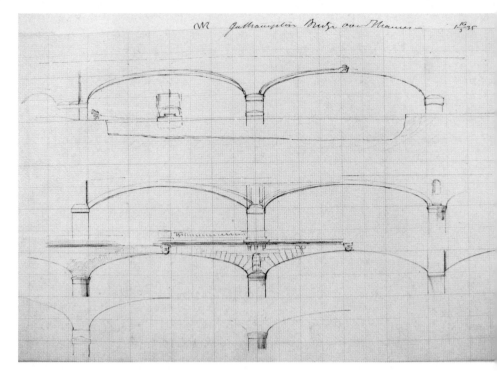

Various, more or less decorative, designs for bridging the Thames at Gatehampton, dated 3 October 1835. 44 miles from Paddington, this is the second crossing of the Thames by the railway. There are four spans, each of 64ft 4in, on a slight skew angle to the river. *With permission of the University of Bristol Library Special Collections*

The Gatehampton bridge in 2008. *Author*

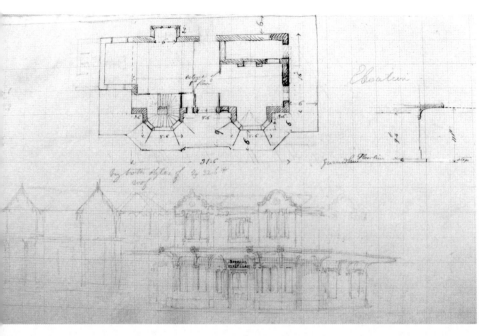

he decision of the London and Bristol Committees to place the headquarters of the railway at the very
cient village of Steventon, approximately halfway between London and Bristol, was nearly as odd as the
cision, taken in 1833, to build only the two most populated ends of the railway and leave the rest for
other day. Brunel went to huge trouble to design a magnificent executive village here in a Jacobean style.
Boardroom and Committee Rooms house, a Superintendent's family house, a Station Master's house, and
inn were erected on the up side and workmens' cottages on the down side. The drawing here shows the
nate station building Brunel intended to build. Notice that he has drawn two styles of roof and marked
e drawing 'Try both styles of roof.' These sketched plans went to the architect John Gandell of Wolverton
be reproduced in formal form. Brunel would then decide which style of roof and which sort of chimney
ack he preferred and send the drawings back for the alterations to be made. Everything was built as
anned except the station shown here. Instead a very plain, single storey, wooden office was provided,
ving he appearance of a temporary expedient. An identical building was provided at the Faringdon Road,
ter re-named Challow. This was intended to serve both Wantage and Faringdon. These were the only two
ach stations on the line and quite unlike the standard, brick,flint and stone buildings provided elsewhere.
suppose that Brunel intended something grander in due course. Steventon station remained as built until
s demolition in 1965, Wantage got its own station in 1845 and the wooden Challow station was replaced
1933. *With permission of the University of Bristol Library Special Collections*

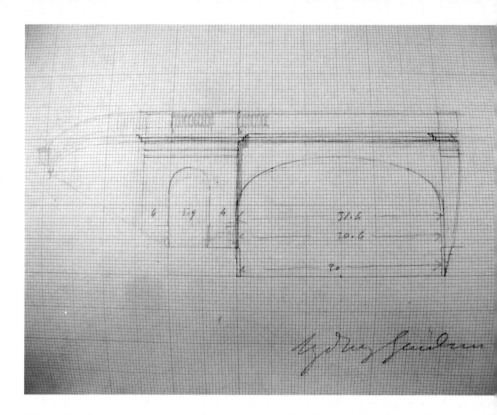

Major civil engineering works were required to bring the railway into Bath from the east. The railway was carried along the side of the valley above the rive Avon and parallel with but 20 feet lower than the Kenne & Avon canal. When the canal got to Hampton Row, approaching Sydney Gardens, it swung to the right and then performed a sharp, 'u'-shaped, bend around the swelling contour of the valley sides. The railway was designed to cut through both side of this 'u' bend. Brunel at first thought he would make a 'cut and cover' tunnel but then decided to persuade the K&A company to carry their waterway onwards, in an gentle curve, and tunnel the hillside. The GWR would have to pay for the work which would improve the line of the canal. To carry the railway through the ornamental and elegant Sydney Pleasure Gardens, Brun willingly agreed with the Trustees of the Gardens to create the railway in a form quite as elegant as the gardens. The canal too, now to pass through the higher level of the Gardens, was given elegant iron bridge and carved stone tunnel portals and I suppose that Brunel would have had some informal influence on those designs.

Here we see his sketch for the stone arch which now carries a 22ft wide walkway across the railway, connecting the higher and lower levels of the Gardens.

With permission of the University of Bristol Library Special Collections

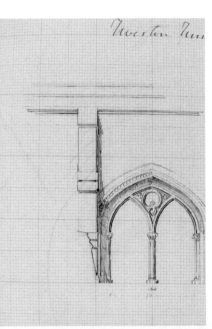

Tunnel portals were of great importance to Brunel. They were the perfect opportunities for grandeur. The sketch shows the embarrassing lengths that Brunel thought of going to – a huge 'Early English' style church window. *With permission of the University of Bristol Library Special Collections*

My photograph shows the rather more conventional design he finally adopted. Twerton tunnel, west front, as built. *Author. 4 June 1974*

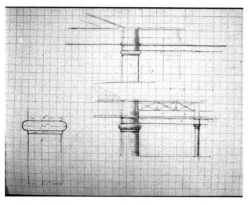

Brunel's sketch plans for a viaduct leading up to the crossing of the Thames approaching Windsor station. In volume 1, page 97, of the official history of the GWR, by E.T. McDermott (Ian Allan ed. 1964) it is stated that the viaduct was of timber. This plan shows cast iron columns. Of course this plan may not have been used. The same book states that the 'timber' viaduct was replaced by brick arches between 1861 and 1865. *With permission of Bristol University Library Special Collections.*

The Windsor bridge across the Thames has a span of 202 feet. This was Brunel's first 'bow and string' bridge and his first use of the tubular principle which Robert Stephenson pioneered for the Conway bridge in North Wales – except that Brunel's use of the tube principle was far more effective, lighter and thus cheaper. The Windsor bridge consists of two parts – the 'bow' – which is wrought iron plate riveted together in the form of hollow, triangular, arches – and the 'string' which are the horizontal wrought iron riveted plates forming the 'wall' of the bridge'. At the foot of the 'wall' is a continuous, square cross section, iron tube for added strength and at the top a curved 'flange' again to add strength against bending. The Windsor bridge was opened on 8 October 1849 a year after the Conway but the crudity of the latter and the beauty of the former shows in stark contrast Brunel's uniquely perfect combination of engineering and artistry.
Author. 2006.

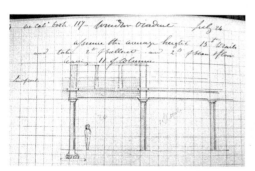

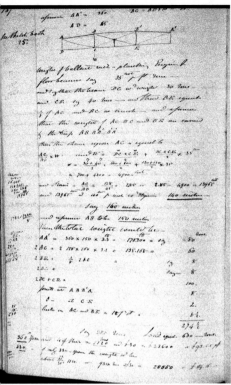

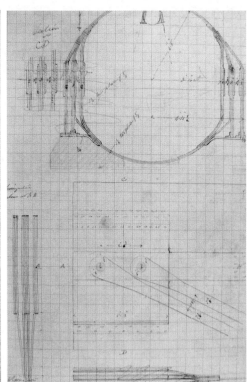

Brunel began to design his bridge and viaduct across the 600ft wide River Wye at Chepstow in September 1848. At that time he was also designing a 202ft span to cross the Thames near Windsor and also to carry the Cornwall Railway 100ft above the River Tamar on a bridge/viaduct 2,200 ft long. His calculations for all these bridges was based on his educated guesses – 'assume that' – concerning the weights to be carried and the strength of materials. Based on these assumptions he made mathematical calculations and when he had arrived at an answer he would increase the figure - just to be on the safe side.

This page from his Calculation Book No. XX show him calculating the weight to be carried by the tubular truss he is designing. The pages begins with the word 'assume'. Below the sketch of the 300ft truss he writes:

"Weight of ballast xxxx - planking xxx & floor beams say 35cwt per foot run and say that the beams DC [woul]d weigh 30 tons and CE say 40 tons - and that BE equals 1/8 of AC and BC as much and assume that the weight of AC BC and BE are carried by the truss AB BBi BiAi
then the strain upon AC is equal to……………"

With permission of the University of Bristol Library Special Collections

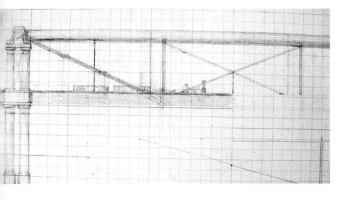

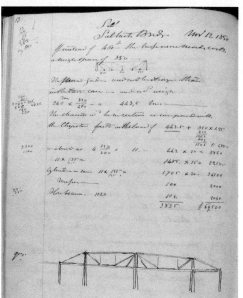

Brunel made painstaking plans to cross the actual waterway of the Tamar on two 450ft. trusses. (He eventually built these 455ft long. Having spent much time – and I am sure not inconsiderable pain and worry – getting this idea drawn out and costed, he spared himself not at all but at once started to work out whether it would be less costly to bridge the river with a single mighty span. At this time he was still thinking of using a Chepstow-like truss design. He wrote his thoughts in a great haste and they are very difficult to decipher. He began:

Saltash Bridge   12 November 1850

If instead of a 450ft the truss with made with a single span of 850

The dimensions of the sketch of a Chepstow-style span, a tube supported by verticals dividing the span from the: 250ft., 350 ft., 250ft.

Under the top sketch the first one or two words are illegible but the next part reads:

Girder need not be stronger than in the last case - and wd. weigh
Tons
240 x 850   =   443.5 tons
      460

Below this he might have written

The chains wd. be in section as compared with the Chepstow first as the load of   and he enters into the arithmetic laid out on the right hand side

At the foot of the page he has drawn a double Chepstow-type span.
It looks awful. The Chepstow system would not work here, and with that, his mind re-thought and produced the superb solution his greatest design - the Royal Albert Bridge, Saltash. He completed that design in 1852. It was opened to traffic in May 185⁹ and is, of course, still in use in 2010.

as you can be that there should be no occasion for repeated complaints or any interference on our part & also to remind you that if the work does not proceed satisfactorily no objections or notices of yours will release you from that responsibility which by your contract is fairly thrown upon you. Proper centring must be provided and bad work must be replaced and if this causes any delay upon you must fall the consequences.

It is the interest of the Company of course to render that delay as trifling as possible and if Mr Glennie finds you improve the quality of the work and proceed to supply new centrings he will under my direction allow you as much time for replacing the effective work as he can but entirely as an accommodation to you.

I am, Dear Sir,
Your obt. Servt.
I. K. Brunel

G. Burge Esq

18 Duke Street,
Westminster.
14th September 1838

Sir,
In reply to yours of the 12th I can only repeat what I stated in my letters of 11th – that if delay is caused by your centrings being insufficient and requiring to be replaced by better you are liable for the consequences of that delay – but that I will endeavour to assist you in rendering that delay as slight as possible particularly if I find that you exert yourself to remedy the defects complained of as quickly as you possibly can – if every exertion is made in constructing new centrings I will allow the old ones to be used until the others are ready – more care must be taken however in securing them.

I do not know to what you allude when you request that Mr Glennie may furnish you with a plan of what I require to do but I have no objections to the construction of the present ribs but I consider they should be 6 inches thick instead of 4 inches and at intervals of 3ft with intermediate braces – any assistance that I or Mr Glennie can afford you in designing or drawing these will be rendered most willingly if you wish it.

A Committee of the Directors had been appointed at my request to visit the Box tunnel on Monday next and we shall be glad to see you on the Works.

I am Sir,
Yours very truly,
I. K. Brunel

G. Burge Esq

In November Brunel reported to Thomas Osler, Secretary to the Bristol Committee of the GWR (Rail 1149/5, p25):

18 Duke Street
28 November 1838

Dear Sir,
Shaft 6 – nothing doing nor any attempt making to pump the water or to provide any means for doing so.
Shaft 5 – to the east the work last completed is so bad as to require to be immediately pulled down and rebuilt to the west no work has been done since Thursday the 22nd – and there is no evidence of any intention of resuming the work.
The Contractor pretends that the brickwork cannot be erected without being subject to injury from the blasting of the excavation and that the centres are unavoidably struck and thrown down by the same operation – yet at shafts 2 and 3 under similar circumstances the excavation is blasted without injury to either brickwork or centres.
At Shaft 4 the same subcontractors are employed and the same evil exists the brickwork is bad and some of it ordered to be removed.
At shafts 2 & 3 there is much less subject of complain – the rate [of progress] is insufficient.

I am dear sir, yours very truly,
I. K. Brunel

Thos Osler Esq

The Bristol Committee evidently responded, and early the next year

Brunel wrote to Burge (Rail 1149/5, pp55-56):

Box,
Wilts.
January 19th 1839

Sir, I enclose you a letter from the Secretary of the Company. The measures to which it refers as necessary for the progress of the works are the following.

First. That immediate steps should be taken towards the erection of an engine and pump of sufficient power at Shaft No 6. It is necessary that I should be informed exactly of what steps are taken in order I may satisfy myself upon the point.

Secondly. That a force of horse power be provided for the works generally.

Thirdly. That you commence immediately the driving of headings for the purpose of opening additional faces or adopt some other means equally effective to enable you to regain the time already lost.

Fourthly. That the additional centres which will be required for these new faces be immediately put in hand and proceeded with as fast as possible and that the timber required for these faces be also provided and brought upon the ground.

Your active adoption of these measures can alone satisfy the Directors that you are about to proceed with energy in the future prosecution of the work and you must distinctly understand that unless I can report satisfactorily upon these points as well as upon the general progress during the next fortnight no further confidence will be placed in you.

Certificates for the work measured up to last week will be paid on Tuesday if on the day I can report to the Directors that you have up to that time made exertions to proceed with the work.

Yours very truly,
I. K. Brunel

G. Burge Esq

However, delays persisted, so that Brunel had to write thus to Lewis & Brewer (Rail 1149/5, p100):

18 Duke Street
23 March 1839

Gentlemen,
Mr Glennie has just informed me that the works have again been
delayed by the breaking of your machinery.
This has been of such frequent occurrence and the consequences
are likely to be so serious that I must insist upon some decisive
steps being taken to remedy the evil. It is not my business to point
out to you where is the principal defect. Whether it be in the
designing of the machinery or in the construction, or in the use of
it, it is evident that it cannot be depended upon. I never knew a
work in which the failure of the machinery was so frequent – when
the Directors desirous of affording you every encouragement
agreed to postpone for the present leaving the 1/5th of the amount
of penalties due by you it was upon my representation that the
works were now in such a state that great progress might be made
and that I had hopes that you would soon regain the arrears which
had accumulated. It is evident that no such hope can be entertained
while the works are subject to be stopped weekly and almost daily
by accidents to the machinery and I feel that the Directors will be
compelled to enforce the penalties immediately and that I must
withhold any certificates until I can report that the machinery
upon which everything depends is put into an efficient state of
repair – your most serious attention must therefore be immediately
given to this subject.

I am, Gentlemen,
Your obt. servt.
I. K. Brunel

Messrs Lewis & Brewer

In April George Burge gets 'gunfire' again from Brunel. Box Tunnel was
a nightmare for him – and for the poor devils slaving away in the freezing
cold and the wet. Brunel had to verbally lash him hard from the day he
started till the day the work was completed. And with the 'en avant'-style
spurrings-on came also the withholding of payment – which can only
have made the tragic man's worries the greater. Burge's invoices for work
done had to be compared with Mr Glennie's measurements – and, of
course, Mr Burge came off worst (Rail 1149/5, p111):

18 Duke Street
April 2nd 1839

Sir,

In reply to your letter of the 27 ult. I have to express my regret that the progress of the works is not such as to give any encouragement to me to recommend to the Directors any other course than that pointed out by the strict terms of the contract.

While you are wasting so much valuable time at Shaft No 6 in a bungling attempt to make the present machinery do that which it is totally unfit for, while you are neglecting to drive the headway between shafts 5 and 6 which would have shewn some intention of providing against similar difficulties next winter. While such a total want of management continues I shall certainly not recommend the Directors any further payments.

The side headings instead of advancing the work rather delay it, in consequence of their not being pushed forward enough and always remaining just in the position to interfere with the other – this great want of management which I had vainly hoped was about to be remedied and the total inefficiency of the machinery at shaft No 6 are points upon which not one moment must be lost in effecting a total change and until great improvement be made I doubt whether I can be justified in sending in any certificates. In the statement of accounts which you sent me some time back, although the measurements of quantities agree nearly with those of Mr Glennie, there are many items which are inadmissible and others omitted so that the result of my statement is very different and the payment already made to you was as liberal as the circumstances would admit of – Mr Glennie will shew you this statement as corrected.

I am Sir,
Your obt. Servant,
I. K. Brunel

George Burge Esq.

William Glennie was injured while working inside Box Tunnel in June 1839. Brunel was truly concerned about his Assistant, as he was about all his closely acquainted 'right-hand men' (Rail 1008/35, folio 36).

June 14th 1839

My Dear Mrs Glennie,
I am much obliged to you for your letter and am delighted to hear
that Glennie is improving I had expected to see you today but have
been prevented leaving Town by an accident last evening from the
effects of which I feel rather stiff – will you have the kindness to
let me hear again on Monday morning.

Yours very truly,
I. K. Brunel

Thomas Osler, Secretary to the Bristol Committee of Management of the
GWR, was a man who often irritated Brunel. Just now he has found a
letter addressed to Brunel in the Bristol Office and has mistakenly
returned it to its author, Charles Saunders. This letter also shows the
origin of the track layout for 5 miles between Standish and Tuffley, on
the Swindon-Gloucester line, where the Midland and the Great Western
routes ran side by side.

Tuesday
31 August 1839
Private.

My Dear Saunders,
Our friend Osler chose to take it into his head that I was gone to
London and has returned your letter to you – I really am teased
out of my life by the man – he expects to know every day when I
am to be every next day and because I <u>do</u> <u>not</u> <u>tell</u> <u>him</u> [Brunel's
emphasis] *that I was to be at Clifton on Sunday he not only*
absurdly sent my letter to London but even now pretends to be
angry at my '<u>uncommunicativeness</u>' because I didn't tell him I was
to be here <u>in</u> <u>case</u> <u>he</u> <u>should</u> <u>want</u> <u>to</u> <u>come</u> <u>to</u> <u>me</u> – as it is, unless
anything should occur to lead me to suppose I am wanted in
London on Tuesday I shall not come –
    I was at Gloucester yesterday and we effected what I consider to
be an excellent arrangement with the B&G [Bristol & Gloucester
Railway] the line is to be split down the <u>middle</u> and each to have
half to do what we like with – single or double (for which there is
just room) they to pay half – and lay their own rails – we save a
full £20,000 – no mean sum and get all the independence I have
been long striving for.

If you have occasion to write to me Monday night address it to Shrivenham.

Yours sincerely,
I. K. Brunel

Right to the end, Brunel had to push Burge to get on (Rail 1149/6, p212):

Bristol
3 March 1841

Mr Burge
I am sorry that now we are so nearly arrived at the completion of the great bulk of our work that I should have to complain of the backwardness of some parts and particularly of the Tunnel front which ought a long time to have been completed – as I explained to you the other day upon the ground I have no alternative – the work must be finished and if you don't do it I shall and without a moments hesitation or a day's delay.

I therefore give you formal notice that unless you immediately use the greatest exertions and proceed to my satisfaction I shall take the work out of your hands – your delay also leads to delay in the completion of No 6 Extension and consequently <u>prevents</u> <u>your receiving so much money</u> as you otherwise would do – I hope however instead of compelling me to take such a step as that referred to – you will enable me to express my satisfaction – and to certify accordingly.

Your obt. Servt.
I. K. Brunel

After all the labour, George Burge then had to extract final payment from Brunel. When he signed up he agreed that Brunel would be arbitrator in any dispute and agreed to be penalised financially for failing to keep up his contracted rate of tunnelling. Even after taking into account deductions made by Brunel for his not completing on time, Burge still considered that the GWR owed him £29,000. Two years after the trains started to run through the tunnel Burge is still trying to be paid (Rail 1149/7, p277):

18 Duke Street
11 July 1843

Mr Burge,
Your offer made this day I find on reference to my papers to be
exactly the same as that made by you in February last and to which
I have already told you I consider as not admitting of consideration
– In arriving at your estimate of a balance of £29,059 in your
favour you make an error of £3,000 in the amount of payments
actually made by the Company for you – you include claims which
altho' you may have diminished them by half are still perfectly
groundless & the amount of £10,759 after which […] your
estimated balance would be reduced to £14,000 against which still
remains the whole amount of the penalties which if […] would I
believe approach £10,000 and yet you propose that the Company
instead of bringing an action against you for £40 or £50,000
should pay you £20,000 – how can I propose such a settlement to
the Directors let me have a reasonable proposal and I will do my
best to carry it.

Yours very truly,
I. K. Brunel

G. Burge Esq

Brunel had to deal with extortionists all the way along the line from
Paddington. Here (Rail 1149/2, p88) he needs a bit of field owned by a
Mr Wiltshire, who hires lawyers to make the most of his supposed
opportunity to hold the GWR to ransom. 'Chapman' was Captain
Chapman, Secretary to the Bristol Committee of the GWR.

18 Duke Street,
Westminster.
31 August 1836

My Dear Chapman,
I unfortunately missed Mr Wiltshire the other day at his home but
met him upon the road and agreed to see him in a few days. In the
meantime I wrote him a note requesting that he would allow a few
levels to be taken in order that I that I might be better prepared
when we meet.
*   I sent my letter through Glennie. Mr Wiltshire returned my letter*

with the accompanying note [not in the record]. The conclusion I draw is not favourable and I want to know your opinion because you know the man better than I. I believe Mant wrote the other day as his solicitor to say he would not object to afford us any reasonable accommodation. I am to see Wiltshire in a few days and should wish to have a cue if you have an opportunity before you go to see him and without bringing him formally to the subject try and learn whether he is still practicable at all events let me hear from you addressed to the Bath Hotel where I shall be on Saturday morning early. I have received your letter with the copy of Mr Dicks. I believe nothing can be done, however I shall see the Directors on Tuesday.

Yours very truly,
I. K. Brunel

18 Duke Street
Feby 6th 1837

My dear Chapman,
Several negociations [sic] connected with our Great Western Railway Bills detain me in Town tomorrow – I am rather disposed to be angry with Messrs Paxton & Orton for the application for money – I saw Orton on Tuesday evening and no application was then made to me and I think that up to the present time their works has been profitable – however we took them knowing them not to be men of capital and I have to thank the Directors for acting in my absence upon the emergency.
On the subject of Mr Wilkins Appeal to us on the score of a promise made the first year that promise taken a' la' letter would certainly preclude touching a square inch of Mr Wiltshire's ground even if at miles off from Shockerwick but this was not the spirit of the promise and the case here is very little different, still, however, the Directors will prefer incurring any inconvenience (and it is a serious one) to raising the slightest doubt even in the mind of this most capricious Gentleman of our good faith. If they should determine to abandon in Committee the right of touching No 74 and to carry the line outside of this field – if required so to do by Mr Wiltshire – I trust they will at the same time pass a resolution expressing this feeling 'that by the spirit of the promise they are not called upon to do so – that considering the taking this course does not really cause any injury to Mr Wiltshire while the avoiding it

will cause irreparable injury to the railway and thereby the public by increasing a more already sharp lug [sic] do not think that Mr Wiltshire out to require it.' To gratify a caprice we are called upon to make a serious sacrifice.

I have made some experiments with coal tar by a good heat above boiling water I have evaporated [...] in small quantity a fatty very fusible crystallisation, very stincking [sic] substance rather abundantly and left the coal tar very fusible but hardening to the consistency of glue just before it set.

The result does not alarm me I think if the tar is admitted hot and the vessel warm no further heat will be necessary – our first step will be, I think, to get the air pump to work and a small vessel – I have written to Babbage through Mr Frere about it.

I am, my dear Sir,
Yours very truly,
I. K. Brunel

Negotiations have evidently dragged on to September, when Brunel writes to Thomas Osler (Rail 250/82, p85):

Sept. 7th 1837

My Dear Sir,
The proposal of Messrs Clark & King is a specimen of their grossly extortionary intentions and their notions of the necessity of our case – such as I fear precludes all hopes of arrangement. It is very difficult to estimate in money the advantages to us of encroaching on that corner. I think it well over £500 to you in actual diminution of work and I should say £300 or perhaps even £500 well bestowed in reducing the depth of cutting in slippery ground which independent of the expense allowed for in the first £500 might be troublesome and ugly and in increasing the radius of the curves already small and I suppose we must not allow the feeling of disgust at being cheated and robbed to enter into the calculation. My figures therefore reach £1,000 or even £1,200 but I hope Messrs. Clark & King's charges will not be left to us to pay. It may as well be understood by Mr Wiltshire that if we don't take the corner it makes no difference in the nature of the works and of course we shall take no pains to prevent there being a nuisance.

Yours etc.,

I. K. Brunel

Thos. Osler Esq

A dispute with the Trustees of the Corsham turnpike road causes Brunel to write to Osler again:

18 Duke Street
10 December 1838

My Dear Osler,
On the subject of the Trustees of the Corsham Road it is right that the Directors should be aware that I have long endeavoured in vain to convince the Surveyor [William McAdam] *that some improvements might and ought to be made by the Trustees when we build the bridge and although I never committed the Company to any thing they have been given to understand that any arrangement whatever would accommodate them without involving the Company in expense and be cheerfully acceded to but they always seemed to have rested on the supposition that we wanted something and that they could drive a bargain with us – what they now ask is not quite reasonable & I much fear impracticable even if modified –*
First there appears to be mistake –
In the copy you sent me it says 'to place the <u>bridge below</u>' (that must mean towards the valley or westwards) but adjoining 'on the <u>north</u> side to the site of the present road.' I suppose it must be <u>South Side</u> or else above.
The expense of widening the bridge to 24ft and raising it 6ft would even if built square [ie not at a skewed angle] *be considerably more than the cost of a temporary diversion – so far therefore I think the proposal unreasonable but I think we might propose to make the bridge 20ft wide – to be placed square to the railway and 4ft higher (every foot in height adds considerably to the expense) but price causes what I fear will be found the difficulty – they must undertake to have the new road intended to be made by them, so far completed as to lead over the bridge by the time the bridge is finished or else we shall be worse off than ever and our works quite end-off [sic].*
It will be desirable to request them to mark on the plan which was sent them – the position of the bridge as they propose it subject

to the above or such other connections as the Directors may determine upon.

The increased expense of the bridge as they propose would I should think be of £200 more than the temporary diversion.

The increased height would be no advantage whatever to us as we have plenty of headroom.

Yours very truly,
I. K. Brunel

Thos. Osler Esq

Brunel wrote to William McAdam a couple of weeks later:

Bath
21 December 1838

My Dear Sir,
I am told that the Committee appointed by the Trustees on Saturday last have met but have not come to any conclusion upon the subject of the temporary diversion and that they were disposed to mix up the question of the arrangements which may be made with reference to the Holloway Bridge. I can hardly believe that my information is correct particularly as I understand you were present.

The diversion of the road as amended by you and was <u>agreed by the Trustees</u> was settled and that the Committee would meet on the ground to see it and <u>confirm it</u>.

The question of any arrangement for an alteration of the permanent works was clearly <u>postponed</u> until I could meet the Committee and the meeting of yesterday was expressly for the purpose of settling the diversion which as I stated <u>must not be postponed</u>. The other question can have nothing to do with the present diversion and as I hope we are now going to work amicably I caution you not to allow the question of diversion to be postponed because with every desire to continue that courtesy which I think in this business we have shewn and received I cannot allow our works to be stopped and if we don't agree upon a diversion we must make it without agreeing – and give up all idea of improvement at Holloway and if the public suffer as well as us upon the Trustees must be the blame – we have entered upon it *with every desire to settle points to our mutual advantage – you for the Road Public, I for the Railway Public, if you break through the understanding upon you must rest the discredit in every sense of the word.*

Yours very truly,
I. K. Brunel

Mr Wm McAdam Esq

The following letter (Rail 1149/5, p58) ends in mid-sentence, probably because the copying clerk was unable to decipher Brunel's writing as his anger got the better of him after being messed around by McAdam and the Turnpike Trustees.

Bath
No day. January 1839
Private.

My Dear Sir,
I trust you will admit that I have met you fair and frankly on this business and stated what we could do to accommodate you and what we require in return and I feel that I have a right to call upon you as a professional man to use your best exertions to prevent this line of conduct being met by a different one.

It does seem to me that the Committee were bound to come to some opinion upon the propositions laid before them which was to guide the Trustees at the General Meeting that such was my object in meeting a sub-committee instead of the General Body and the Chairman and Mr Hine certainly then told me that although the proceedings or rather the recommendation of the Committee must be confirmed by the General Body yet that this was a matter of course and if you remember I adopted every suggestion made by you or the Committee and I pledged my word to stand as firmly by what I asked for and by what I promised to do to the very letter.

I need not go into the merits of the bargain you know as well as I can tell you that it is all gain to the Trustees and no loss while on our side it is a mere point of apparent rather than real proportion in our case for which we are willing to pay in money in the improvement at Holloway and elsewhere but as we can do perfectly well at Cross Post Gate as we are the case stands thus –

as at present set out the line is within 16ft from the summit of the road agreed upon if we give you 1 foot 6 inches of metalling and 2 inches of cast iron plates for whether we raise the road or not we shall only have cast iron plate – this leaves us 14 feet 4 inches of headway and the engines chimneys are only 14ft and our gauge by which everything is limited is only 15 feet so that if we chose even to adhere to this which is I think 2 feet more than other railway we should only have to lower our rails 10 inches near London we have in our place.

I pointedly observed that I should consider the decisions of the Committee quite sufficient and leave the confirmation to their convenience as a mere matter of form. Now I may be wrong but it appeared to me yesterday as if the Committee were not going to pass any specific resolution but after my experience of what I may call the highest price I could offer – the matter seems to be referred to the General Body where again the bargain was to be fought and probably rejected – for let it be clearly understood not one inch will the company stir from my proposition...

The railway running past Box village cut the Box-Bath main road (the modern A4) on the east and the west of the village. This letter (Rail 1149/5, p80) mentions 'wing walls' and is therefore concerned with the bridge to the west of the village. Brunel is writing to the Secretary of the Trustees of the Turnpike.

18 Duke Street
26 February 1839

My Dear Sir,
I have no objection to place the proposed new bridge for the Corsham Road at Box on the north side of the present road but as this will involve the purchase of land for the approaches, the Directors must of course pay for that land the materials required for the approach we can supply at a trifling expense and therefore that need not enter into the calculation but the position of the bridge must be determined upon and I believe that shown on the accompanying tracing is what the Trustees wish but as this will require a diversion of the road which I understand forms part of the improvements proposed by the Trustees it must be clearly understood that this diversion is not required by us and that we shall not execute it or incur any part of the expense of forming the

road except immediately over the bridge and to the extent of the
wing walls and the Trustees must undertake to have so much of the
diversion as may be necessary ready to carry the road as soon as
the bridge is finished so that we may cut through the old road.

I am, My Dear Sir,
Yours very truly,
I. K. Brunel

Meanwhile Brunel continues to wrestle with the Surveyor of Bath roads, William McAdam, over the construction of the 'Holloway' bridge, an arched opening, wide enough for a double road, through the viaduct leading west from Bath station, where the Holloway road and the Wells road meet at the foot of the hill, close to the River Avon. When Brunel wrestles with someone in writing, his wording tends to writhe. This letter (Rail 1149/5, p56) is just such a one. Brunel wants to make a partial diversion of the road, which he thinks will inconvenience the public less, but McAdam will not agree, so Brunel is offering a total diversion, which means building a new, temporary, road. McAdam is being stubbornly obstructive, refusing to allow any diversion as far as one can tell from Brunel's convoluted constructions. Brunel has the power of the law to push his railway through, but he always tries diplomacy and politeness first in these situations. He is attempting to persuade the reluctant road-mender, and subtly points out to McAdam that, in standing in the way of the railway company, he is not hurting the GWR but the contractor, an innocent third party. However, at the end of the letter he threatens him with the GWR Act of Parliament, then an olive branch – a very common Brunellian device.

Bath
28 November 1839

Dear Sir,
The object of the Great Western Railway Company in making the
arrangements which they had recommended for the purpose of
constructing the Holloway Bridge seems to have been greatly
misconstrued by some persons. A complete diversion of the road
which would have the progress of our work uninterrupted would
have much better answered every purpose and would be preferred
by the contractor upon whom alone by the terms of his contract
the whole expense would fall. A decided opinion which I still
entertain and of the correctness of which I had conceived there

could not be a reasonable doubt, that the public convenience would be much better studied by having the diversion of the road the same as at present and by merely enclosing a part first on one side and then on the other while the foundations of the piers were being built, induced us to adopt the plan which has been partially acted upon and which as you must be aware would have put us to considerable inconvenience and increased expense on the centring when the westwards foundations are built and the centring being constructed so as to leave a headroom of 15ft during the construction. I need hardly say after thus describing the process that such a plan would be very inconvenient to us and would have been adopted and is now proposed only from a strong desire to study the convenience of the public and with a clear understanding that it is not met by an equally liberal spirit on the part of the Trustees (of the Bath Turnpike) and that our attempts to study the interests of the public at an increased expense to ourselves will not be frustrated by unnecessary interference.

It is necessary that we should commence without delay the required diversion of the road and shall feel obliged by your immediate attention to the subject and your reply after the meeting of the Trustees on Saturday on the subject of the proposal now made. Have the goodness to address any comments to me at this office as I shall be in the neighbourhood for the rest of this week.

If you think it will at all forward the arrangements I shall be happy to attend the meeting.

I am, Dear Sir,
Your very truly,
I. K. Brunel

William McAdam Esq., General Surveyor of the Bath roads.

I now forward a plan showing a proposed road marked A-B to be formed according to the terms of our Act the surface of such road will be a straight line between the points of junction with the Wells road and the Lower Bristol Roads the level of which you possess.

I will still leave you the option of adopting that which I am convinced the public will prefer namely a partial diversion of the present road in the manner shown at C-D such diversion to be of the same width being shifted westwards.

Brunel became, reluctantly, stern with Mr McAdam, who is apparently going back on his agreement with Brunel (Rail 1149/5).

18 Duke Street
8 March 1839

My Dear Sir,
The arch at Twerton will particularly be raised upwards of a foot the point at the centre will be raised six inches and the haunches raised 6 inches more by making the arch much flatter.

However whether much or little I can assure you that it is all we can do and it will be an expensive job as it is. But I must protest against you mixing up the question of this bridge and the road at Cross Post Gate – I expressly refused to unite the two questions – the latter was part of a bargain between the Trustees & myself on the part of the Company we shall perform our part of the bargain at the Holloway bridge and while the technicalities required by your Act be all completed with or part we shall be quite satisfied with the assurance of the Trustees and if I feel convinced that you would not sanction a breach of faith on the part of the Directors – I must come down I should wish to see you on the subject of the water at Saltford – think the parishioners are not possessing a wise course in holding out threats to us while we are really anxious to do all in our power and have succeeded far beyond my expectations. Compulsion depend upon it won't make the water come so freely as good will, and the latter at present exists.

I am, dear Sir,
Yours very truly,
I. K. Brunel

J Batchelor, Corston Lodge, Bath

Brunel had a huge problem when bringing his line into Bath from the east. The Kennet & Avon Canal and Sydney Gardens lay in his path. The canal made a sharp, almost pointed loop around the hill to the south of the line that the railway would take so that the railway would cut it twice, while the Trustees of the Gardens did not want to see the railway running through their grounds. Brunel overcame these formidable obstacles with magnificent diplomacy. He persuaded the canal company to allow him to divert its canal through the hill, improving its line by removing the sharp bend, and persuaded the Trustees that the Gardens could be improved with fine architecture if the railway came through in the open.

The following letters (Rail 1149/2, p132, and 1149/5, p53) follow Brunel's meeting with Henry Goodwin, representing the Trustees of Sydney Gardens. The first is a covering letter, explaining the second. Brunel is generous with words. In spite of the time it took to write a score of letters a day, when he had people appointed to see him throughout the day, or after a long day out on site, sitting in an inn or hotel, he wrote each, never cutting down on the words, as if it was the only letter he had to write. There are, of course, exceptions – his rebuke to the contractor Shedlock is a masterpiece of brevity.

The canal was contoured around the projecting 'nose' of the hill, making a sharp U-shaped bend that required either the railway to tunnel under the canal or the canal to be diverted to allow the railway a reasonable curve into Bath. But tunnelling would require a very untidy 'dip' in the otherwise beautifully even gradient of his railway. Brunel composes a most kind and diplomatic letter.

18 Duke Street,
Westminster
31 October 1836

Dear Sir,
Amongst their deviations and amendments of the line which the Great Western Railway Company intend to apply for powers this next Session is one which will carry our line across the Kennet & Avon canal (under it) for the purpose of avoiding the sharp curve which the canal takes just after passing through Sydney Gardens at Bath – these crossings will not necessarily involve our interfering with the canal as we pass at a convenient depth below it but as the Parliamentary Notices next month may refer to 'powers to divert' I thought you would be glad to have this previous explanation.

I believe that while attending our own diversion we may benefit you by assisting you in cutting off your sharp curve at the same time. If your Engineer will turn his attention to this I shall be very happy to confer with him or you upon the subject.

I am,
My Dear Sir,
Yours very truly,
I. K. Brunel

Bath
January 23rd 1839

My Dear Sir,
The enclosed is the substance of what I propose but there was one
or two points requiring explanation.
First. I have taken 28ft for the width of the bridge as being about
that of the present walk eastward of the proposed bridge – this is
however considerably constricted in a very short distance and is
only 20ft at the canal bridge. I think therefore that 28ft will appear
very wide and certainly as a promenade is a very splendid roadway.
With respect to the gravel it is absolutely necessary that a definite
quantity should be fixed upon as at many points of the cutting
where it is in thin beds or mixed with marl it may cost more to
separate it than it would be worth – and the quantity I have named
I should think would gravel your walks for the next ten years and
would of itself form a heap that would be inconvenient to you in
the Gardens – by fixing the quantity it becomes an object with our
contractor to select it & save it as the excess would be used with
the gravel from the other excavations in ballasting our road if there
were no such object gained the chances are you would not really
get more as unless there is an interest to keep it separate it would
probably be allowed to fall in and get mixed with the marl.

I am, My Dear Sir,
Yours very truly,
I. K. Brunel

Mr Goodwin Esq

Bath
January 23rd 1839

Dear Sir,
I now forward to you according to your request a memorandum
of the proposal made by me this morning on the part of the Great
Western Railway Company of a modification of the Terms of
Agreement existing between the Proprietors of the Sydney
Gardens and the Company.
It is proposed that the railways should be carried through the
Gardens by an open cutting instead of a Covered Way. The ground
on the upper or east side being secured by a retaining wall and on

179

the lower side to be sloped down towards the railway with a terrace & wall at the bottom. The slopes to be trimmed and soiled and returned to the Proprietors of the Gardens. A bridge to be constructed for the present centre walk of not less than 28ft in width between the parapets. The surface of the walk over the bridge to be made level with the present surface at the east end of the site of the proposed bridge with so many steps at the west end as may be necessary to connect the surface of the bridge with the level of the Walk. Two smaller bridges of cast iron or wood to be constructed at such points as the Proprietors may determine.

So much of the top soil not required for the slopes or before described and one thousand cube yards of any gravel obtained from the excavation to be laid aside and deposited on any part contiguous to the line of railway which may be selected by the Proprietors.

The bridge and retaining walls to be constructed according to the general character of the designs submitted this day to the Committee of Proprietors.

I am, Dear Sir,
Yours very truly,
I. K. Brunel

Henry Goodwin Esq

The railway west of Bath station had to squeeze through a narrow strip of land between the River Avon and steeply rising ground to the south. The Lower Bristol Road already occupied this strip, and the village of Twerton lay directly in the railway's path. The village was for the most part the property of the largest employer in the area, the textile mill owner Charles Wilkins. The railway was on an embankment from Bath station to Twerton and to take up as little room as possible the embankment was contained within vertical stone walls. The village was, to a great extent, demolished and rebuilt to the north of the line. The contract – for the demolition of 50 cottages, the construction of the 638-yard-long walled embankment, the diversion of the Lower Bristol Road and the construction of a new road to run along the northern edge of the railway – was given to Charles Wilkins.

Note that these office copies of Brunel's letters to George Frere (Rail 1149/2, pp62, 73 and 50) do not appear in chronological order in the pages of the ledger.

January 21 1836

My Dear Sir,
Plans do not contain all you suppose or you give me credit for
perception I do not possess. No material discrepancy between
general tracing and small precedent [sic] – no means of comparing
general directions of lines which I suppose must be wrong. Suspect
that they must be wrong from the IKB who took the angles. I can
do nothing till your corrected plan comes up.

Directors have authorised me to take advantage of Mr Wilkins
offer and I propose to write to him, thanking him and accepting.
But I wish to know from you that Mr Wilkins clearly understands
it to be a gratuitous offer to let me occupy at once free of expense
a house we propose to buy. Any pictures? – just see to all this and
let me know.

If you would wish to reside in it you can have such portion as
will make a comfortable residence at a small rent – of course small
but a rent there had better be – it giving you a possession free from
intrusions.

Yours faithfully,
I. K. Brunel
G.E Frere, Esq.

PS. I have sent a cheque for Bell addressed to you.

18 Duke Street,
Westminster.
25 Feby. 1836

I send you £130 which you do not deserve to have for not sending
your account and I am consequently obliged to allow today's
General Bond to pass and to hear the complaints of the Directors
for my not sending in my account. Am too late for bank and so
shall send cheque tomorrow.

I. K. Brunel

G. E. Frere, Esq

Great Western Railway
18 Duke Street
April 3rd 1836

Dear Sir,
Accompanying this is a plan of Twerton with the boundary lines
of the width which will be required for the railway and the
proposed diversion of the turnpike road. The houses shaded with
Indian ink stand in our book of reference as belonging to Mr
Wilkins, those shaded pink as held by him under the Kennet &
Avon Canal Company in consequence of some peculiarity in the
tenure which Mr How will explain to you. These must be valued
separately from Mr Wilkins property there is also some other
property which I believe Mr Wilkins has purchased since our Book
of Reference was made. This Mr Wilkins will be able to point out
but I should suggest that it will be better to keep these valuations
quite distinct.

I do not know whether you have received any instructions as to
the sale or value you should attach to these species of property
particularly Mr Wilkin's houses as compared with mere value if for
sale each individual piece or lot and inclusive of severance or other
immediate damage if not it must be a matter for consideration after
you have made your survey and Mr Osbourne will be able to give
you every information as to the understanding existing between
Mr Wilkins and the Company upon this subject.

I have only to add for your guidance that these boundary lines
include all we shall want when passing amongst the houses where
the railway will be upon masonry work and upright walls but in
the present garden of Mr Wilkins there slopes both to the Lower
Bristol Road and the railway which I cannot at present exactly
determine. The viaduct will be 14 or 15 feet high through the
village.

Yours truly,
I. K. Brunel

G. E. Frere

As we have already seen, Brunel had to allow William Ranger to give up
his contracts at the Bristol end of the line early in 1838, as he was in great
difficulties with the contract for excavating Sonning Cutting. Brunel
asked Hugh and David McIntosh to take over Ranger's contracts. David
was against this, but his father over-ruled him. Hugh died in 1840 and
David's worst fears became a reality by the time the contracts were
complete. Short of money because of continuing arguments with Brunel

over pay, David seems to have been trying to save money by omitting to use scaffolding on his masonry work. Here (Rail 1149/5, p205) Brunel writes to him in what must have been very great agitation. Luckily his letter was copied by a clerk with very good handwriting – there are two words in this copy that are plain to read but I cannot help wondering if the clerk, in deciphering Brunel's writing, got them wrong.

18 Duke Street,
Westminster
2 October 1838

My Dear Sir,
From letters I have just received this morning since I saw you I learn that the east face of Twerton tunnel is very badly secured that in fact they are trusting to the chance of the brown snail [?] standing at a very slight slope without any timbering.

I consider this very dangerous and must strongly caution you against running such a risk – the expense and delay which may be caused and the possibility is already for want of a little timber is too great to be trifled with

If is [sic] true it falls upon you – but the delay might be irretrievable and the Company will then be the sufferer and you can expect no indulgence when it arises from your own neglect – let me beg you to send to Twerton immediately.

Yours very truly,
I. K. Brunel

D. McIntosh Esq

On 26 May 1840 Hugh McIntosh asked for his surety bond to be returned but the Directors had minuted Brunel that no moneys were to be released. This indicated to Hugh that Brunel was not an 'arbitrator' under the terms of his contract but subject to the orders of the GWR Board of Directors.

Here (Rail 1149/7, p23) Brunel writes to Timothy Tyrrell, David McIntosh's lawyer, in a letter emphasising his – Brunel's – importance, making cunningly disguised insults and delivering a lecture in manners – 'gentlemanliness'. But Brunel's view of gentlemanliness and good manners did not extend so far as to pay McIntosh for the work he had done.

18 Duke Street
24 November 1841

Sir,

I am in receipt of yours of the 22nd and I should prefer silence alone induces me to notice the singular manner in which you take upon yourself to fix the day upon which you are to receive replies to your letter and assume the right of ascribing motives for delay if any should occur. If I may take more time in replying to your letters than that which a man having many occupations may fairly be expected to take in a business of some importance it arises from the course you have pursued being unusual and therefore requiring much consideration and still more from the singular character of your correspondence.

It is not my practice to assume unavowed motives and then to endeavour to interpret the letters or motives of my correspondents by fitting them to these assumptions and I have occupied and I fear wasted much time in endeavouring simply to <u>understand</u> letters very different from anything I am in the habit of receiving from Gentlemen and professional men and to discover what parts could be related to the business in hand and which admitted of or required a reply and from any want of acquaintance with such style of letter writing .

I have found great difficulty and consequently spent some time in replying to observations which appeared to me neither pertinent or relevant without being drawn unintentionally into any criticism of a style which I considered so faulty or saying anything which could be offensive and therefore ungentlemanly.

Confining myself now simply to the question which you have raised the matter seems to me to stand thus – After going into the accounts of No 9L and bringing them nearly but not quite to a close after allowing so long a time...

It is a great shame that these letters from Tyrrell have not been kept. Brunel accepts Tyrrell's apology but still continues with his sarcasm (Rail 1149/7, p25):

18 Duke Street
29 November 1841

Sir,

I have to thank you for your expression of regret that your letters should have given me any annoyance, the language was certainly such as to induce me at last to observe upon it but I can relieve your mind from the fear that any other or greater source of annoyance existed in those letters from any statement of facts as I have never discovered in any one letter since your first dated 14 October anything that can be correctly called a statement of fact.

Your obt. servt.,
I. K. Brunel

And whilst on the subject of Brunel's sarcasm this letter was published by his grand daughter, Lady Celia Noble on page 147 of her book 'The Brunels: Father and Son' (British Library shelfmark 10858.e.11)

The Manager of Swindon Refreshment Room
December 1842

Dear Sir,
I assure you Mr.Player was wrong in supposing that I thought you purchased inferior coffee. I thought I said to him that I was surprised that you should buy such bad roasted corn. I did not believe you had such a thing as coffee in the place. I am sure I have never tasted any. I have long since ceased to make complaints at Swindon. I avoid taking anything there if I can help it.

Yours faithfully.
I. K. Brunel

8: Personal Relationships

'I am not a habitual fault finder'

Very few letters from Brunel to his wife have come into the public domain – I have seen only two. He wrote this (DM 1282/2) to her early in 1841, from an inn at Wootton Bassett, 7 miles west of Swindon.

My Dearest Mary, I have walked today from Bathford Bridge to here, 20 miles along the line and I am really not very tired. I am going to sleep here. If I had arrived half an hour earlier I think I could not have withstood the temptation of coming up by the 6.30 train just to see you. However I will write you a long letter instead. It is a blowy evening, pouring with rain and I arrived rather wet and found this <u>Hotel</u> which is the best of a deplorable set of public houses and here I am at the Cow and Candle Snuffers or some such sign, in a large room or cave for it seems open to the wind everywhere, old fashioned with a large chimney in one corner. But unfortunately it has one of those horrible little stoves just nine inches across. I have piled fire on the hobs but it is no use. There are four doors and two window. What's the use of the doors I can't imagine for you might crawl under them and they seem too crooked to open – the two with a not bad looking bit of glass between them seem particularly friendly disposed. The curtains are wisely not drawn or if they were they would be blown across the room and probably over two greasy muttons which are on the table giving just enough light to see the results of their evident attempts to outvie each other as to which can make the biggest snuff. One is a quite splendid fellow, a sort of black colliflower.

There is a horrible harp, upon which, really and honestly somebody has, every few minutes for the last three hours been strumming these chords – always the same.

Goodbye my dearest love,
Yours, IKB

Lady Noble wrote in her book *The Brunels: Father and Son* 'Relations between Brunel and his children were particularly easy and friendly, especially for the period. Their old nurse recalled "their Dear Papa" charging upstairs to play with them, when he could get away from his office, while their "Dear Mama" only received visits from her children when she sat rigidly upright in the Drawing Room.' In spite of all the easy friendliness and devoted love Brunel was happy to send his oldest son, Isambard, (1837-1902) away to boarding school at the tender age of seven. From the letter below, published on page 189 of Lady Noble's book , it is evident that both little Isambard and his mother were very upset at this. It is, in fact, arguable, that tearful words were spoken by Brunel's wife, Mary on the subject. But Brunel was adamant. On his way to Exeter he wrote this breezy letter dismissing all concerns with, possibly, exaggerated statements about the far greater 'pain' of his own start away from home

Taunton.
April 17 1844.

My Dear Love,
Here I am on my way to Exeter. I have every reason to believe that, although I may be at home on Thursday, I shall be away again on Friday.
I hope, dearest, you are feeling well and happy. You are wrong in supposing that I cannot feel your parting from dear Isambard. I hope the poor little fellow is not very unhappy but it is what all must go through and he has infinitely less cause for pain than most boys in beginning. I made my beginnings in ten times worse circumstances and now he will soon get over it. Give my love to the dear boy and tell him I have smoked his cigar case twice over. Adieu, dearest love to Baby,

Yours devotedly,
I. K. Brunel.

'Baby' was their second son, Henry, then two years old.

Isambard Brunel (Jnr.) went to Harrow College on 22 November 1852 had a shuffling walk due to a birth defect which could have been cured by surgery but his mother, although she was disappointed in not bringing forth a perfect child, refused to have surgery done. She was even proud of her refusal. See page 190 of Lady Noble's book. I. K Brunel was disappointed that his son was not able to walk properly and the boy was subjected to a great deal of harsh exercise in a doomed effort to correct the shuffle. In the words of Lady Noble, page 190: 'Many of the letters from Brunel to Isambard are taken up with injunctions to profit by his drilling master and try to walk properly. At the end of one such letter Brunel wrote: *"If I could have you under my care for three months I feel sure I could cure you. I wish I could do it, my dear fellow but you must do it for yourself.*

Brunel not only liked to chain smoke good quality cigars, he enjoyed his beer and whisky. This comes out occasionally in his letters and never better than in this letter to his son, Isambard, now a pupil at Harrow school. (*The Brunels: Father and Son.* Page 191.)

Young Isambard is in for a very happy Christmas, badgered about 'walking properly' and being given maths lessons during the festivities.

November 22nd 1852

My Dear Isambard,
I send you Dr Scott's reply.
How for arithmetic? I think I must take you in hand at Christmas for I fear very much that the quality of your arithmetical knowledge is very queer, whatever the quantity and that is probably small. Half a pint of poor small beer is not nourishing and cannot be called a malt liquor diet, neither can I imagine Harrow arithmetic to be much better. It is very distressing but one must put up with it as one would if brought up in a country where it was the practise to put out one eye.

Your affectionate Father,
Isambard Kingdom Brunel.

Brunel was the Engineer-in-Chief of the Bristol & Exeter Railway (B&ER), but he delegated a great deal of responsibility to William Gravatt. Gravatt was a close and trusted friend from the days of their involvement with the Thames tunnel. Gravatt was the only example, on railway construction, of Brunel delegating. Unfortunately for him he had chosen the wrong man and Gravatt was to cause him a great deal of worry.

William Gravatt was an engineer and mathematician, verging on genius; he was of great assistance to Charles Babbage in the design of Babbage's mechanical calculator, his 'Difference Engine'. He was the same age as Brunel and, with Brunel and Beamish, had been a Resident Engineer of the Thames Tunnel. They were close friends: Gravatt attended Brunel's wedding, and Brunel really trusted him, delegating to him a great deal of the design and construction of the Bristol & Exeter line. However, Gravatt had his own strong ideas on design and, coupled with what was a very difficult, anti-social personality, he caused Brunel a great deal of worry – and the situation went from bad to worse as the months and years passed.

The 'Hemmings' referred to in this letter is a contractor building a section of the B&ER. The fifth, sixth and seventh paragraphs of the letter are a wonderful example of double standards from Brunel (see his letters to George Burge at Box Tunnel). In the 14th paragraph, extensive underlining shows the root of the offence for which Gravatt would eventually be dismissed.

There are 1,757 words in this letter (PLB 2A, p379), and it took me two hours to decipher it and type it out. It must have taken Brunel rather longer than that to write it, having also to think about what he wanted to say. That is quite a large bite out of his day – or night – of writing letters to manufacturers, contractors, assistants and Directors. At some point he would have to put the worry of Gravatt from his mind and attend to engineering design.

15 April 1839

My Dear Gravatt
Hemmings complains that undue severity and harshness have generally been used towards him by you and your assistants and that lately and particularly the other day at Gloucester you have shown such a decided feeling of hostility that he does not feel safe in your hands. He has written a letter to that effect to the Directors and claimed to be relieved from his contract on those grounds.

The letter to the Directors was sent but has not been seen by anybody but Mr Badham [Chairman of the B&ER] and myself. I therefore requested Hemming to write to Mr B, withdrawing the letter as the course he had adopted would effectively prevent any amicable arrangements for the future. Whether he might prove right or wrong is unimportant compared with the effect which the raising of such a question must have upon the interests of the Company.

It is impossible to prove or disprove the past existence of feelings or manner or the precise necessity of any particular measure which may or may not at the time have constituted harshness and it would lead to much ill if all the past acts of your assistants were to be raked up and enquired into. The mischief of seeking the remedy would be greater than the disease and I very much doubt whether in a case depending on opinions rather than facts the truth would in the slightest degree be elicited by any enquiry.

The works must proceed quietly for the interests of the Company and I shall not enter upon any such enquiries. For the sake of frankness I will state briefly my impression of the past state of the case and shall then point out the course which for the future I must strongly urge upon you and must request you to adopt.

You must be quite aware that unless a contractor is managed with great care and unless he feels confidence in those placed over him by the Company the works cannot proceed satisfactorily. When a man like Hemming – of no great strength of [... – pride?] and from ill health. Not over strong in mind or body, he has in his hands such an important part of the whole line and where the progress of the works depends entirely upon him, the interests of the Company require that he be handled with the utmost tenderness – his losses become the Company's, in fact, through him – and if he is harassed by order difficult to obey, or by what he only fancies is harshness, the work suffers.

Now Hemming is peculiarly a case in point. We know that he has not a large capital that if he loses very much it will be beyond his means and upon the company will necessarily fall the consequences. If he loses time we are all the sufferers – he cannot compensate us. If he should be entirely stopped the loss to the Company would be immense, in time irretrievable. He is the horse we have in harness and upon which we must depend – and therefore his weak point or his vices or whatever our rights to treat him as we choose it is in our interest not to over-drive him or starve him and to be contented with his utmost although this may fall short of what we originally calculated on.

I am far from saying that any injustice has ever been contemplated towards Hemming but I do not think that either you or your assistants have been aware of or have sufficiently considered the harassing nature of a Contractor's business – the peculiar position of Hemming and the great necessity of dealing very delicately with him in all money matters – and I think there has been gradually growing up a prejudice against him which although you may think will not influence your actions does at least influence those beneath you.

The fact is – Gravatt – that you like others in your position and still more your assistants, though you may work hard, like a comfortable life of peace and comparative irresponsibility and do not know what real anxiety is. When you have tasted one tenth part of what has been my share you will feel how essential it must be for the management of an extensive contract that a contractor should have his mind at ease and above all that he should be able to calculate with confidence upon all payments and upon the fairness of those whose arbitrary decisions govern those payments.

The object can be attained by constant watching on your part and by your keeping a strong check over your assistants to counteract that unavoidable tendency to abuse their power and to save the trouble of watching the works by severe discipline when they go wrong – which, without much fault on their part, is the natural consequence of their position. Whatever may have been past practice it must never, in future, be at all in their power, by the mode of measurement or by the proportionate prices, to influence the amount paid – we know how easily a difference of £200 or £300 may be made by a liberal or a strict measurement, by a full or a bare allowance and yet give no ground for complaint.

No discretion whatever on these points must be left to an Assistant. You must insist upon a simple, strictly correct, measurement or estimate and an impartial representation of facts being made to you – and you alone must then consider and determine the rate of payment or the <u>allowances</u> or <u>deductions</u> <u>to be made</u> and when you see any reason for departing from the actual schedule of prices or for <u>suspending any</u> payment or when Hemming makes any claim or as you suppose is likely to make any claim for a different rate of payment from that previously adopted or which you propose to adopt, you must consult me upon it.

You must adopt the same principle in issuing any orders for the mode or time of proceeding with any works which in their results can possibly affect the interests of the Company.

Following these rules and endeavouring to instil into the minds of your assistants a kindly feeling towards the Contractors and if possible a conviction of the fact that they themselves are of much less importance to the Company than the Contractors over whom they are placed there will be no opportunity for any further complaints whether well or ill founded.

You must let your assistants know that I do entertain the opinion that some of them have occasionally been unnecessarily severe and that although I expect them to look as closely as possible after the interests of the Company, I wish them to endeavour to render the strict performance of his contract as early as possible to the Contractor. You will let them know this by a circular in writing.

And now as regards yourself. Some change must also take place or rather return to the more careful observance of the relative position in which we stand. I have no doubt that you have frequently refrained from referring matters to me from a desire to save me trouble. This has undoubtedly led to inconvenience of a serious sort. Without referring to the past – for the future your communications must be more frequent and detailed. It is difficult to define exactly the frequency or the extent of the detail which should be referred to me but if you bear in mind that it is necessary that I should be kept informed of the general state of the works – the doubtful questions arising from time to time between you and the Contractor – if any proposed departure from the plans agreed upon or from the usual course – in order that I may decide such points if I wish to do so. That it is desirable that in your communications with the Directors you should avoid as much as possible advancing you own opinions upon new subjects until you have communicated with me. If you bear in mind that upon me must ultimately fall, in the event of any difficulties, the responsibility for any acts of yours or your assistants and the failure of any plans they may have difficulty with – recollecting all this, your own good sense will tell you on each case as it arrives what it may be necessary to write to me about.

I have said nothing of what I am told passed at Gloucester because although it seems to have been the more immediate source of irritation and as Hemming states an example of prejudice on your part against him, I do not see that it affects the position and I have no wish to go into it. Whatever appearances have been I have no doubt that you acted conscientiously and as you thought right but what I have heard amounts to this – that you refused on principle to give the calculations on which you founded your award and that you were provoked by the Counsel's doubting you.

Direct communication with the solicitors of one of the parties calls for this observation – that you should recollect that the necessity of appearing just and impartial is hardly inferior to the necessity of being so. The latter may be rendered useless and even negative by the absence of the former – and no man can with impunity place himself in suspicious circumstances and rely on his character to clear him.

Your refusal to give the details of your communicating with the other party was sure to be attributed to wrong motives by many – it was courting difficulties and the bad effects on people's minds will not easily be removed. It would have been wise to have sacrificed your feelings and your idea of rights to the opinion of others.

However, as I said before it is useless going into the question of past grievances, it is now desirable for the interests of the works that you should quiet Hemming's fears in order that we should make a fresh start and leave no doubt of just proceeding very easily doing this. Whether you prefer to do it alone or for us to meet on Friday morning I leave you to say – if the latter, make an appointment accordingly at the stroke of 9 o'clock.

Yours very truly,
I. K. Brunel

Lose no time in letting me have the different things I wrote for last week.

Brunel found it necessary to write to Gravatt again the following year (PLB 2A, p31):

Bristol
23rd July 1840

My Dear Gravatt [Brunel wrote, then crossed out, 'My Dear']
Communications have been made to me within the last 24 hours referring to a course of proceeding said to have been pursued by you which absolutely calls for enquiry.

Unless the statements made to me are totally untrue or so highly coloured as practically to be untrue they must entirely destroy all confidence in you.

It appears that you entertain opinions differing very much from my own on important engineering questions which have been discussed and which have been belittled as forming part of the plan of construction of the Bristol and Exeter Railway. In this there might be nothing extraordinary but that connected as we have been as intimate friends of long standing, acting as my assistant for 4 or five years constantly at my side when these subjects have been discussed in public or at the Board that you should ever have

193

hinted to me that you differed and that I should hear of it now for the first time and indirectly is extraordinary.

If (as I before said) the statements made to me are not entirely untrue it would appear that you have for some time past imparted these views – these expressions of doubt as to the correctness of my view privately to others – that you have furnished figures and calculations which you must have known differed from the calculations which I have positively advanced and that you should never have discussed the points with me, have asked for information or a [...] on which you are ignorant, have informed yourself or if your sense of duty tell you that [...] notwithstanding the decision of the Board founded on my advice notwithstanding your position as my assistant in my absence my [...] representative it was still your duty to express an opinion – that you should not have openly addressed to the Board! Can this be true? Is it the conduct of a friend, of a gentleman, of a subaltern trusted and confided in by the man above him?

Representations to this effect were made to me once before and as a prudent man I weighed in my mind their probability – I failed to believe them and I drove the recollection of them from my mind. I would do the same again but combative circumstance crowd upon me and statements come to me from Directors and the course if followed is most injurious to the company. I would submit to the insult that it would be to myself and should not mix up my own feelings but I must call upon the Board to enquire into the circumstance as affecting the interests of the concern. I shall request to do this at a special meeting may be called for tomorrow Saturday at 3 o'clock.

In bringing the matter thus immediately before the Board I give you every advantage. Comparatively speaking I am but slightly informed and might have delayed for a week and in the meantime have collected much information but I could not keep up the appearance of friendship and intimacy while secretly engaged in collecting evidence against a man.

I have taken steps to ensure a full meeting of Directors I have written to Dr Miller, Mr Tyrell and Mr Beardon and I have seen [...] and [...].

I was on the line yesterday and have much to say to you as there appears to be many points of dissatisfaction some of which you could probably remove by explanation amongst them was the singular state of the permanent way at Uphill but all such matters must now stand over.

I have had to introduce some punctuation into the following letter (PLB 2A, p38) because Brunel was so agitated when he wrote it that without some intervention from outside it would be close to incoherent. Even with some punctuation, it is difficult to understand in places. Gravatt had been his very close friend and Brunel is exceedingly hurt by his betrayal of him. Gravatt had found that he could not be a loyal Assistant – that he could not 'play second fiddle' to Brunel.

Clifton
4 August 1840

My Dear Gravatt,
I enclose you a copy of the resolution adopted by the Directors on 25th ult. and a copy of a letter addressed by me to them this day. Having assumed doubt, if not of your fidelity towards me as a friend or of your integrity as a man, yet certainly the degree to which the [...] operates to control your other feelings and the correctness of your views as to your duties – it may appear contradictory that I should now appeal to those feelings in the hope that you will adopt a totally different course in future – but I never did and cannot support you destitute of them – although I fear that other feelings – and particularly a vanity almost incapacitating you from occupying the place of second to any man – has been too powerful.

You will see by my letter to the Directors the course I propose to follow for the present – the future must depend upon the line of conduct you prove yourself capable of following. By this management nothing need be known to your assistants and if after the works between this place and Bridgewater are completed and the Company is in a position to proceed towards Exeter you shall have regained the whole [...] a position of the confidence I formerly placed in you and if it shall appear to the Directors consistent with the interests of the Company I shall be most anxious to continue you in the same situation you now hold.

It must be understood for the present that you give your word that you will neither directly nor indirectly either by your acts or by the mode of omitting to act express opinions or raise doubts against me or my views individually or against those which either *under my orders or contrary to them are adopted by the Bristol and Exeter Company and that you will serve me faithfully according to <u>my</u> notions of fidelity and if you find you cannot or think you ought not to do that which I require you will tell me so.*

Your sincere well wisher,
I. K. Brunel

Gravatt's manner continued to cause Brunel problems the following year (PLB 2A, p58):

6 April 1841

My Dear Gravatt,
Penistone has written to me about his leaving. He has enclosed a copy of your letter to him. It is not exactly the sort of letter I meant you to write. There is nothing on the face of it to indicate that he is not singled out to be dismissed and that this was a circular leaving it doubtful whether he or anyone was to remain neither did I authorise you to tell him that there was no probability of his continuing. You should be more careful Gravatt to gather one's meaning remembering in such cases that you are acting as the agent of communication not as the principal. I trust you <u>have</u> to the others [...] was the only one that I have made up my mind to keep on as yet and in consideration of his circumstances I wished him to know it. Let me know exactly what you wrote to [...] and the others.

Yours truly,
I. K. Brunel

6 April 1841

My Dear Sir,
The letter you received from Mr Gravatt was in consequence of my requesting him to inform the assistants generally on Bristol and Exeter Railway that their services might not be wanted as new arrangements would be required. It grows uncertain whether all [...] might be required. This uncertainty will reign for some little time to come – but you shall know as soon as you possibly can what I determine upon.

Yours truly,
I. K. Brunel

Mr Penistone

Matters come to a head (PLB 2A, p63)...

Bath
15th June 1841

My Dear Gravatt,
It is with great reluctance and regret that I have come to the
conclusion which I now communicate to you. I feel that I cannot
with justice to myself or the Company take upon myself the
responsibility of continuing to conduct the works through you as
my Assistant you do not represent me in any respect and without
questioning your integrity in the ordinary sense of the term or your
talents I cannot confide in you in the least degree either for carrying
out my views and following my directions or for keeping me
properly and correctly informed upon all matters which ought to
come under my observation.

This conclusion is neither hastily formed in consequence of
recent circumstances several of which however have been quite
sufficient to have justified it nor was it a determination come to
when I wrote to you in August last [...] remaining unchanged but
as I then stated to you I should do – I have tried you until this time
– the completion of the works to Bridgewater – and as far from
having recovered any part of the confidence in you which I then
stated I had lost – I have radically and reluctantly come to the
conclusion that we must part and have determined that nothing
shall ever again induce me to attempt to carry on the work through
you.

My past conduct towards you for nearly 15 years and
particularly on several occasions must satisfy you though you may
not admit the justice of my decision that nothing but a very strong
sense on my part of it justice and necessity could have driven me
to this – I have not communicated this determination to the Board
nor do I now enter into a series of the numerous circumstances
which have influenced me because I propose to leave you the
opportunity if you wish to avail yourself of it of resigning without
entering into enquiries before the Board and because my course

*being resolved upon I should be most anxious to avoid a useless
discussion or correspondence upon so painful a subject.*

*If you determine upon resigning it must be in terms as simple as
the following:*
*'that the works upon which you had been engaged and in which
you felt interested being now completed you begged to tender your
resignation'. If you resign without raising a question as to the case
you may depend on my silence and you may consider this letter as
private. If you determine otherwise you must let me know that I
may follow such course as I may think advisable and I must know
your determination without fail before Friday morning's Board as
it is a subject which cannot be allowed to pass over a meeting of
the Directors and one for which for both our sakes it is desirable
to settle quickly.*

Yours truly,
I. K. Brunel

Brunel wrote that on the day of the opening of the B&ER to Bridgwater,
with a branch line to Weston-super-Mare. That same evening, at the
celebratory dinner, attended by Brunel and Gravatt, Mr Badham
proposed a toast to Brunel and another in equally glowing terms to
Gravatt. I suppose Brunel raised his glass for the sake of appearances.
Three days later (PLB 2A, p66) he writes:

Bath
18 June 1841

My Dear Gravatt,
*I received your note by which you decline to avail yourself of the
opportunity I proposed to leave you of [sic] resigning. I regret this
determination and I consider that you act very unwisely. I would
strongly urge that you reconsider it. It seems to me that you
mistake your position altogether and that you would act the part
of one standing upon much higher ground than you can pretend
[sic] to do.*
*In August last, upwards of 10 months ago, I informed you that
you must consider yourself engaged only until the completion of
the work between Bristol and Highbridge and that your further
employment under me would depend upon my regaining that
confidence which I told you I had entirely lost, such having been
the circumstances and conditions under which you remained.*

Since August 1840 and the period fixed having now arrived I do not feel called upon to account for the decision that I have come to, that I do not wish to continue you in your present situation as my Assistant & that nothing will induce me to take upon myself any responsibilities through you.

I have no charge to bring against you and I do not intend to bring any. My ground is simply this, that so far from having regained any lost confidence in you I have lost the little that might have remained or rather the hope that you could ever improve. I have no objection to repeat what I have frequently said that I find that you cannot feel or represent or carry out my views & particularly that you do not keep me fully – or even truly – informed upon all those matters (with) which I ought to be intimate acquainted with – that I believe you, as I have repeatedly told you, (are) incapable of acting as second – at all events, under me or any person who has opinions and views of their own.

This is my view of the general defects in your conduct & character which render it impossible that I should place confidence in you. That that has been my opinion can have been no secret to you as I have repeatedly told you of it when urging you to cure yourself of such serious faults.

I will remind you of three instances which you will clearly understand. I make no charge upon or even complaint but I mention them only as the most recent of numerous specimens of the general conduct which has made me determine that I never again will trust my character or my interests in your hands.

I directed you to send a circular to all the Assistants giving them notice that their engagement after June was uncertain. I told you at the same time that you might inform Froude that he could certainly remain. On 6 April or thereabouts, in consequence of a letter from Penistone I wrote to you that your letter to Penistone was not the sort of circular I had meant. I recapitulated my instructions to you as to the circular and as to the single exception of Froude and I stated in my reply to Penistone which I sent open, through you that your letter to him was similar to those sent by my directions to the other Assistants.

You allowed me to tell this to Penistone and to one of the Directors whereas I apprehend you never did send back a circular, that Penistone was the only person you did write to – that you not only regularly dismissed him without any authority from me and – by some misapprehension as I understood you to say – it was you appointed Froude – *who has actually taken a house* – *about whom I certainly never gave you any directions and consequently there could have been no misunderstanding* – *and not only is all this totally contrary to my directions but it is concealed from me & I learn it only long after and by accident and not through you. In the meantime I had precluded any possibility of any misunderstanding by my letter.*

Again – *all the bridges are built much lower than the standard long since fixed for the Great Western & several even lower than the standard which seems to have been adopted on the B&ER. I am positive that I have frequently & very long ago told you that the standard of the Great Western had been made 15ft 3in over the outside rail. However, I will admit for the sake of argument that the original fault rests with me that I ought to have examined the contract drawings* – *that I ought not to have trusted to any verbal communication to you upon such a point* – *that originally there was no neglect or fault of yours* – *yet you admit that you remember my speaking about the Bath Road bridge, before it was built, & yet you knowingly built that one low because you knew the others were low* and never told me of it. *Had you told me then of the apparent discrepancy between the height required and the height you had built the bridge (assuming it to have been a mistake this discrepancy must have struck you) the rails might have been laid accordingly and this disgraceful exposure of mismanagement avoided.*

On the 1st May I have a report that the centres of the Exeter bridge have been eased and that the settlement has not exceeded what was allowed for. No doubt a true report as far as it goes but was there nothing more to tell me! [sic]

A month passes, nothing is told me about the bridge – *you allow me to fix the opening of the line for the following week and I afterwards discover* quite *by* accident *that this bridge is and had been in an alarming condition, that the settlement is most unequal, that the stones of the bridge are crushed in a frightful manner, that this has been going on for weeks and not a word hinted to me* – *altho' I had previously expressed anxiety in consequence of the centring being removed against any orders and I firmly believe that but for the precautions I have since taken to prevent the vibration from the trains, the bridge would have been in the river or condemned as unsafe.*

After such a course of deception or concealments such constant neglect or perversions of any orders, I should act the part of a fool towards myself and a knave towards the Company if I pretended that I had you for an Assistant. I have had only a screen that has prevented my seeing what was going on and a medium that has entirely intercepted or perverted all my instructions and plans.

I cannot allow old feelings of friendship so entirely to dispense all sense of prudence or duty to others as to induce me to continue such a state of things. I should have wished that you knowing my feelings would have resigned and precluded the necessity of my laying the whole matter before the Board.

You have not chosen to do & I having received two resolutions from the Board relating to the past and future conduct of the engineering establishment no alternative was left to me but to explain the state of things to the Board and I enclose you a copy of the resolution paper by the Directors.

I have now to inform you that referring you to my letter of August 1840 you must consider that you cease from this day to be in the service of the Bristol & Exeter Railway Company.

I shall, of course, rely upon your giving every assistance in preventing confusion and inconvenience in the transfer & rearrangement of papers and other documents.

As the Minute of the Directors refers to a verbal communication from me – to prevent the possibility of any future misapprehension of the statements then made by me I shall send to them a copy of this letter and the preceding one to you.

I shall still hope that you may upon consideration see that it will be more agreeable to all parties, certainly more advantageous to you in your future course, that this charge should be made in point of form by your resigning which you can still do by addressing it direct to the Board and not through me or in reply to this.

Yours very truly,
I. K. Brunel

Brunel has only just finally dealt with Gravatt when he is upset by a young sprig – S. J. Tucker – in his office. Brunel appears to have reprimanded him and Tucker has sent in his resignation. Brunel writes a long letter (PLB 2A, p72) informing him of his failings, never using the shortest form of words, and while we do not know the entire story, a reading of Brunel's letter might convey an idea of why young Tucker has decided to leave his service. Brunel may well be genuinely concerned for the young chap's future – but, my goodness, he does *go on*. He is difficult to believe when he writes that he 'is not a habitual fault finder'. For an man claiming to be easy-going, he is too frequently to be found informing people – at length – of imperfections in their character. He is angry with the young man. He has taken some pains with his education and the young man is actually quite useful. But now he has taken offence merely because he has been reprimanded and is throwing away a good career because he is unable to take criticism.

Bath
22 June 1841

My Dear Sir,
I have been too busy to reply to your letter expressing a wish to leave. A young man in your position would have shewn more wisdom and modesty if he had waited till I had intimated to him that his services were no longer required instead of assuming without any real ground for such assumption that he was no longer of any use and if I thought it was only foolish or a bit of temper I should pass it over and tell you to still do your work and not be surprised to find that your particular work was not the most important that I have and consequently that it might without damage to the concern be somewhat neglected while I have very pressing business to attend to elsewhere but I see in this a strong proof that you have not and cannot without infliction cure yourself of that which I have seen to be the ruin of most young men who notwithstanding good abilities good qualities have not succeeded.
You cannot even see yourself in fault and we are constantly forcing yourself into a little higher position than the one you are placed in. I am not a habitual fault finder on the contrary I fear I am to blame for some of the failures of my Assistants because I dislike complaining I have not very often finding fault with your engineering proceeding – it would be much easier with so many young men hanging about me to dismiss than to attempt to care.
The probability is that I am in the right when I do complain and you would do much better to look at yourself and try to discern and cure the faults I complain of than to take the huff like a child and cast away your present means of support and for a good introduction to future work as you would a top because you could not spin it as well. I shall do you a kindness and relieve myself of much trouble which I have taken with you by letting you feel the consequences of your folly – you will remain to the end of the

quarter as you wish and I may want you for a month more. I have
appointed Ward to succeed you at the Engine House.

Yours truly,
I. K. Brunel

S. J. Tucker

The next letter was written to Herschel Babbage, son of the great
mathematician Charles, in Italy. Herschel was Brunel's agent in his
attempts to become Engineer of the Maria Antonia Railway from
Florence to Pistoia, as well as the Modena-Ancona *and* the Genoa-Turin
lines. Brunel's lobbying for this work has got in the way of Jackson and
Bonfil.

Herschel Babbage was not tied in any formal way to Brunel, but the
two men were close friends. Brunel could not forbid Herschel from
having any dealings with Bonfil and Jackson and, market forces being
what they are, those two struck a strong blow against Brunel's ambitions
in Italy by the simple expedient of luring Herschel Babbage into their
employ by offering him much more money than Brunel. And Herschel
took it. In the end, however, Brunel and the 'Sardinian' Board of Works
found it impossible to work together – he would not build the railways
according to their specification – and he achieved very little in Italy (see
my *Isambard Kingdom Brunel: Engineering Knight-Errant* [John
Murray, 1991], pp190-93).

Brunel refers to the 'Sardinian' Government, but since 1815 the correct
term was 'Piedmont-Sardinian', or 'Piedmont' for short. This
Government controlled the island of Sardinia but also the territory of
Piedmont, in north-western Italy, with the major industrial cities of Turin
and Genoa, and Savoy, in what is now a part of France, including Nice.

William Jackson was a highly energetic and very successful
entrepreneur. He was the 'Father of Birkenhead', but, creating the large
industries of that place – and the employment that went with them – was
only a small part of the successful schemes he initiated.

18 Duke Street
31 March 1845

My Dear Babbage,
You will probably shortly hear of some English gentlemen – Mr
Jackson and Mr Blake accompanied by Mr Bonfil, a Neapolitan,

who are Directors of the Modena & Ancona Railway but the
Company have also given them the powers to treat for any & all
railways in Italy or Austria – and they are going to try their hand
at the Sardinian. In this I have told Bonfil I don't think they will
succeed.

As respects their other railways I am their Engineer – As regards
their negociations [sic] for this I have told them I can take no part
and you will have to act a very prudent part . I have given them a
letter to you merely stating that if circumstances should have left
you quite free of the Sardinian Government or Company that you
could go and commence the survey of the Ancona line – Jackson is
a clever, spirited man who has made Birkenhead a rival to
Liverpool. Bonfil is a clever, very clever, stockbroker speculator –
they would wish to identify me and you with their application to
the Sardinian Government – this you must studiously avoid
without offending them – My position with the government (I
daily expect the decision as to my employment [by them]) will be
your excuse. If any really authorised member of the Government
– the Minister – wishes to know your instructions from me you
may freely tell them – but never volunteer anything – my position
is this – that if the Government or the old Company make the
railway and unless they both give it up I cannot whether employed
by them or not have anything to say to any new company but if
any circumstances should arise to render you free at the present
time and this new company wish to prosecute the survey of the
other lines in Italy I wish you to undertake them. Of course I
should be glad for you to give every friendly assistance to Mr
Jackson and Mr Bonfil perfectly consistent with you being really
apparently neutral in their Sardinian matter – and in this
suspicious country to appear neutral you must avoid very frequent
interviews.

Yours very truly,
I. K. Brunel

Brunel loved to party and socialise. He dined with various groups of the
leading people of the railways he was engineering when he was in their
town – London or Birmingham or Plymouth – and felt under an
obligation to return the favour from time to time. The original of this
letter written to W. H. Bond was sent to me by a descendant of Mr Bond
for translation and with permission to use it here. W. H. Bond was

Company Secretary of the Cornwall Railway and was also Secretary of the Reform Club in Pall Mall. The Reform Club building, next door to the Tories' Carlton Club, was built for the Liberal Party by Grissell & Peto. Brunel joined the club as soon as it opened, in 1836, and remained a member until 1858. Bond was Club Secretary from 1844 to 1846, and from 1849 to 1852. Although he was not an official of the club when Brunel wrote this, he was clearly a man whose wishes carried great weight in the club.

Private
July 11 1847

My Dear Sir,
I just remember a very important point on which I haven't consulted you – and on which if you could drop me a line by return of post you wd much oblige me and several of our Great Western Directors.

I owe Mr Russell [Chairman of the GWR] and five others a dinner on Saturday next and it has been held out to them that it wd be at the Reform Club and of the best – I am going tomorrow to see what are the requisite forms to be gone thro' – I am an old member – (my visitors are all conservatives) – a note from you to some of the officials recommending me to their kind attentions of the cooks and cellarmen I daresay would make the dinner work.

Yours faithfully
I. K. Brunel

W. H. Bond Esq

John Calcott Horsley RA (1817-1903) was Brunel's brother-in-law, and was a very successful painter of people – he made two portraits of Brunel – and landscapes in rural Kent, in a style of romantic glow that pleased the nostalgia of the burgeoning industrial middle classes. He was elected an Associate of the Royal Academy of Arts in 1855, and was Rector from 1875 to 1890. The year is not given on the following letter (DM 1281/1), but it is very probably 1848. The letter contains some startling admissions by Brunel. The underlinings are his own.

Wednesday night
23 August

My Dear Horsley,
You consulted me the other day as to you giving up the school – or rather as I look upon it – giving up the <u>salary</u>.

All I could say was that if you felt sure that you could nearly make up the loss of income by this means I agree with you and the propriety of doing so you have probably made up your mind before this but my reasons for having any doubt upon the subject may not be useless to you in your future proceedings. I am disposed no doubt to look at things with a concerned but doubtless gloomy eye at present but the reason for my doing so must also be a reason for you to do the same

My spirits are positively broken by the proceedings which I have been compelled to adopt and which have occupied my thoughts and time for many weeks past. The state of trade and money in England at present is such that in my particular department of business I have been entirely engaged for weeks past in cutting down salaries and dismissing assistants – I have been obliged to do this to an amount equal to more than £10,000 a year – imagine the situation of unfortunates – and the extent of disappointment pain and misery that I have had to inflict and you will easily understand the anxiety I must feel for anybody who has to give up <u>any certainty</u> however small –

I have been with large families who have been <u>luxuriating</u> upon their £300 [a year] which appears to them as certain as your income does to you. – receiving their quarterly payments from me so regularly that they looked upon it by habit as certainly as the day of the month – who never troubled themselves about financial matters potato blights or anything suddenly deprived of all means of existence

The extra quarter or so that I squeeze out of the Company for them perhaps not covering their common outstanding debts. Young men who have just married on the strength of a handsome salary of 500 or 600 a year suddenly told that after another quarter they will have <u>nothing</u>. All this arising from the very same causes which indirectly affects you and all men who minister to the enjoyment or expenditure of surplus capital.

Really at the present moment I do not think that I would give up £250 a year unless I felt very certain that I could replace it – now do you feel confident in yourself that you will <u>slavishly</u> occupy the time you will thus gain – your proposition is one which <u>admits</u> of great industry but does not compel it – and I believe that

compulsion near to irksomeness induces wholesome habits –
If you give up the school let me entreat of you to slave. To compel
yourself to complete certain things by certain times – and let me
entreat of you also to produce somehow or other more in quantity
each year whether for commission or not – what I dread is the
effect of your being left without any irksome compulsory duty –
nothing induces a more time spending (I must not call it idle) habit
than the absence of compulsion. I feel it strongly because I believe
that I am naturally idle but – all my life is one of slaving and
compulsion you and many others may think my life a pleasant one
– I am of a happy disposition and therefore it is a pleasant one –
but from one end of the year to the other, from morning to night
it is the life of a slave – I am never my own master and I have
always an overwhelming quantity of work which must be done by
certain days and hours – knowing the effect of this – and how
artificially industrious it makes a man – I confess I dread a man's
being left always his own master. As I said before though if you
give up the school for God's sake take to working not industriously
but like a slave.

Yours faithfully
I. K. Brunel

9: NAVVIES

'The ordinary operation of supply and demand'

On 16 June 1846 Brunel gave his thoughts on the treatment of the railway navvy to a Parliamentary Select Committee (1846, vol xii 570). My understanding of Brunel is that he was not greatly concerned for navvy welfare. They were not his employees, therefore not his concern. They were a nuisance, rather disgusting for most of the time, uneducated, uncivilised – not 'Gentlemen' – an unfortunate necessity. He wishes this was not so; he would prefer it if they behaved themselves in an orderly way. He had no idea how to achieve that, yet he is oddly dismissive of Morton Peto's methods, which did produce orderly navvies. Morton Peto stated that his methods of navvy control produced for him a greater profit and the work was done more quickly for the client.

Brunel deplores the 'evils' of the system but is convinced that it is the only way to get railways built 'cheaply' – yet his railways were not built cheaply. He is extremely wary of any laws to assist the navvies, even if those laws might produce an improvement in their behaviour – he, as an employer, does not want his actions restricted by laws or to have his costs increased because of laws. It does not occur to him that a more orderly workforce would get the work done more quickly and cheaply.

Brunel is on his best behaviour when answering to the Committee. While his favourite law is the Law of Supply and Demand, he is forced into ambiguity. He has to 'play to the gallery' and try to show concern for social improvement. He expresses a desire for that, but not for any law that would move in that direction. Railway navvies were not protected by the Truck Act of 1831 – nor were any description of railwaymen under that protection until about 1900. On this one point only is he clear – the men ought to be paid with coin of the realm. How and when they were paid is another matter, but when they were paid it should be only in real, cash, money. He states that in all his contracts he forbids the contractor to pay wages in food, or to set up shops to sell food. He talks of the company policing contractors' shops to prevent the 'truck'. He even seems to suggest that the men should form a trade union. But in his daily dealings with contractors all this seems far away.

Brunel was concerned only with the interests of the company he represented. He states to the Committee his opposition to any law to govern the relations between employer and employed, navvies to contractors, contractor to company – no laws governing safety, no laws on compensation for injuries sustained due to a negligent employer. He was aware of deaths from premature explosions of gunpowder and said he approved of copper ramrods instead of iron so as to avoid sparks generated when iron ramrods struck rock. He approved of the use of safety fuses of known burning time; he believed these devices should be used but he disapproved of laws forcing their use. He was to be in sole charge of the works and the sole arbitrator of any disputes between his company and the contractor. He wished for his perfect freedom to do exactly as he wanted. The other side of the coin was that, ultimately, the workmen had to endure whatever befell them because that – according to Brunel – was the cheapest way to get the job done.

In the end the entire enquiry achieved nothing because nothing was done in law, following the Committee's Report, to make life better for the navvies, not even a very simple thing – an extension of the Truck Act to make it apply to the 'railway labourers'. Brunel's *laissez-faire* instincts triumphed over Morton Peto's regulations.

Members of the Committee were often sympathetic to the plight of the navvies, but they were not the entire Parliament assembled. The Chairman was the Rt Hon Edward Bouverie (1818-89), Liberal member for Kilmarnock 1844-74, the second son of the Earl of Radnor and a lifelong Whig. Such was the strictness of his morals that he found his Prime Minister, William Ewart Gladstone, to be insufferable. In 1872, when a charge of evasion of the law was made against Mr Gladstone in connection with the appointment he made to the rectory of Ewelme, Bouverie expressed regret 'that the prime minister should amuse his leisure hours by driving coaches-and-six through acts of parliament, and should take such curious views of the meaning of statutes' (Hansard, 8 March 1872, col 1711).

Sitting on the Committee was Viscount Ebrington, Earl Fortesque (1783-1861), first cousin to the great Tory Duke of Buckingham. Ebrington had a sympathy towards the labouring poor. He became MP for Buckingham, but his sense of fair play took over when he was asked to vote against the reduction in the money paid as a sinecure to one of the Duke of Buckingham's sons. He resigned the seat. He had previously outraged his Tory uncle by voting against the suspension of *Habeas Corpus* in 1817. Ebrington became the Whig MP for Marylebone.

Other members included Sir Thomas Acland (1787-1871), of an ancient North Devon family. He was a paternalistic landowner of vast acres, and Tory MP for North Devon 1837-57. Ross Mangles was Liberal MP for Guildford 1841-58, and William Deedes, described by Hansard as 'of Conservative principles', was Member for East Kent from 1845 to 1857 and from 1858 to his death in 1862.

Isambard Kingdom Brunel Esq, called in and examined.

Mr Deedes asked:
2046. Have you had great experience in the conduct of the labourers generally upon railway works?
IKB. *Yes.*

2047. With regard to the system of payment by the truck system. What is your opinion on that?
IKB. *I think it is a very bad system and one that it would be desirable by some means or other to prevent. By that I mean strictly payment by means of the truck system. I do not include within that the system of having some means of providing the men with provisions. I believe the whole mischief arises from that which is, strictly speaking, paying in anything but cash, the current coin of the realm.*

2048. You think it necessary to have some mode by which the men may get at time provisions or rather get money to provide themselves with provisions at first, when they come to undertake the work – that there would not always be found a supply at the place?
IKB. *I think it very necessary frequently that there should be means of providing men with provisions in localities where there is not a supply by shops or the ordinary means but even in those cases I do not think it necessary or desirable that they should actually be paid by tickets or by provisions. If you can trust a man with a shilling's worth of provisions you may as well trust him with a shilling and pay him in advance the money you wish to help him with.*

2049. Suppose a man to come to work and to state at once that he has no means of providing for himself with what he wants – you think there would be no objection to advance him the money for his immediate necessities?
IKB. *No – I think what slight objection there may be would be counterbalanced by the following out the principle of not paying in*

anything but money.

2050. You would not imagine that such a thing could be enforced by law? IKB. *I am not particularly fond of laws for enforcing such things. Upon that point I am not familiar with the law. The Truck Law I have always understood to have been an attempt to render illegal the paying in provisions and I do not see but that a law, if it does not already exist, might exist to prevent the payment of labourers and workmen in anything but cash.*

Viscount Ebrington asked:
2051. You would have no objection to an extension of the same principle to railway labourers which has already been extended by the Truck Law to particular manufacturers?
IKB. *No. I brought with me, knowing this was a point likely to be referred to, a printed form on which the specifications are prepared by me and then the contracts drawn up and in that I have a clause expressly against the truck system which is afterwards embodied in legal phrase in the contracts with the contractors. It is as follows: 'The contractor shall truly and strenuously endeavour, to the utmost of his power, to prevent the introduction of the truck system upon the works and to this effect he shall not, by himself or his agents, directly or indirectly, allow of the sale of provisions, or any other articles, to the workmen, either by parties exclusively privileged, or in payment of wages, or for any other consideration than money and shall not in like manner allow of any control or inducement being exercised over the men with reference to their choice of market or of prices or of the mode of payment. And moreover with the same view, the contractor and his agents shall cause all men employed directly or indirectly, under him, to be paid at least once a fortnight and in cash, and on no account shall the whole or any portion of wages be paid or any advance made to men by tickets or orders upon victuallers, or in any way whatsoever except in cash.*

2052. With regard to truck, you would see no objection to these conditions being enforced by the Legislature, which in your own dealings you have thought it desirable for your own sake and the sake of the men to insist upon?
IKB. *No – if it can be done. I do not know whether it is easy to be done.*

2053. Is it your belief that under particular circumstances it is necessary that steps should be taken by contractors or companies to provide supplies for the workmen or take active steps in setting up a shop and that that cannot be left safely to the laws of supply and demand?

IKB. *I think if the parties, companies or contractors, would endeavour to bring fully into effect the ordinary operation of supply and demand, it would be sufficient but the simplest way very often is to bring the supply at once – in fact, for the contractors to set up a shop it would be sufficient but the simplest way very often is to bring the supply at once – in fact for the contractor to set up a shop.*

Mr Mangles asked.:

2054. Is that not liable to abuse?

IKB. *Liable certainly to great abuse but I think if the truck system were kept down that the abuses would not counteract the advantages. In many cases there are great advantages and if the companies would endeavour to prevent the contractor using any undue influence, to give privileges to his shop, I think that combined with any law or any contract against the use of the truck system the two together would prevent the abuse.*

Viscount Ebrington asked:

2055. I suppose that a contractor keeping a shop would have greater facilities for transporting supplies at a very slight cost because opportunities might be taken for conveying goods by means of the carts and tramroads laid down for the use of the works which could not be enjoyed by independent shopkeepers setting up on their own account?

IKB. *I do not think that would apply to any great extent. The provisions will always be brought by the common carts. No doubt the contractor has a great number of these carts and can send them to market towns at the least possible expense but the consumption will be sufficiently large in all cases to pay well for the carriage of provisions.*

Mr Mangles asked:

2057. Mr Peto has stated that he had had works in all parts of the country, many in parts removed from large or considerable towns and villages, and he never found any difficulty in supplying his men upon the ordinary principle of supply and demand. By giving notice to the nearest market town or village that payment to the men would be made at such a time?

IKB. *I think that agrees with what I said – that if a company and the contractors will assist the ordinary process of demand and supply it will be quite sufficient.*

Sir Thomas Acland asked:

2063. Describe the different classes of contractors essential to executing these works – supposing you had not the good fortune to employ such a man as Mr Peto [which Brunel had not done for six years].

IKB. *There are a great number of grades of contractors. I will endeavour to describe them. I would mention that I believe all these grades, the lower ones also, are necessary for the protection of such contractors as Mr Peto – but for the competition of the small contractors I do not think the public would have the advantage of these large contractors and large capitalists disposed to execute works at low prices. We have contractors very much below Mr Peto in point of capital, in point of education and character, but who take works costing on the whole £10,000 to £15,000 and requiring £1,000 or £1,500 of capital and the way that class of contractors get their work cheap is by sub-letting the different portions of the work to gangs of excavators and small bricklayers who have their working bricklayers under them. The consequence is therefore that on these works a very small class of contractors is necessarily employed because the ganger or sub-contractor under the principal contractor is in fact the very contractor for the work, running the risk of the price at which he has taken it being sufficient or not. That leads frequently certainly to defaulters and to distress among the men and to a great many evils but I do not see that it is possible to prevent it. I do not believe it is at all desirable to prevent it because but for the fact that we can get works executed at moderate prices, we certainly should not get large capitalists, who would very soon have a monopoly of all these works, to execute works at low prices. The price at which railways are constructed, compared with those at which large government works were constructed thirty years ago, is a strong instance of that. In those days there was a monopoly by the large contractors.*

In the case of Peto and Brassey, many of the sub-contractors were their own navvies who, by following the encouragement of their employees had saved their wages and accumulated capital and were given sub-contacts. If, during the course of the work, the agred price was found not to be profitable to the 'subby' Peto or Brassey would increase it. A *loyal* workforce was of utmost importance to these great contractors

Viscount Ebrington asked:
2064. Do you conceive that all the evils that have attended railway works are the necessary and inevitable consequences of the employment of small contractors?

IKB. *No. I think they might be very much mitigated. I think the truck*

213

system alone is one very great source of evil. Another great evil is the irregularity of payment of wages.

2060. Do you not think some arrangement might be made by law with respect to the payment of wages?
IKB. *I think that would be very difficult indeed. I do not see how you are to make such a law.*

Mr Deedes asked:
2067. Do you think that any law that might be made between master and man might easily be evaded?
IKB. *Yes. I cannot conceive how you could make a law compelling the master to pay the man for work, payment for which he does not claim. For instance if a man chooses to enter into an engagement and to do a certain quantity of work for £20 to be paid when the work is done, I do not see what law would provide against that. There would be a small contractor who takes £10 or £20-worth of work who would only be paid when that work was done which may take three weeks or a month. If his men are paid so much a yard it is frequently impossible to measure up the work in its rough state, week by week. They might be paid something on account but that would be optional, merely a nominal sum. It might be only a shilling a piece. The law cannot fix the amount. If it were convenient for the Ganger and the men to be paid once a fortnight I do not see how the law could reach such a case.*

Viscount Ebrington asked:
2068. By doing away with the truck system and giving shopkeepers a claim upon the contractors instead of the men for the supplies given to them – if the wages were not paid within a certain time – do you think that greater frequency of payment could be practically enforced? [What Ebrington probably did not realise was that the contractor was often unable to pay his men because Brunel had not paid the contractor.]
IKB. *You must make it the interest of the men to get frequent payments and then if you take care that the masters employ no improper coercion over the men, the men will get frequent payment.* [His implication is that he thinks the men should band together and he would support them should their employer use 'improper coercion' against them. Nothing could be more alien to Brunel's practice in life.]

Mr Deedes asked:
2069. Do you think that many works are sub-let at an unfair price so that

the men do not get a fair return for their labour?
IKB. *I do not think so. The men are quite independent.*

Viscount Ebrington asked:
2071. There have been many cases of men suffering from the refusal or inability of the sub-contractors to pay them for work done. Do you see any objection to giving these men a claim upon the contractor [for whom the sub-contractor was working] or upon the company in those cases?
IKB. *I think there would be great objections to that. In the first place it is unjust. If five men agree with a sixth that he shall take a piece of work and that they shall join him in executing it and they let him receive the money it is perfectly optional on their part and I cannot myself see the justice of almost inducing him to be a rogue by giving them a claim upon a third party who has no claim on him for the money owed. Practically – it would lead to preventing this sub-contracting because the company would give notice that they would not be answerable for such acts and you could not after that enforce payment from them. If the sub-contract is not taken with the authority of the company you cannot make the company liable for the debt incurred by one man to five others.*

The reason Acland asked this question was because the Commitee had heard from other witnesses, clergymen and magistrates that these problems has frequently arisen.

2072. Do you not see also that there is great injustice – on the other hand – in saddling parishes where these works may happen to be undertaken with the support of persons left destitute and chargeable upon them in consequence of the neglect of due precautions on the part of the company in choosing sufficiently solvent persons. [It could be the case that the person was solvent until he came to take a contract from Brunel.]
IKB. *I must say that I never knew a case of a parish suffering from a railway company having works in that parish. Upon the whole the parishes are very great gainers in increased trade and eventually they gain by the introduction into them of an additional quantity of rateable property* [the money paid by the railway company in parish rates towards the upkeep of the workhouse and the roads].

2073. Do you not conceive that parishes may sometimes suffer from having thrown upon them the temporary support of a large number of men who have been defrauded of their wages by persons in the employment of a contractor?

IKB. *I do not believe that such cases have occurred. I have never heard of them. There may be a momentary demand upon a parish for some support but I never heard of a case where, taking six months and six months, any parish was otherwise than a great gainer by the large sums of money spent in the parish and ultimately by the very large proportion of poor rates paid by the company after the works have been completed. But assuming the possibility of the case put ... if a company have done their best to get as responsible a man as can be found, if the process of sub-letting is necessary – and I believe it is – it is impossible that the contractor can pick out all his gangers as men who are perfectly responsible in purse, even if they are perfectly honest. If a man does make a mistake in the price at which he takes the work, or if a man in that rank of life, as in many others, turns out to be a rogue, I do not see how it is justice that the main contractor or the company should be responsible and if held responsible it would lead to no good.*

2074. Would not such a law as that stimulate persons who might otherwise not be particularly anxious to promote frequent settlements of accounts?

IKB. *The principle seems to me so strange of inflicting a punishment merely for the sake of bringing about an effect that I do not feel capable of offering an opinion on it.* [In the case of William Ranger and George Burge, and probably others, Brunel constantly inflicted punishments in the hope of producing the effect he required.]

2075. These contractors may be looked upon as agents of the company?

IKB. *It may be so considered if you use the word 'agent' in a much larger sense than usual. You mean an authorised agent. I do not see why the company can be more liable for the conduct of that agent than your Lordship could be for the blacksmith who shoes your horse. Because you generally employ that blacksmith, if that blacksmith did not pay his men, you would not feel yourself called upon to do so. I believe it would lead to mischief and to attempts to evade it. Sub-letting is very essential and you could not hope to sublet for the instant the ganger found that the work did not pay him he could go away and leave the company to pay. There would be combinations between gangers and the men to get paid twice over.*

2076. Is it impossible to take security [a financial bond] from that class of men?

IKB. *It is impossible Ten or twelve men take a piece of work and they name one of their group as their leader. He becomes the sub-letter. He has no means of giving security, he is merely the leader of a certain number of men.*

Mr Deedes asked:
2077. Is he not the man who employs these men?
IKB. *You may call it so but he is one of the same class – he does it by agreement with the others. He gets a little more money than them and he creeps up but this ordinary ganger, who occasionally commits fraud, is merely one of the men.*

Sir Thomas Acland asked:
2078. How often are the men defrauded?
IKB. *At the present money it is not worth consideration as an evil that may be said to exist. During bad times for contractors, when wages got very high, there was difficulty in getting money and that led, very frequently, to frauds on the part of the sub-contractors but where there is a good demand for work and a tolerable labour supply as at present the cases of fraud are very rare.*

2080. Does not delay and irregularity of payment lead to much improvidence on the part of the navvies?
IKB. *I think so. Where there is delay they get tickets on the truck shop.*

Mr Mangles asked:
2083. Mr Peto has paid once a week for years.
IKB. *Mr Peto has immense capital. He takes very large works so he can apply over a considerable extent of country a very first rate system of account keeping and superintendence and he can ascertain on Saturday morning what is due to his men and pay them in the afternoon. That requires a system which very few men are capable of and there are very few men like Mr Peto for managing large works and no law would enable a man who has not an aptitude for business and who does not conduct his affairs with the extreme regularity that Mr Peto does, to pay his men with that extreme punctuality and I do not know how you can do more than is doing now. A man has a right to claim his money at the end of a day or a week under common law and if he has not I would give him that.*
[Morton Peto had to borrow £100,000 to pay his men and buy materials while working for Brunel, who was refusing to pay him.]

Mr Deedes asked:
2084. Where to do you consider that remedy to be?
IKB. *It is difficult to say. If the common law of the land is not sufficient, not merely for the railway labourers but labourers generally, if there is a want of remedy to enable the labourer to recover his wages it would be difficult and I do not know how you are to give it to him.*

Sir Thomas Acland asked:
2085. Would there be any difficulty in calling a magistrate to hear a case between workmen and their ganger and determine between them how much payment was due to them on a Saturday evening if a dispute arose as to the nature of the work which was incapable of being established in a plain way?
IKB. *I believe it would be utterly impossible to get that evidence to enable the magistrate to safely determine what was due to the men.*

2087. The difficulty of getting what they have fairly earned does not exist to a great extent?
IKB. *No. Not where there is the ability to pay. If there is no money there is no law that can touch the case – if a contractor fails the money is not forthcoming and if you went back to the company for the money it would be impossible to pay the men and if you did do that it would destroy the whole system of contract throughout England.*

2088. Must you not require security?
IKB. *We do take security in cases where contractors have failed to a large amount and the men have by that means been left unpaid, in all the cases I am aware of the companies I have been connected with have paid the money but then that was a case that could only occur rarely. The company was not compelled to do it and therefore it was not likely to occur except where an absolute necessity arose but if you made the company liable for everything and if they were to require sufficient security to meet such liabilities the contractors would directly raise the prices at which they took the work. There are no doubt great difficulties in all this. The system of free competition for contracts is what enables us to execute works in England so extensively at a moderate price.*
[Brunel estimated £2.5 million to build the GWR. It cost £6.5 million.]

Brunel takes a deposit from the contractor for the due performance of his contract, but Ebrington and Acland want to press him on who pays the workmen. Brunel thinks that the best guarantee of the men being paid is

the men themselves, contradicting his answer to Question 2084 – and several others before that.
    Acland continues his questions.]

2089. Do you take security for the execution of the work from the small contractor?
IKB. *We take down as low as £1,000.*

2090. In what way will you have security for the payment of the men?
IKB. *I think such security as that might lead to mischief – the men would cease to have the same watchfulness over the contractor that they had before.*

On Saturday 26 May 1838 the navvies employed by William Ranger in Sonning Cutting had not been paid for two weeks. Brunel had refused to pay Ranger because his men had not excavated a sufficient amount and the navvies had been slow because the ground was waterlogged. The 'watchfulness' of the navvies made them down tools, and with their wives and children they marched hungrily to Reading where they took up camp in what is now the Forbury Gardens. They made known their problem to the townspeople, who gave them food, and sent messages to Mr Brunel to come and see that they were paid. Brunel never came. On the following Friday the Dragoons arrived and they were turned out of the Gardens, at sabre point, back to the cutting, each man receiving sixpence as he left.

Viscount Ebrington asked:
2092. Because with this system of long deferred payments and of contracting without much capital, much expense is thrown upon the public of the maintenance of the men defrauded of their wages and on the Poor Rate or by their arrest and prosecution if they take to vagrancy or crime.
IKB. *I know of no system of deferred payments. That payments occasionally are too much deferred is the exception and is an evil that exists but no general system on the part of any company or any contractors that I have ever heard of.*

Brunel's contracts had provision for withholding payment for work which was so little as 'not to be worth paying for', and also fines to be inflicted if the work did not progress at a pre-arranged rate. There were no excuses – Brunel was the Arbitrator.
    He begins now to appeal to 'general principles' – that is, 'the way these

matters have always been arranged', so there is no possibility of improvement. He absolutely opposes the payment of wages as amounts of food but he agrees with the idea of the employer owning the shop where the navvies buy their food for money. He says that the company should 'endeavour' to police the shop to prevent an abuse of this (see the last sentence of Question 2054).]

2093. There would not be so much inconvenience if you had regular payment of wages?
IKB. *I should like to have regular payment but I doubt the possibility of doing it by law. If by any means whatever you can enforce it, I would do it but I deny the possibility of your doing it except by a piece of machinery as would produce great inconvenience to the whole system of contracting.*

2095. Do you think the reason sometimes given for long deferred payments – that every payment will be followed by a period of idleness and debauchery on the part of the men – is a valid one and that the works really would be delayed in their construction by a system of frequent payments?
IKB. *In the present very bad state of things with all the evils that at present exist [but not on the works of Peto, Brassey and Betts] no doubt frequent payments would produce still greater mischief but assuming – which I hope will be the case – that we get rid of the present evils then the more frequent the payments the better.* [But Brunel did nothing to improve matters and did not believe matters could be improved.]

Sir Thomas Acland asked:
2096. What evils do you allude to?
IKB. *Drunkenness, irregularity and various other evils that are in existences. I believe that deferred payments are one of the causes of the evils being produced. It certainly is true what many people say, that if you paid once a week you would lose still more time but nevertheless I would pay as often as possible and endeavour to diminish all these evils. I doubt the possibility in all these extensive works, undertaken as they must be by small contractors, of arriving at such an excellent state of management as that of Mr Peto but I would seek to draw the greatest possible approximation.*

[Viscount Ebrington asked whether 'general principles' could be applied to extraordinary circumstances.]

2098. You spoke of 'general principles'. Do you not conceive that some exception may be made with regard to the application of 'general principles' when parties come asking Parliament for extraordinary powers to carry on works of an exceptional nature, bringing large masses of men together on one spot for a short time and employing them under very different circumstances from the ordinary circumstances under which the mass of the labouring population of the country are employed? IKB. *I believe that that general principles if they are good ones will apply perfectly well in these cases as in all others. I do not think an exception can possibly arise simply because you have the power to enforce them. If the principle is a good one by all means enforce it.* [Here the principle was to improve the navvies' living conditions and thus speed the work of construction, but Brunel, while wanting this, denies that any law can be brought to create that effect.]

2099. Do you not think some of these cases might require more interference (from the law) because hardly sufficient time elapses for the operation of the (existing) laws which in the long run regulate the employment of labour and the adjustment of prices? IKB. *I do not think the departure from general principles will be productive of good. Where, as you say, large masses of men are brought together on one spot they are certainly within the ordinary operation of the laws governing society.* [Brunel cannot help the men improve, but when their neglect leads them into 'evils' the police will be there to arrest them.]

2101. Do you not conceive that particular regulations, made by law, would be advantageous with regard to making provisions for lodgings which, in the case of permanent work, might safely be left to the law of supply and demand? IKB. *I believe it would be desirable indeed if more provision were made but I cannot conceive the possibility of doing it by law. I cannot conceive how you are to define all the cases, all the various shades of difference which will arise between works carried on in a great town, works carried a few miles from a town or where the work is to be carried out in a perfectly barren place.*

2102. You mean a law vesting some persons with discretionary powers? IKB. *If you vest a power in some individual that gets over the difficulty as far as the law is concerned but I doubt the result being satisfactory. I remember perfectly well the large works carried on at Hanwell, Grissell*

& Peto were contractors for the viaduct and Mr McIntosh, one of the largest contractors, was contractor for the earthwork. They were not able to obtain lodgings thereabouts. There were 700 or 800 men and large numbers were sleeping under the hedges while a considerable number would walk from lodgings in London. There was lodging in the neighbourhood but owing to the fine weather and a desire to save money large numbers of labourers used to sleep under the hedges.

Sir Thomas Acland asked:
2109. Are you familiar personally with the habits and condition of the men?
IKB. Yes.

2110. Have you been able been able to observe any change or improvements in their habits since these kind of works first commenced? IKB. No. [He deliberately ignores the good done by Peto and Betts, Jackson and Brassey.]

Edward Bouverie asked:
2116. Are you generally aware of the French law with reference to the liability of the employers of labour in case of accidents to the employed. IKB. I believe I am.

2117. You are aware too that the construction of these works is accompanied with a very large amount of fatal and serious accidents? IKB. A large amount.

2118. Are you able to express any decided opinion whether a similar liability would or would not be attended with beneficial effects in diminishing that amount of casualty?
IKB. I should assume in the first place, that if applied to one class of work it must be applied generally throughout the country. [A dodging of the question – the Truck Act was a labour law designed to apply only to factory labour – it could have been extended.]

2119. It is the general law in France?
IKB. Yes. I should be sorry to see it in England. I do not think that it would be productive of a good effect.

2120. In what way?
IKB. I think that, unless the minds and habits and feelings of Englishmen

222

and English labourers are very much altered and become more similar to those of the French or natives of the Continent generally, that the skill and activity and independence of the labourer would be injured by that reliance on his employer.

2121. If it became the employer's interest to protect the men from accidents would it not operate as an advantage to the skilled and careful labourer that the master should have a direct interest in employing him rather than the careless man?
IKB. *That would be one advantage, of course.*

2122. Would that not be a premium to the skilled and cautious labourer rather than to one who was careless and incautious?
IKB. *No. I think not.*

2123. Suppose that the cautious labourer was more preferred than he is now in comparison with an incautious labourer. Would that not be an inducement to the labourers to become more cautious?
IKB. *Yes. But the system of piecework and contract work which pervade the whole of iron making and mining would be materially interfered with by a law such as that.*

2124. In what way?
IKB. *A man who is working piece work at the bottom of a mine is thrown entirely upon his own resources and his success depends upon his own care and throwing the liability of any accident to him upon the master would necessarily involve a much greater interference on the part of the master with the mode of proceeding and the whole detail of the work of that workman. It would alter the present position of things by which every department from the highest to the lowest is sub-let to men who are free agents and who seek to execute the work in the cheapest way. Some risks I admit are run as a consequence but I do not think that the results of those risks are at all to be compared with the advantage attained in our manufactures generally by that system, the independent efforts of the workmen and of every class of men employed in manufactures.*

2125. Then, as I understand you, you would limit your objections to this liability to those accidents where the employer has no co-operation with the employed?
IKB. *I would say that [employer's liability] cannot be employed in any case where the man is more than just the mere tool of the employer. That*

would be the general principle. There would be exceptions, of course.

2126. In a large organised system of industry, where the employer largely cooperates with the exertions of individual labourers, do you think that any amount of intelligence and independence on the part of the labourer can guard them against an accident – over the causes of which the labourer has no control?
IKB. *Not entirely but to a great extent – an extent which I should say is quite sufficient.*

2127. In the case of iron stemmers [ramrods] being used to pack home gunpowder charges for blasting which are supplied by the employer to the labourer. Do you think that the employer has no part or share in a fatal result arising from the use of iron stemmers?
IKB. *I think he has and I think that this is a case where, if there is to be any interference, it might be tolerably safely applied. I believe, still, that the non-interference will lead to much better results and that men who have a constant opportunity of doing it will discover improvements in working much quicker and better, according to the present system in England than according to the system more common abroad of regulating and controlling by a higher authority the exact mode in which everybody is to proceed. Still I admit that if an employer wilfully compels his men to act in an unsafe manner that might be a case where he would be liable for the consequence of the compulsion – but if carried far I think this would produce a bad effect instead of a good one.* [Amen to that!] *I have found that the men prefer very much and require the patent fuses. I never allow anything else to be used in work under my direction.* [These burned for a definitely known time per foot of fuse, giving time for men to take cover.]

2129. So far as the employer cooperates in the performance of work with the labourer, you think the employer might be liable for risks occurring from negligence on his part?
IKB. *I think if there is to be any liability it should be restricted to those cases where the employer actually increases the risk by some act of his own.* [The Committee has got Brunel somewhat penned in now, and they press their point.]

Sir Thomas Acland asked:
2130. Accidents are not infrequent – are they – from falling in of earth and excavations?
IKB. *No.* [They are not infrequent.]

2131. And those accidents are very often occasioned by want of attention on the part of the workmen and those immediately superintending the work?
IKB. *Yes.*

2132. In the case of work being rapidly pressed on – so as to continue night and day – are not the accidents increased?
IKB. *Yes.*

2133. In such a case is not the employer virtually cooperating with the labourers in the causes of such extraordinary accidents? [This is very close to home for Brunel, who constantly urges his contractor to go faster to make up time lost through bad weather or machinery breakage.]
IKB. *Not unless he insists upon an unsafe way of proceeding with the work. But a certain number of men take the excavation of a piece of ground at the contract price. They choose to then excavate that with a high face, as we call it. They then choose to undercut it very much before they allow it to fall. That is the fault of the operatives and not of the principal contractor who, if he lets work by piece to the men, could not properly prevent it because they understand it a great deal better than he does. In 99 cases out of 100 they are much more able to judge the safest and best way of working down that piece of earth.*

[Here is a classic example of where the least cautious men are of the greatest value to the contractor and thus to the company. They agree to take down so many cubic yards of earth in a very fast time and to be paid accordingly. They must dig a horizontal undercut to the vertical face, in order to bring down the greatest amount in the shortest time – and they must judge how much weight of earth will remain stationary, unsupported, and they bet their lives on their judgement for the sake of a few extra shillings. They choose to take this risk *when it is offered to them by their master.* If they bury themselves alive their erstwhile employer nonchalantly writes them off and looks for some other group of men to be lured to try their luck. Brunel always puts the main responsibility on the labourer. Employers in Brunel's eyes seem to have very little responsibility towards their workmen.]

Edward Bouverie asked:
2134. I understand your objection, put generally, is that such a law on employers liability would tend to put the labourer into leading strings more than he is now?

IKB. *Yes.*

2135. You admit that liability would stimulate employers to make regulations and take precautions that they do not now take? [Better leading strings than a coffin, Mr Brunel?]
IKB. *It would depend on how the liability was enforced. In many cases it would tend to evasions which, I think, would be easy, unless there was to be a similar responsibility as there appears to be in France where, without inquiry into the cause, the master has to provide for his servant.*

2137. Do you not think that being the immediate sufferer from the consequences of an accident will be sufficient stimulus to the labourers to take proper care to prevent an accident?
IKB. *I think it the most effectual stimulant you can possibly devise.*

2138. Do you not think that with a stimulant to the employer likewise to do his part in protecting the life of the labourer, that together you have as perfect a safeguard as you can get against these casualties?
IKB. *Yes – if you assume that the mode of assessing the damage on the part of the sufferer can just be justly and properly carried out – which I doubt. If it is to be left to anything like the tribunal we have now, called a 'Coroner's Jury', I think that could only lead to mischief. I cannot believe it would be safe to leave it in the hands of neighbouring magistrates from my experience of their decisions.* [This was a bold shot because Acland was a magistrate, and maybe other Committee members also.]

Edward Bouverie asked:
2148. Was there any return made to you during the construction of the Great Western – or to any other Officer of the Company – of the accidents that took place?
IKB. *Yes – every one was always reported.*

2149. Was any inquiry made by the Company into the causes and nature of the accidents?
IKB. *Not on the part of the Company. I used always, as a matter of duty, to inquire into the causes.*

2150. Did you ever take any further steps to prevent a recurrence of similar accidents?
IKB. *I have no doubt that I have – such as insisting on stronger ropes or*

using greater precautions in tunnelling.

[In all my reading of Brunel letters, which is extensive, I have found only one that was concerned with the safety of the work.]

2152. Have you ever seen a list of the accidents being taken into Bath hospital from the Great Western? Here is a list. [Thomas Gale, who worked in the excavating of Box Tunnel and who went on to spend his life as a porter at Bath station, produced a pamphlet of his recollections of the excavating. He it was who wrote that 'upwards of 100 men were killed'.]
IKB. *I think this is a small list – considering the heavy works and the immense quantity of powder used in that district which contained the heaviest and most difficult works. I am afraid that this does not show the whole extent of accidents incurred in that neighbourhood. [Bouverie was probably a little ruffled at Brunel's way of dismissing the list. The list has never been found, but it was clearly a large one. Bouverie continues:]*

2153. Do you not think, *prima facie*, that a list like this is not a startling thing?
IKB. *No. I think it would be a small number of accidents considering the large number of men employed for between two to three years and doing a very large quantity of work. I believe if the same number of men had been employed in twos and threes on parish roads, scattered over the country, the number of accidents would have been as* **large, if not larger** *[my emphasis].*

2160. Do you find any difference of conduct on the part of the regular navigators and the agricultural labourers from the neighbourhood of the works?
IKB. *No. They each have peculiar habits. I do not know that one is better than the other.*

2161. Have you ever had any difficulties with them?
IKB. *No, very little indeed.* [See Question 2096.]

2162. If well treated they are a manageable set of people?
IKB. *Yes. Very manageable.*

Mr Brunel was permitted to withdraw.

10: THE DAILY GRIND

'Engaged in consultation and committees'

Brunel lived life at a terrific rate and pushed his small body to the limit. With all this business to attend to and long-distance travel thrown in, it is quite remarkable that he had any time or energy to design his railways with their stations and bridges. The following are the complete entries, day by day, from his office diary held at Bristol University Library, Special Collections.

1848

1 January. Saturday
Mr Brunel left London by the express train 9.50am for Bristol. [The fastest train in the world – the 'Flying Dutchman'.]
Engaged there during the day and returned to Duke St about 9pm.

3 January. Monday
Mr Brunel with Capt Claxton RN, Mr Brereton and Mr Whitcombe left Euston Square station at 6.15am for Chester – arriving at Chester at 2pm.
Left Chester at 4pm posting [travelling by horse-drawn coach] to Holywell, St Asaph and Abergeley (sic).

4 January. Tuesday
Left Abergeley at 7am posting to Conway. Inspected the Tubular Bridge and engaged on the Works until 1 pm. Examined Sea Wall at Penmaen Mawr. Went along Chester & Holyhead line to Bangor. Remained the night at Bangor.

5 January. Wednesday
Left Bangor at 7am posting to Holyhead.
Inspected Holyhead Harbour and went on board Packet at 4pm
Left Holyhead Harbour at 5pm

6 January. Thursday
Arrived in Kingstown [Dun Laoghaire] at 3am.

Engaged in morning with Mr Muggeridge and Mr Pindon on Waterford, Wexford & Wicklow Railway business generally.

7 January. Friday
Mr Brunel went to Dublin at 1am [sic] and attended Board Meeting there with Mr Pindon.
Returned to Kingstown in the evening.

8 January. Saturday
At 6am went to Bray with Mr Pindon, Capt Claxton, Mr Brereton and Mr Whitcombe. Examined the WWWR Works there. Returning to Kingstown in the afternoon.
Went on board Packet at 6.30pm. Leaving Kingstown at 7pm, landed at Liverpool at 10.30am on Sunday morning 9th.

9 January. Sunday
Left Liverpool by 11.15am train to Birmingham and on to London by Special Train from Birmingham arriving at Duke St about ¼ before 8.

1848
1 May. Monday
Mr Brunel left London by the 6am train for Bristol.
Returned to Duke Street by afternoon express train.

[Mr Brunel was engaged at Bristol on Bristol Dock business and also engaged at the steamship works inspecting the testing of an iron girder.]

4 May. Thursday
Mr Brunel left London by the Express Train for Devonshire – engaged previously at Duke St at 7am with Mr Fisher on PGW Dock contract.

5 May. Friday
Opening of the South Devon Railway from Totnes to Laira Green near Plymouth.

[Mr Brunel was engaged with Mr Carr, Messrs Glennie, Harrison and others at the Totnes station previously to going with South Devon Directors down to Laira Green by the 10.15 Train.]
[Mr Brunel saw Mr Power at Plymouth and arranged with him at Mill Bay respecting the works of the PGW Docks.]

Returned to London by the Mail Train from Totnes.

7 May. Sunday
Mr Brunel left London for Paris.

[In Paris on 23 February 1848 the Government of the Bourbon King of France, Louis-Phillipe, fell and the King abdicated. Armed uprisings and counter-measures created a riotous situation, which continued for many months. The situation was something like that which greeted Isambard's father, Marc, when he was in the French Royal Navy and returned from Martinique to Paris in 1792. Marc had had a very exciting time, fighting as a Royalist against the Revolutionaries.]

[On 7 May 1848 Isambard Kingdom Brunel went to Paris to witness the violence – and maybe he hoped to take part in some fighting. He loved dangerous situations and was, I have no doubt, very envious of his father's exploits in Normandy in 1792.]

10 May. Wednesday
Accident on Great Western. Mr Brereton on train.

[This happened at Shrivenham at 3.03pm when the 12 noon Exeter express train to Paddington collided with a horse-box that had been left on the up main line. See my *Grub, Water & Relief* (John Murray, 1985), p100.]

12 May. Friday
Mr Brunel returned to Duke Street at 11 o'clock and engaged with Mr Seymour Clarke at ¼ to 12am respecting the accident to the 2.5 Express Up Train on the 10th inst.

Engaged with Mr Varden shortly afterwards on Ox & Worcester. Parliamentary. Preparing for Committee.

Also with Mr Saunders and Mr Danvill on matters connected with the Windsor Rly.

At 1pm engaged with Mr W. O. Hunt, Mr Whatley and Mr T. Smith, Ox & Wos Business.

Mr Brunel attended Oxford & Worcester Committees at ¼ past 1pm. Preamble of these Bills proved.

Saw Mr Miles and Capt Claxton for a few minutes.

Engaged with Mr Muggeridge and Mr Glodale [?] at ¼ to 6pm on Wexford Waterford & Wicklow matters.

Engaged with Mr Rennie [?] South Wales contractor also with Mr Sharpe, also South Wales contractor shortly afterwards.

[Mr Brunel left London by the Mail train for Devonshire.]

13 May. Saturday
Mr Brunel attended Cornwall Railway Board meeting this day at Plymouth and returned to London by the Mail Train.

14 May. Sunday
Mr Brunel saw Mr Bedford, Mr Millett and Mr Hemmings (Contractor) at ½ past 12pm.

15 May. Monday
Mr Brunel was engaged with Mr Hemmings at ¼ past 7am.
   Saw Mr Whitehurst at ¼ past 9am and Mr Skymes shortly afterwards with who he was engaged for a considerable time on McIntosh matters. [Brunel was refusing to pay the contractor McIntosh what he was owed.]
   Engaged with Messrs Hunts.
   Saw Mr Varden and Mr Bedford Ox & Worcester and with Mr Saunders afterwards.
   Mr Brunel was engaged at Committees [Parliamentary?] between 1 and 4pm.

17 May. Wednesday
Mr Brunel and Mr Richardson before breakfast on Monmouth & Hereford Railway matters. [Charles Richardson was one of Brunel's very important assistants. He engineered the Bristol & South Wales Union Railway, 1857-63, and became the Engineer of the Severn Tunnel in 1872.]
   Engaged with Mr Humphreys 10 to 10 respecting Rennie's [stationary pumping] engines South Devon Railway.
   At ½ past 10am Mr Brunel attended a consultation at Messrs Hnts. Saw Mr Muggeridge afterwards.
   Mr Brunel went to the Lobby of the House of Commons to hear the decision of the 'Audit of Railway Accounts' Bill. This was thrown out at Committee.
   Mr Brunel attended Board meeting of South Wales Railway at 4½pm.

31 May. Wednesday
Engaged with Mr Skymes at 9am.
   Saw Mr T. Smith at 10 and went with him to Messrs Hunts.
   Engaged in consultation and Committees.
   Returned to Duke St at ½ past 4pm with Mr Mereweather and went to consultation at Messrs Hunts afterwards.
   Windsor Railway. Preamble of this Bill provisionally proved. Clauses to be gone into on Friday next.

B&O Jcn Rly [Birmingham & Oxford Junction Railway]. Date of Line and gauge questions. Bill proved.

Mr Brunel was engaged between 6pm and 12 with Special Constables J. C. Talbot and others. [A great movement for democracy in Britain was reaching its climax from April to July 1848. The Chartist leaders were demanding the vote for working people. Huge rallies were held and an uprising was planned for July – and foiled by the arrest of the plotters. Brunel joined a force of Special Constables and received instruction into how to fight with a truncheon. He and his friends went out to patrol the streets. He was certainly hoping for some excitement, but none came his way.]

11: THE ATMOSPHERIC RAILWAY

'A good and economical mode of applying staionary power'

Brunel visited the 1¾-mile single-track atmospheric railway by which the Dublin to Kingstown (Dun Laoghaire) railway had been extended to the village of Dalkey. By atmospheric pressure three carriages were propelled at 28mph up a 1 in 57 gradient from Kingstown Harbour to Dalkey. He saw that it worked and was deeply impressed. George Stephenson famously called this 'A Rope of Wind', likening the atmospheric system to the well-known system of rope haulage on steep inclines. Brunel decided that the system was equally applicable to haulage on a trunk main line. He entirely overlooked half a dozen fatal disadvantages that made it entirely useless for working any main or branch-line railway. A great many eminent engineers were opposed to the system – Brunel's great friend Daniel Gooch, Joseph Locke, George Parker Bidder and Robert Stephenson, to name but a few. For the benefit of Parliament, Robert Stephenson entered into extensive running trials and mathematical calculations with which he filled a large pamphlet, when all he needed to have done was point out that atmospheric haulage depended on the pressure of the atmosphere to drive the train – approximately 14.7psi.

In this very remarkable Report to the South Devon Railway Directors (Rail 631/44), Brunel says that calculations can be made to prove anything, so he has approached the question of the atmospheric system as 'a practical man'. A practical man would have seen at once that trains would have to be of standard weight in order to maintain the timetable; if more coaches were added the train would go slower, because there could be no increase in the force available to move it along he track. He would have seen that, at a junction, the suction tube could not cross the rails; trains would have to stop short of the junction and be towed across until the power car's piston could enter the next suction tube. As an aside to this, it is interesting to note that when Brunel was faced with the problem of launching the SS *Great Eastern*, he steadfastly refused to listen to the practical advice of highly experienced shipbuilders in Britain and the USA and instead relied entirely on experiments and mathematical calculations.

South Devon Railway

August 19th 1844

Gentlemen,

I have given much consideration to the question referred to me by you at your last meeting – namely that of the advantage of the application of the Atmospheric system to the South Devon Railway.

The question is not a new one to me as I have foreseen the possibility it arising and have frequently considered it. I shall assume, and I am not aware that it is disputed by anybody, that stationary power, if freed from the weight and friction of any medium of communication as a rope, must be cheaper, is more under command and is susceptible of producing much higher speeds than locomotive power; and when it is considered that for high speeds such as 60mph the locomotive engine with its tender cannot weigh much less than half of the gross weight of the train, the advantage and economy of dispensing with the necessity of putting this great weight in motion will also be evident.

I must assume also that as a means of applying stationary power, the atmospheric system has been successful and that, unless when under some very peculiar circumstances it is inapplicable, it is a good and economical mode of applying stationary power. I am aware that this opinion is directly opposed to that of Mr Robert Stephenson who has written and published an elaborate statement of experiments and calculations founded upon them the results of which support his opinion.

It does not seem to me that we can allow the minute data required for the mathematical investigation of such a question: and that such calculations, dependent as they are upon an unattainable precision in experiments, are as likely to lead you very far from the truth as not.

By the same mode Mnsr Mallet and other French Engineers proved the success of the system and by the same mode of investigation Dr Lardner arrived at all those results regarding steam navigation and the speed to be attained on railways which have since been proved to be erroneous.

Experience has led me to prefer what some may consider a more superficial but what I should call a more general and broader view and more capable of embracing all the conditions of the question – as a practical man.

Having considered the subject for several years past I have cautiously and without any cause for a favourable bias formed an opinion which subsequent experiments at Dalkey [the Kingstown Harbour atmospheric railway] have fully proved to be correct – viz:- that the mere mechanical difficulties can be overcome and that the full effect of the partial vacuum produced by an air pump can be communicated without any loss or friction worth taking into consideration, by a piston attached to the train.

In this point of view the experiment at Dalkey has entirely succeeded – a system of machinery which even at the first attempt works without interruption constantly for many months may be considered practically to be free from any technical objection. No locomotive line that I have been connected with has been equally free from accident.

That which is true for one railway of 2 miles in length is equally true for a second or third, altho' they may be placed the one at the end of the other. The chances of an accident are only in proportion of the number or in other words the length – a proportion which holds equally good with a Locomotive may be affected by the distance it has previously run while a stationary Engine and its pipes cannot in like manner be affected by the previous working of the neighbouring Engine and pipes.

In my opinion the Atmospheric system is, so far as any stationary power can be, as applicable to a great length of line as it is to a short one.

Upon all these points I could advance many arguments and many proofs; but I shall content myself with saying that as a professional man I express decided opinions that, as a mechanical contrivance, the Atmospheric apparatus has succeeded perfectly as an effective meanings of working trains whether on long or short lines at higher velocities and the less chance of interruption by stationary power than is now effected by Locomotives.

It will simplify the discussion of the question very much if it is considered as a comparison between a double line worked by locomotives and a single line of Railway worked by stationary power – the only peculiarity of the present case being that upon four separate portions of the whole 52 miles stationary power would in any case have been used – these four inclines forming together one fifth of the whole distance. [Brunel has said that the atmospheric system is as applicable to a long line as a short one. He now says that a long atmospheric line has to be a single track because of the expense of building a second line of pumping stations. A single-track main line is restricted for ever in its capacity to carry trains. If a stationary engine failed it would create a blockade on the single track until the engine could be repaired, but if a locomotive engine failed a second engine could quickly come to the rescue to push the train to its destination.]

It is necessary to consider it as a question of a single line on account of the expense – the cost of the pipe for each line being about £3,500 per mile, an addition of £7,000 per mile [his arithmetic is at fault – the additional cost in making a double line would be £3,500 per mile] or about £330,000 in the first construction could not be counterbalanced by any adequate advantage in saving in the works on the South Devon Railway and probably not by any subsequent economy or advantage in the working; but the system admits of the working with a single line – certainly without danger of collision – and I believe also that, considering the absence of most of the causes of accident there will even be less liability to interruption and delay on the average resulting from accidents than with an ordinary double [-track] locomotive railway.

By the modification of the gradients and by reducing the curves to 1000 feet radius where any great advantage can be gained by so doing and by constructing the cuttings, embankments, tunnels and viaducts for a single line, a considerable saving may be effected in first cost. In the permanent way and ballasting this reduction will be about one half. I should propose to make the rails about 52lbs per yard weight and the timber 12ft 6in, the quantity of ballast would probably be rather more than half but at the present price of iron and timber the saving could not be less than £2,500 per mile.

From a careful revision of the work generally I consider that a reduction may be effected in the following items and in the amount specified in each.

Ballasting Gradients & Curves	
Reduction in earthwork	*£16,500*
do. in length of principal tunnels	*£14,000*
Savings by making single line	
Earthwork	*£25,000*
Tunnels	*£11,500*
Viaducts	*£15,000*

Permanent-way & ballast to allow for
Sidings 50 miles @ £2,500   £125,000
                                                     £207,000

Atmospheric costs
Pipe on 41½ miles   £138,000
Increased pipe on 10½ miles inclined plane   £6,500
Engines for the 41½ miles   £35,000
Patent rights, say   £10,000
                                                     £190,000

Difference in first cost is £17,000

To this however must be added the cost of locomotive power with attendant expenses of engine houses etc
Which cannot, I think, be put at less than £50,000
Making a saving of £67,000.

I have not included in the expense of the Atmospheric apparatus that of the telegraph because at its present reduced cost of £160 per mile I am convinced its use would repay the outlay in either case.

It would appear then that the line can be constructed and furnished with the moving power in working order on the Atmospheric system for something less than the construction only of the railway fitted for locomotive power but without the engines and that taking into consideration the cost of locomotive power a saving in first outlay may be effected of upwards of £60,000.

But it is in frequent working that the advantages will be most sensible.

In the first place with the gradients and curves of the South Devon Railway between Newton and Plymouth a speed of 30mph would have been for locomotive engines a high speed and under unfavourable circumstances of weather and of load it would probably have been found difficult and expensive to have maintained even this and with the dimensions of pipes I have assumed that a speed of 40-50 miles per hour [but that could only be achieved by a strictly observed restriction on loads to permit that speed.] may certainly be depended upon and I have no doubt that from 25 to 35 minutes may be saved in the journey.

Secondly. The cost of running a few additional trains as far as the power is concerned is so small, the plant of engines, the attendance of the enginemen remaining the same that it may be neglected in the calculations so that short trains [ie those running short distances] or extra trains with more frequent departures adopted in every respect to the varying demands of the public can be worked at very moderate cost and I have no doubt a considerable augmentation of the general traffic thus effected by means of which with locomotive engines would be very expensive and frequently unattainable particularly as regards one class of short train whether for passengers or goods which from the inconvenience of working them by locomotive are hardly known.

I refer to trains between intermediate stations.

By many means, which the easy command of a motive power at any time, at every part of the line, must afford, of accommodating the traffic, I believe the traffic may be increased [sic].

It appears to me also that the quality of the travelling will be much improved that we shall attain great speed less the noise and motion and an absence of coke dust which is certainly still a great nuisance and will be inducements thus held out to those (the majority of travellers) who travel either wholly for pleasure or at least not from necessity and who are mainly influenced by the degree of comfort with which they can go from place to place.

Lastly. The average cost of working the trains will be much less than by locomotive with the gradients of the South Devon Railway and assuming that not less than eight trains including mail and goods trains running the whole distance and certainly one short train running half the distance to be the least number that would suffice I think an annual saving of £8,000 a year in locomotive expenses (allowing for depreciation of plant) may safely be relied upon.

For all the reasons above quoted I have no hesitation in taking upon myself the full and certain responsibility of recommending the adoption of the Atmospheric system on the South Devon Railway and of recommending that as a consequence that the line and its works should be constructed for a single line only.

I have the honour to be
Gentlemen,
Your obedient servant,
I. K. Brunel

The 'Atmospheric principle' was roundly condemned by the 'Associated

Companies' – the GWR, the B&ER and the Midland Railway – all of whom were supplying capital to the South Devon. This letter (Rail 631/44) is from Charles Russell, Chairman of the Board of the Great Western Railway Company, to Thomas Gill, Chairman of the South Devon Company. It very politely says: 'Do as you think best – but on your own heads be it.'

Charles Street
24 December 1844

My Dear Sir,
If you will call to mind the discussion which took place at the South Devon I am sure you will remember that the Directors who represented the Great Western Company always resisted the adoption of the Atmospheric principle without further experience – I myself took that course at a Board held at Plymouth stating that my reasons for not dividing the Directors present were that the subject had at a previous Board been decided by a large majority and that I saw from the opinion then expressed that the same result would ensue if the question were again put to the vote –

Under such circumstances it would not only have been useless to agitate the question at the first general meeting of our proprietors but it would have been quite inconsistent with the friendly & amicable spirit in which we were desirous to act with our colleagues to raise such a discussion – It has always seemed to me that the legitimate way of exercising the influence of the Associated Companies is that which we adopted thro' our own representatives at the South Devon Board.

The question took a different form as regards the Cornish line. It was not then one on which the Cornish Directors were in that capacity deliberating; but it was one between the Cornish Company & the Associated Companies as to the terms in which the agreement between them should be drawn up & it was surely competent to the latter to require as one condition of their assistance that the line should be double & applicable to locomotive engines & that the atmospheric principle should not be finally resolved upon until it had been established by fuller experience.

Nothing would be further from my wish then to embarrass or obstruct the proceedings of the South Devon Company or to disturb the good feeling which has prevailed at their Board but we did feel it due to ourselves to let it be clearly understood that the atmospheric principle had been adopted on your line on the judgement of the South Devon Company and not on that of the Great Western Company.

I remain, My dear Sir,
Yours sincerely
Charles Russell

Brunel wrote the following letter (PLB 4, p33) to one of the Royal Commissioners, Lord Kilgour:

18 Duke Street
31 March 1845

My Dear Sir,
I object very much to giving evidence upon the abstract point of a particular system and thus furnishing general opinions which others are to apply as they may choose to particular cases & if I could I would refuse to give evidence at all before the present Committee whatever might be the consequences to the promoters of the Atmospheric system. Circumstances however render such a refusal impossible but I am equally anxious not to be drawn into becoming an advocate of the system.

When I gave evidence last year – altho' it was then very much against my inclination – it was in support of a particular case and it was only incidentally that my opinion was advanced as to a system. The evidence is now avowedly sought in support of a system and I do not – as I before stated – intend to become an advocate of this or any other system. I mention these my views to prevent disappointment.

If the following facts & opinions are likely to be of use to the Committee I can give evidence of them.

I made experiments upon the portion of railway laid on Wormwood Scrubbs – those experiments were made for my private satisfaction & not made public in any way.

They satisfied me of the mechanical practicability of the system.

In 1843 & 1844 I made several experiments upon the Dalkey Railway.

The results of my observations & of those experiments is an opinion that the mechanical difficulties may be overcome and the whole as a machine made to work in a very perfect manner – that as a mechanical power for locomotion it will generally but not in every case be more economical than what is strictly termed locomotive power – that high speeds may be more easily attained – that from the absence of the locomotive engine the rails may be constructed & maintained in more perfect order – and as a consequence the carriages may be constructed & worked in a more perfect manner & so run more smoothly & that in all respects the travelling may be rendered more rapid – more luxurious & more safe – as regards the last, viz:- safety, collisions may be rendered altogether impossible to most remotely possible which all other sources of danger now very small may be almost entirely removed by the increased perfection of the rails.

As regards first cost – a single line may be made to answer all the purposes of a double locomotive line for most lines except main lines in immediate connection with a locomotive line in immediate connection with the metropolis – or forming trunk lines for others not under the same control and a single atmospheric line will generally cost less than a double locomotive line without the engines.

I am now constructing a line of 52 miles in length for the Atmospheric System – I already see many advantages to be attained in the setting out and constructing of a railway if originally designed for this system – but the principal advantages can only be attained and above all the principal difficulties in the system can only be properly provided against where the line is originally designed for the system – the choice of gradients and curves and levels and above all the arrangement of stations will generally be totally different in the two systems & the difficulties to be avoided will equally differ.

Yours very truly
I. K. Brunel

A few days later Brunel writes on the same matter to the Rt Hon Mr Bingham-Baring, Chairman of the Parliamentary Select Committee on Atmospheric Railways:

18 Duke Street
3 April 1845

My Dear Sir,
I am summoned to attend your Committee and as it is known that
I have expressed opinions favourable to the Atmospheric system
and that I am actually applying it upon a line of some length it
would be considered an absurd affectation and would moreover be
useless to attempt to avoid giving evidence when called upon – but
I am a most unwilling witness – I think it rather hard upon a
professional man who wishes to be cautious that he should be
called upon to express general opinions which if written down
even in the most [...] careful language cannot be so worded as to
be applicable to every case that may hereafter arise – or to be proof
against unfair [...] [...] attack of the paid writers on these
controversies – I mention these difficulties which I feel – that you
may make some allowance for them if my feelings should appear
in my evidence or if that evidence should appear to fall very short
of the opinion I am known to entertain & which I must entertain
to induce me to apply the system extensively as I am doing.

I find it difficult to define the points upon which it would be
desirable to examine engineering witnesses – and I really believe
that entering freshly upon the subject and feeling as one of the
public you are more likely to elicit the useful points than one who
like myself has been turning his whole attention (lately at least)
solely to the mechanical construction, however I enclose a copy of
a letter I addressed to a party interested in the patent which refers
to my opinions on the several points – opinions however expressed
without that caution to which I referred as so necessary.

I am dear Sir,
Yours very truly,
I. K. Brunel

The following letter is written to an unknown person – possibly Charles
Saunders. Brunel, a great protagonist for individual liberty, has just
returned from Italy where he hopes to engineer railways and, in this letter,
expresses astonishment at the spectacle of individual liberty in full flight
– and this at only the start of the 'railway mania'.

October 29 1845

My Dear Sir,
I returned only this afternoon and am endeavouring but very
ineffectually as yet to comprehend the present extraordinary state

of railway matters – when everybody around seems mad – stark, staring, wildly mad – the only course for a sane man is to get out of the way and keep quiet and as a general rule I think it may be safely followed – whether the Topsham & Exeter concern is to cause an exception is most difficult to say – I am half inclined to think it ought to be – that is to say that if you can unite the really respectable & powerfull interests of Exeter & Exmouth & and the landowners & bring them to Countess Weir (or rather as much below as possible) it will no doubt be a great protection to all our interests & a good public work, the B&E Company are particularly interested in it. The value of the Ferry is not of course worth a moment's consideration – as to Starcross I apprehend the question would always and will still depend upon the merits of the site as regards deep water etc, etc.

There is one thing that strikes me however, the names on the prospectus don't seem to imply any great local strength – & we should be sure that we acquire strength and a good deal to compensate for the risks in meddling with such a project.

I am my dear Sir,
Yours very sincerely,
I. K. Brunel

With respect to the Bridport or any of these new schemes my present intention is to have no connection personally with them – unless where the interests of my present clients require it and the lines are also bona fide proper lines I don't intend to be the Engineer to any more – I don't intend to go mad & I should soon at the rate others are going.

By the latter part of 1847 thousands of people were bankrupt owing to gambling in railway shares. The 'Collins' in the next letter (Bristol University Special Collection, Private Letter Book 5, p239) might have had some position in Brunel's office. Maybe he has fallen into debt and is trying to lever money out of Brunel. We do not know – but this note is are among the most extraordinary notes in the Brunel collection.

13 August 1847

Collins,
I have been induced to put up with the repeated instances of your

unequalled insolent, self-confidence because it has generally displayed such extra-ordinary folly and impudence to the prejudice of your own interest that it excited one's pity.

Your last letter, however, is so purely selfish and displays such bad feelings towards those who have really befriended you that I cease to take any interest in you and have nothing left but disgust at your conduct.

I must plainly tell you that you are to me an expensive nuisance and that you appear to Mr Babbage a most ungrateful slanderer.

I have forwarded your letter to Mr Babbage and must leave him to deal with you as he thinks best and which I suppose will be to get rid of you as quickly as he can.

Brunel

Returning to the vexed question of the use of the atmospheric system on the South Devon Railway, Brunel wrote the following (Rail 631/44) to the Company's Directors:

27 August 1847

Gentlemen,
It is a subject of great regret and to no-one more than myself that we have yet been unable to open any portion of the line to the public with the Atmospheric apparatus although a considerable distance has for some months been in a state to admit of frequent experiments being made upon it. This delay has arisen principally if not entirely in that part of the whole system which it might have been expected would have been least exposed to it – namely the construction and completion of the steam engines. It is due to Mr Samuda that I should say that, so far as regards the mere pipe and valve and other details which may be said to constitute the Atmospheric apparatus, we might have since commenced but the engines, although designed without interference with their plans and finished by the finest makers in the country and although differing so slightly from the ordinary construction of steam engines have proved sources of continued and most vexatious delays both in the unexpected length of time occupied originally in their construction and in the subsequent correction of their defects in minor parts. While the engines were imperfect it would not only have been unwise to have commenced working the line, even had

244

it been practical, but the present interruption to the continuous working of the engines rendered impossible to test and complete the different portions of the Atmospheric.

There are still some defects to be remedied in one or two of the engines and I am using every endeavour by persuasion and every other means in my power to urge on the manufacturers in their work of completion. Within the last week or two only have we been able to work at all continuously between Exeter and Teignmouth so as to have the opportunity of trying the different parts and getting the various details requisite for actually working trains tested and brought to sufficient perfection to ensure efficiency and regularity.

Since the beginning of last week however four trains a day have been running regularly, stopping at the stations and keeping their time as if working for traffic. The tube and valve appear in good order and the whole has worked well but running in this manner can alone show the deficiencies which may still exist in the details necessary for stopping and starting quickly from the stations and all the other minor operations incidental to working the traffic in the ordinary course and until all these arrangements are completed and the engines in perfect order I think it would be better to defer for at least a week the substitution of the Atmospheric for the Locomotive working.

Trains in addition to those now running may perhaps be advantageously worked for the public after a further short continuance of the present practising.

The two engines completing the number to Newton are nearly ready for trial and it is to be presumed that after the experience of the past the makers will be enabled to put them at once into an efficient state.

The delay and difficulties attending the bringing into operation the Atmospheric upon this portion of the railway have been beyond all anticipation and beyond what any previous experience would have justified anybody in anticipating. The difficulties have all been seriously aggravated by the necessity (consequent certainly upon the original delays) of working the line with locomotives during the construction and completion of the Atmospheric. Not only has the constant occupation of the line interfered with the progress of the work but it has been necessary to devise all the arrangements so as to admit stations, sidings and line to be worked either by locomotives or the Atmospheric or both in succession or even at the same time.

These difficulties added to those always consequent upon the introduction of any new system have been most wearying and incessant that I myself have more than once repented having ever made the attempt [words crossed out by Brunel] and I am not surprised that the public and proprietors should have been impatient.

I trust the ultimate result will however remove any grounds for disappointment.

With respect to the state of the works generally I can report satisfactorily. On the entire distance from Totnes to Laira Green at Plymouth there remain only some 5-6,000 yards of earthwork to excavate, the ballasting is everywhere else almost finished, the bridges and viaducts wait only the parapet and minor accessories to be completed and generally the works are so far advanced that the opening of the line will now only depend upon the laying of the permanent-way which together with the construction of a temporary station at Laira Green will be proceeded with rapidly and I cannot see any reason to doubt that the whole may be completed by the end of the year.

The works of the Torquay branch are also drawing near to completion and by erecting a temporary station at the present extremity may I think be opened to the public at the same time as the line to Plymouth.

I remain, Gentlemen,
Your obedient servant,
I. K. Brunel

To the Directors, South Devon Railway

12: CHARLES SAUNDERS

'Your exceeding kindness in relieving me of everything
you possibly can'

Charles Saunders, the GWR Company Secretary and General Superintendent (General Manager in modern terms), was Brunel's lifelong friend. He provided Brunel with the 'shoulder to cry on' – the moral support anyone needs, especially in the stressful situations in which Brunel put himself all his life.

Brunel is very tired and worried, and after an all-night letter-writing session he writes to thank Saunders for his unwavering support (DM 1758/15). Because he is exhausted a certain self-pity comes through – and also a very rare apology.

18 Duke Street,
Westminster
December 3rd 1837

My Dear Saunders,
None of my certificates have arrived yet, although the mail is in and I therefore cannot start until tomorrow. I have just received a letter from Osler expressing the great disappointment of the Directors that I was not there yesterday although I wrote to them on the subject of Ranger and he (Osler) knew I was going out of Town – Meeting adjourned till tomorrow and expect a 'report'. I shall therefore be at home if you call on your way to the City.

A hint or two from the other end is useful now and then to remind me of what however I am fully sensible and always thinking of – your exceeding kindness in relieving me of everything you possibly can and still more strongly shown in your silence and the absence of complaint.

In my endeavour to introduce a few – really but a few – improvements in the principal part of the work I have involved myself in a mass of novelties. I can compare it to nothing but the sudden adoption of a language familiar enough to the speaker and in itself simple enough but unfortunately understood by nobody about him – every word has to be translated – and so it is with my work. One alteration has involved another and no part can be copied from what others have done [he was supplied with plans for brick arch overbridges by Robert Stephenson].

I have cut myself off from the help usually received from assistants [which seems unfair to his loyal, hard-working and very patient Resident Engineer assistants]. No one can fill up the details – I am obliged to do all myself and the quantity of writing in instructions alone takes 4 or 5 hours a day and as invention is something like a spring of water – limited – I fear I sometimes pump myself dry and remain for an hour or so utterly stupid.

As regards the company, I never regretted one instant the course I have taken – on the contrary the conviction which daily grows stronger that eventually they will profit immensely by the changes is my only consolation for my own annoyances – and as regards myself, if I get through it with my head clear or at all I shall not regret it but I certainly never should but for your kindness and the corresponding kindness and forbearance of our Directs.

I have spun the long yarn partly as a recreation after working all night, principally to have the pleasure of telling a real friend that I am fully sensible of his kindness although he hardly allows me to see it and partly because I want you to know that if I take things coolly it is because I feel them so acutely that I am obliged to harden myself a little to be able to bear the thoughts of them – and also because I do feel conscientiously that I am doing my utmost to lead the Company safely through the temporary difficulties I have got them into [these underlined words are a rare example of Brunel apologising. This passage was left out when L.T.C Rolt published this letter. See his 1st Ed, p114].

If I ever go mad I shall have the ghost of the opening of the railway walking before me, or rather, standing in front, holding out its hand and when it steps forward a little swarm of devils in the shape of leaky pickle tanks – uncut timber – half finished station houses – sinking embankments – broken screws – absent guard plates – unfinished drawings and sketches of details will quietly and quite as a matter of course and as if I ought to have expected it – lift up my ghost and put him a little farther off than before.

What a note I have written you – well I do not think it is altogether time wasted. I hope you will think the same.

Yours sincerely,
I. K. Brunel

Mary wishes a word to say how Florence is.

The Clarke brothers, Seymour and Frederick, were the Traffic Superintendents at Paddington and Bristol respectively. Seymour had been Brunel's Chief Clerk at 18 Duke Street and was appointed in May 1838 – in time for the opening of the GWR line from Paddington to Maidenhead in June 1838. Frederick was appointed in May 1840 in time for the opening from Bristol to Bath. He writes to Saunders regarding them (Rail 1008/35):

18 Duke St
5 August 1842

Great Western Railway

My Dear Saunders,
I have as you know very frequently called attention to the state of the different carriages which I find defective as I make a rule of always trying each carriage in the train I travel by. The result being that these carriages are taken off work and the defects rectified – generally also I have pointed out the cause of the defect and suggested the best mode of remedying them.

Both the Clarkes have always shown the greatest desire to ask my advice as to the work to be done – and I believe are always anxious to adopt that advice – thus I have frequently seen what I have considered very injurious and un-mechanical things done – and I don't think a mere coachbuilder however good is for the engineering of railway carriages – for instance the ironwork and fittings of our framework are by no means what they ought to be and one great defect which has annoyed us so long namely that awful thumping of the wheels when going fast I think would not have occurred had an ordinary millwright or engineer examined and received the wheels – after a great deal of trouble and very close examination I discovered the causes – an inequality in the thickness of the tire which threw the wheel out of balance – when the wheel is clean and new this would have struck the eye of a tolerably good mechanical workman when deliberately inspecting the wheel – and a large expense saved to the company. Besides the 'thumping' I believe the defect is principally in a certain size of wheel and is rather peculiar to our railway as the 'thumping' taking our wheels of 4ft to the others at 3ft high and our high speeds about same proportion will be about as 2½ to 1.

I think all the constructional parts of the carriages should be in some way under the engineering inspection and further – done at one place. I found a very bad carriage today – bad enough to stop it running to Taunton but I preferred letting it run to telling Clarke because I have found these carriages get repaired first at one [place] and then at the other and have seen extra-ordinary remedies when the physicians call – I think incompatible remedies apply and more than one – they get terribly patched up and a great deal of work is required and not very profitably.

I think all the wheels, axles, springs, oil boxes, buffers, heavy ironwork and bolts should be made (or inspected if delivered under contract) at Swindon by the same class of people as the engine work is – for it ought to be carefully made – to be taken into store there.

I believe that Swindon would also be the proper place for effecting any material repairs – small repairs ought to be effected at Paddn or Bristol if they always draw the parts ready made from the General Store because I would undertake them if the whole was under one management and a proper class of workman, the constant little doctoring now required would cease.

The thumping which puzzled us all and what has caused so many carriages to have something done to them really arose as I before explained from a defect which wd have caught the eye of an experienced workman – these dreadful motions which have shaken our carriages to pieces would never have arisen –

I discovered quite indirectly that the bearings of the axles having worn longer, the pattern [?] of the brasses perhaps shorter, they were in the habit of using brasses ½ inch or more too short – no mechanic would have done that. There are fifty other points I could refer to but they all form the same thing – that a railway carriage requires engineering superintendence and that is quite impossible that Seymour Clarke can conduct such a department while Fredk I don't think is at all competent & altho' the former is very intelligent he has not had the mechanical practice that is required.

Let me know your views and objections when we meet.

Yours,

I. K. Brunel

Of course you will not hint at my opinion of the Clarkes to anybody but think over what I have said.

Brunel is unwell and needs ten days leave, but then, in recounting what needs to be done before he can get away, he loses himself in the worries of his work and the intricacies of railway politics, the latter Machiavellian manoeuvres being, I think, something he really enjoys – so he appears to forget his weary state of health. At the end of the letter (Rail 1008/35, folio 67) Brunel starts to diplomatically change Saunders's mind over using single-line working when track relaying is taking place. He points out the cost of 'deranging the traffic'.

18 Duke Street
31 August 1842

Private.

Great Western Railway

My Dear Saunders,
I had supposed that I should be prevented attending the board tomorrow by being obliged to attend an important arbitration pending in the Euston business but I find myself also prevented by more potent causes – I cannot get out early in the morning, and this evening I feel that it would have been impossible for me to have been at... [this sentence he left unfinished at the end of the last line of the first page of the letter. The second page begins:]
I doubt my attending even the arbitration at Steventon tomorrow – my state of health indeed renders me very anxious to get away entirely for a week or ten days or I see no prospect of ever getting well but I believe that would be sufficient and if you can get the Oxford meeting – and if I can get the Cheltenham business in train – and if this question of the permanent way (as regards the final prices) and the question of cottages can be settled you & I get away by the end of next week – I would be back to see the rails laid which I think is important and to assist in terminating the Cheltenham matter.
As regards the cottages – Rigby is by no means desirous to give them up he has pushed on vigorously and offers to undertake to get 80 more finished by Christmas am I to order them? The present 40 will be ready in a fortnight.

As regards the Cheltenham I believe I shall be ready this week to start portions then that which I estimated at 730,000 may be contracted for at about 620,000 and to this is to be added – land. 70,000 expenses already in arrears on that portion – £ – redemption of Gloucester & Cheltenham line – 90,000 additional rails to ditto – 20,000 – extension into Cheltenham I know not what yet – but say 50,000 & station – making certainly 250,000 so that we cannot assume less than 900,000! £ probably 950,000 – you are of course aware that the Bristol & Gloucester propose to avail themselves of the powers of their Act to enter upon the part between Stonehouse and Gloucester and that attempts are making by the Birmingham & Gloucester to unite with them – & I see nothing to prevent this except the arrangement with the Gt Western which I believe would at once lead the Bristol & Gloucester to treat voluntarily with the GWR even in preference – this is really no false alarm –

You will observe in my report on the permanent way that I have not referred to the possibility of laying the rails without diverting the traffic –

I cannot take upon myself the responsibility of proposing such a plan against the views of yourself and what I may call the feeling of the Chairman and therefore as the idea has not gone beyond the Chairman it was unnecessary to refer to it – apart from my wish not to derange the traffic and alarm the public. I should of course prefer the course I now recommend will you have the goodness to explain this to Mr Russell or to read my letter to him.

I observe on referring to my report I have not carried out the cost of the trial piece I propose to do – it will of course be at £250 per chain [22 yards] £3,250 and upon this piece which is now very bad will save I have no doubt, £500 per year.

I have not referred to the period over which the [...] repairs would be spread as this must be very much a question of finance depending on the result as regards cost of the trial piece – as well as of interference with traffic according to the expedition with which we find we can do any given length.

Yours very truly,
I. K. Brunel

Brunel was Engineer of the Oxford, Worcester & Wolverhampton Railway, formed in 1845. It was to be laid with the broad gauge, the

GWR was authorised to provide a 5 of its capital, and it was by its Act not allowed to sell or lease itself to any railway company except the GWR. The London & North Western Railway and the Midland Railway were anxious to prevent the broad gauge reaching the Midlands and beyond, and tried to subvert the Act of Parliament and take over the OW&WR. Brunel very much desired to finish what he had started in constructing the route and was very reluctant to resign. But the GWR Board insisted and eventually he tendered his resignation in a letter dated 11 March 1852, and it was accepted at a regular Board meeting held on the 17th.

The OW&WR Minutes record the Resolution adopted: 'The resignation of Mr Brunel be accepted and while the Board regret that circumstances should have occurred which in Mr Brunel's mind render such a step necessary they trust that Mr Brunel will equally appreciate the desire of the Directors to repose every confidence in him and which they are fully satisfied has not only been rightly placed but that the duties which have devolved on Mr Brunel have been faithfully discharged.

'The Board thankfully accept Mr Brunel's offer to render assistance to his successor and they will feel obliged by his allowing the party to be appointed to confer with him and that he will have the goodness to furnish him with all necessary information and documents that he may require.

'Mr John Fowler was then Minuted as the new Engineer.'

On 4 March Brunel had written to Saunders (Rail 1008/35) concerning the matter:

18 Duke Street,
Westminster
March 4th 1852

Private

My Dear Saunders,
I gather from W. Hunt that it is considered decidedly that my connection with the Oxfd. Worcester & W'hton Rly may be prejudicial to the interests of the Great Western Company – if this is really desirable all things considered then I should for the interests of the Great Western Rly cease to be the Engineer of the Oxfd W & W'ton or if those who have the best right to judge of those interests assert that opinion I should not hesitate what to do – but as I have great doubts on the subject or rather intention. I entertain a totally different view – and believe the day may come

when we shall regret that I have left them and as the matter affects me in several ways materially – it is natural that I should wish before taking a step which is irrevocable that I should ascertain clearly the opinion of the Directors – of course my opinion on such a subject is to be taken with very considerable allowance for the effect of the strong bias & the desire which I plainly avow to remain if possible the Engineer to the Oxfd. W. & W. Rly.

It is with me not simply the pecuniary question which however I do not make light of – but I feel a good desire to finish works I have begun. I feel a good objection to abandoning a great work simply on what the public will consider a mere party question – and as I have the vanity to believe that my leaving them is … to get the company into difficulties with contractors or routes. I have a feeling (which may be smiled at) of duty which binds me to them – I mention all these views not as arguments against the opinion of the Great Westn but as admitted causes of my opinion being a prejudiced one.

As regards the interests of the Great Western I believe – influenced no doubt to some extent by these prejudices – that my position has not yet and is not likely to prejudice the GWR. I have not done anything as Engineer to the Oxfd, W & W which as Engineer to the GWR I could object to – and I am not likely to have occasion to do so & indeed I should not – because altho' I have guarded myself as well as I could by letters to the Oxfd. W. & W. Rly Co against being assumed to act as Engineer to the GWR yet I should seek to avoid being placed in such a double & separate capacity and I think it more likely that I should never have to do so – on the other hand I believe it to be to the advantage of both companies that I should occupy this position & form a connecting link – I am sure as regards the GWR that I might have been the means long ago of bringing the two together & then I believe & am sure it could have been done easily & securely because the ice had not been broken nor blood tasted of a […] with the L&NWR – I may again effect this – I believe that my connection with the two is just now preventing. I may intervene to prevent a more violent & a total severance & if on the one hand my position may be supposed to compromise the GWR I know that in the minds of many influential men of the public it is looked upon also as a proof that the OWW really means to come again to the GWR – and it is looked upon as a guarantee that altho' there may be great grounds of difference the GWR wish them well – I have gathered the impression from rather a long conversation only talks with two men likely to influence as well as share the opinion of a large number of other public. I refer to Lord Redesdale and to Sir James Graham both of whom I am afraid are strongly opposed to our proceeding northward but who wish us to have the Oxfd. W & Wn. I fear that the instant I leave the O. W. & W. which the L&NWR wish to bring about – will find a more decided hostility adopted in which the O. W. W may certainly injure themselves – but seeing we are suffering enough already by inevitable wars to make even a little neutrality a blessing – all these are points for the Directors to consider – if they think it desirable that under all those circumstances I should resign my position as Engineer to the Oxfd. W. W. Rly. Com I will do so – though with regret.

I remain, Dear Saunders,
Yours very truly,
I. K. Brunel

PS. I have marked this letter 'Private' that it may not be public property but of course I wish the Directors to know the contents.

Below is an extract from Brunel's thinking regarding the design of Paddington station. He is writing a memorandum to himself to get some clear ideas formed from which he can start to design the new terminus. As he is writing to himself it is difficult to make out his words. I have done my best and am grateful for the contributions from Michael Richardson and Anna Riggs of the Brunel Special Collections department of Bristol University Library. The work he undertook at Paddington combined the functions of engineer and architect. I give this painfully deciphered extract to give an idea of the detail of the thought processes he has set himself here – amid all the other huge and continuing problems. This extract from his thoughts is also given to give the background – and greater feeling – to his letter of 17 March 1852 sent via Charles Saunders, to the Directors, complaining about their reluctance to pay him his expenses after over a year of work on this project.

*

BRUNEL GENERAL CALCULATION BOOK 1850-1858

Page 34
Paddington New Station

Plan No 3
Jany. 1st and 2nd 1851

The question between cramping the general dimensions and getting 8 lines under the centre roof instead of 7 –
At Paddington at present by filling departure lines & everything as far as it can be done in practice (except arrivals) we have about 2900 say 3000ft run of covered line including the iron shed beyond the Westbourne Rd. Bridge.
In Plan No 3 with 7 lines – & filling all except the main departure – & arrivals but allowing half one of the arrivals – we should have 7½ x 850 = 6375 + 500 (Iron Shed) = 6875 or if only 7 x 850 = 5950 + 500 = 6450 and in fair uninterrupted line – being considerably more than double the present.
I think therefore there is no necessity for providing dimension for the sake of another line – particularly as it might be got cheaper by an extension over the [...] lines and still less expensively on the west of line between the viaduct and Westbourne Bridge.

The spaces will be then

Page 35
The comparison [carriages under cover] between the present station and the one will be

	Present	New
Length of main Departure platf (hardly possible to use whole length)	380	720
Short-train line	220	720
	600	1440 (thoroughly available)
Length of main arrival platform hardly possible to use all [...])	380	640
ditto second arrival platform	280	850
	660	1490
Spare lines under cover Exclusive of traversing frames Capable of holding carriages 29ft long	58	140

	(very difficult to fill)	
[...]making up line	9	28
Sub-total 67	168	
Departure	18	56
Sub-total	85	224
Auxiliary arrival	(no cover) 28	
Sub-total	85	252
Iron Shed	17	17
Total carriages under cover*	102	269
Goods		
Platform foot run	660	1640

*Assuming <u>comparatively</u> correct they wd both probably be capable of holding more if pushed.

Page 36
The General Offices Required
[...] are numerous such as –

	Present	**Required**
Board Room	30x33ft	28x35 opening into
Antirooms [sic]	30x15	28x20 for public meetings
Committee rooms	none	28x20
	none	28x20
Secretaries room	30x20	28x20
Antiroom		20x15
Accountants Office		
Large room	40x50	25x20 Parcels
		25x55 Passengers
		25x45 Goods
		25x25 Cash accounts
Mr Syke's office	20x15	25x15
Antiroom/strong room	6x10	25x20
Water closet washing room		25x30

Mr Wood's Office
Private room   14x15
3 Clerks' room   14x20
Strong Room [...] below 25x20 35

Mr Ward's office
Two of   40x12   28x15
                                40x12   28x15
Registration   20x40   28x35
                                20x15   28x20
10720

All this might very advantageously be built of two floors with [...] and [...] – Meeting Boardroom and registration on the level of Eastbourne Terrace and Accountants etc above. This wd involve nearly [?] about 5,000 ft area independent of lobby and staircases allowing 1,000 ft for the first and 400 ft for the 2nd wd give 6,400 ft of area for the building.

Brunel finds himself in the unusual position of not having money – which is owed to him. To an outsider, 160 years on, it might look like poetic justice but at the time, after two years of careful and devoted planning, Brunel feels justifiably hurt at what appears to him to be a lack of gratitude from the Directors who appear not to realise how much money he has saved them. (Rail 1008/35, folio 79).

17 March 1852

My Dear Sir,
I have felt myself placed in a very difficult position by the proposal made to me by the Directors through you when I last saw them on the subject of my engineering expenses, the difficulty of the case and my continuous occupation must be my apology for not writing sooner.

I am sure that the offer was made with the intention of meeting very liberally the difficulty which had arisen and consequently to decline it or even to discuss it would appear ungracious and with the interpretation which the Directors put upon the existing agreements I should find myself thrown into a position of antagonism resulting from a difference of opinion upon that most disagreeable of all subjects – money – from which position I see no retreat and no escape which I would willingly contemplate, on the other hand it is not a question of a £1000 but of upwards of 3000 which is at issue and much as I should prefer to disregard the mere money consideration this amount becomes serious to me – If I accepted the offer in the way in which the liberal intentions of the Directors in making it desire to be met – unreservedly and without qualification – I foresee the possibility of the same difficulty arising again because I think the interpretation given (erroneously as I think) to my letter would under many circumstances quite possible if not probable of parliamentary oppositions & other cases leave my liabilities quite unlimited. [This is what he wrote.]

Now I am not exaggerating the question of amount you will easily see when I state that the sums which it is proposed I should pay out if the quarters accounts of June and September last which are unsettled – and including similar amounts in that of December which have been kept back until this question was settled amount to about £650 with reference to Paddington station alone which up to this same date I have paid (or owe the balance upon) £624 to Mr Wyatt for his professional assistance and for his draftsmen making £1274 independent of all their expenses which I considered included in my charges – I cannot hope to get through the current year the completion of Paddington station – of all our Goods arrangements, coal depots etc – and new Engine House etc etc and is at least the same amount for the twelve months that have been expended in the past 9 – and I owe therefore an amount of £2550 for Paddington station alone – the half of this namely all the professional architectural assistance requisite I had taken upon myself as probably coming under the head of original designs now it was certainly uncontemplated when I made the arrangements and if I had requested the Directors to call in an architect as all other companies have done for their stations these charges would have been doubled and tripled and I may safely refer to the Great Northern and the Euston Sq and Camden Town stations as proofs that the building of railway stations by architects instead of engineers involves an excess of expenditure in works in which in our case would not have been less than £20 or 30,000.

The employment of architectural assistants acting under my own control I took upon myself however altho' it was clearly £1,000 to £1500 out of my pocket and was entirely unforeseen & unprovided for in my arrangement now when it appears that the interpretation given to my letter involves another £1500 –

certainly a profitless sum – the question becomes serious – I am prepared to adopt the offer of the Directors to thank them for it and particularly for the intention which decided it – and to submit to the loss – as a contingency of the arrangement I entered into – provided I may consider that this sum is paid in consideration of the circumstances that the present return of works at Paddington were not contemplated by me – and that the acceptance of it will not extend my liabilities whatever they might be in other quarters – that I shall not be expected for instance to employ and to pay an assistant for our Birmingham station – or to incur expenses in the various Parliamentary contests with which we are threatened and that the usual amount of work hitherto done by the assistants and clerks employed in the works and local offices shall continue to be done – as otherwise I might feel called upon to stop all this & have everything done in Town that it might be done on my expenses which would not only increase enormously the amount I should have to pay but would be a serious inconvenience to the works.

I am, my dear sir,
Yours very truly,
I. K. Brunel

Charles Saunders, Esq.

The central drop-down door or flap of an ordinary goods wagon on the broad gauge was tall enough to reach right across the 6-foot space between tracks, and if it was to fall open it could hit a train on the other line. When this happened it caused Brunel a terrible fright, and he contemplates what might have happened in this letter to Charles Saunders (Rail 1008/35, folio 80):

18 Duke Street,
Westminster
November 29th 1853

My Dear Saunders,
The accidents by truck flaps seems to be on the increase although the numbers of defective pins are certainly on the decrease – an accident happened at Melksham on Saturday doing damage & endangering seriously the goods shed which can hardly have arisen from defective points unless they are positively alive – for the train

had not left the station when a flap which had just been well keyed up fell down and carried away part of one end of the goods shed –
With respect to the point being the cause – had it struck you as a singular circumstance that since the opening of the railway we have never heard a flap dropping open on the off side – the side not next to the small station platform. It would be a most serious thing if it did happen as it would cut up a horse box or the Queen's Carriage on the other line. In fact the consequences might be so fearful that I have kept it to myself lest the hint might lead to the result – but it shakes my belief in the effect being caused by the pins.

Yours truly,
I. K. Brunel

The next letter to Saunders (DM 326/29) concerns various station improvements, although Brunel is unable to make any to Swindon station, which is falling to bits; this situation seems to exist because of the contract between the lessee of the refreshment rooms and hotel and the GWR.

18 Duke Street,
Westminster
September 29 1854

My Dear Saunders,

Leamington footpath
I find that a footbridge over the line may be made for about the same cost or perhaps rather less than the tunnel under namely £630 and upon the whole I think it would be more convenient for us – and I presume would be preferred by the public.

Gloucester station
I am continually receiving applications from Mr Ashby and also from Directors travelling the Gloucester road for the extension of the accommodation at this station.
It has always been so and I believe however extensive the station is made there are some superintendents that always find them insufficient but as the representations respecting Gloucester become numerous and some of them come to me supported by the Directors I think it would be desirable before the Hereford line is

opened that the subject should be carefully considered and what is really necessary ordered – and the subject then dismissed.

Swindon station
The question of the platform of the Swindon station about which I wrote some time back is becoming very pressing – something must be done now for immediate safety – but the whole subject of the present state and future repairs of these platforms and of the covering and the condition of the accommodations afforded to passengers at this station requires to be put on a better footing – at present there many serious defects – the works are out of repair and I have no means of enforcing or securing a better state of things.

Yours truly,
I. K. Brunel

The Birmingham, Wolverhampton & Dudley Railway (BW&DR) obtained its Act of Parliament as a standard gauge railway on 3 August 1846 (Brunel usually referred to it as 'the Birmingham & Dudley'). The BW&DR was designed and its construction supervised by John Robinson McClean (1813?-73). McClean was Engineer of the South Staffordshire Railway and of the South Staffordshire Waterworks. Later he was Chief Engineer of the Furness Railway, and was elected President of the Institution of Civil Engineers in 1865. The BW&DR was purchased by the GWR on 31 August 1848 and an Act was obtained authorising the broad gauge. J. R. McClean remained in charge of the works. The financial crisis of 1847-50 and the bitter legal battles between the LNWR, GWR and various other companies in this richly industrial area delayed the opening of the line – as did the collapse of one of McClean's bridges and the unsafe condition of six others. The BW&DR eventually opened to the public on 14 November 1854. (DM 326/12)

18 Duke Street,
Westminster.
7 July 1854

My Dear Sir,
I have seen a letter of Mr Kershaw's as Secretary of the Birmingham Wolverhampton & Dudley Company to you stating that the works of that railway are 'so far completed that if exertion

is made to forward the permanent way the railway may be opened to traffic on 1 August. It is much to be regretted I think that Mr Kershaw should have made such a statement without consulting me. The statement is unfortunately not correct and at the same time it throws a responsibility upon those engaged in forwarding the permanent way which is not fair towards them and which would tend to mislead the Directors; the works have not been (even if they now were) sufficiently completed to render it likely, whatever might be the exertions made in forwarding the permanent way, that the line can be in a fit state to open for traffic on 1 August.

The greatest exertions have been made by all concerned in the laying of the permanent way – and will be continued – but there have been and are now delays caused by non-completion of works which as far as I can judge at present will prevent the opening of the line for traffic on the 1 August – and instead of such an event being dependant only on 'exertion' being made – I believe it to be physically impossible or at all events highly improbable, whatever exertions might be made because even if the rails were continuously laid they could not be in a fit state to run traffic over.

I am, dear sir,
Yours truly
I. K. Brunel

The GWR took over the standard gauge Shrewsbury & Chester, the Shrewsbury & Birmingham on 1 September 1854. Brunel busy with so much of major importance, involved himself in the politics and operational detail of these lines. In a letter to Charles Saunders (DM 326/14) The letter was endorsed by Saunders: 'Rec'd on 31. Ans'd. verbally same day – to try to settle for our signals. If not – for both.' The last short sentence suggests Saunders would have erected both types side by side?

Brunel's general construction of the wording in this letter, especially the afterthought, suggests irritation and impatience – this signal business is a minor detail with which the impending take-over has lumbered him. The way he writes 'semaphores' seems to be dripping with disgust!

18 Duke Street,
Westminster
29 July 1854

Private

My Dear Saunders,
What am I to do – what principle is to guide us – as to signals more
especially I presume that the Shrewsbury lines have hitherto used
what may be called narrow gauge signals – that is semaphores.
  Now to force them to use ours might raise more stories against
mixed gauge and yet I believe ours to be the best as being simplest
– but it is a question of policy requiring consideration.
  Yours truly,
  I. K. Brunel

I wanted to have been on the B & Dudley lines on Wednesday.
Must I give that up for this?

Yours truly,
I. K. Brunel

The following month, the BW&D line is still not open, Brunel advises
Saunders (DM 326/18) regarding the timings of trains between
Wolverhampton and Birmingham, given the poor state of the track.

August 13 1854

My Dear Saunders,
I think there is nothing to prevent our having the permanent way
ready on the B&Dudley Rly for the 1st. – I have swept [?] up all
our rails [...] for repairs on the GW Ry and this will make us safe
after this business is over we must have a reform of the stores
arrangement – at present it is like a relapse from the new Ministry
of War into the old Ordnance and virtually separate departments
– it doesn't work at all but if we are ready to open – we shall not
be ready for high speeds you must time the trains so as to have
ample time at stations and for express trains you must allow 5
minutes more than mileage rate of 25 miles per hour between the
Shrewsbury junction and Wolverhampton Joint station and no less
than 35 minutes from Wv station to Birmingham without
stoppages – and 3 or 4 minutes for entrance into Birmingham –
and I suppose 15 minutes for the interchange at Birmingham – for
ordinary trains you must allow 40 minutes for running and 5
minutes for each station – pray do not try faster at first –
  There are a good many things for MacClean to get done – I will
write to him.

Yours truly,
I. K. Brunel

We got into possession of Hordern's land yesterday.

Later in August 1854 the Birmingham, Wolverhampton & Dudley Railway is about to be inspected by Captain Galton of the Board of Trade. There is great confusion according to this sequence of letters (DM 326/20-23) as to exactly when Galton will inspect. In the Ian Allan edition of the official history of the GWR, McDermott vol.1 page 174, the date is given as 25/26th August. But this does not square with what Brunel writes in these letters. Captain Galton was to carry out some sort of inspection as he passed through, presumably going to other inspections and then to inspect the line fully on his way back. In this letter, (DM 326/20), Brunel warns Saunders only to allow a sparse service until the track has settled down.

Tuesday, August 22 1854

My Dear Saunders,
Galton has misunderstood the form of notice – and has fixed Thursday – I have written to propose that as only a preliminary visit to certain works and to make his final one on Monday – Bertram is much alarmed at the number of trains proposed to be run – at the very outset – the difficulty is this – and mixed gauge has same difficulties – with first opening of a line laid in such a hurry – after the passing of each train through crossings or sidings – the rails require adjusting packing as now with the mixed gauge – great care is required to prevent disturbing the other gauge – and if these adjustments are done in a hurry owing to the shortness of the time intervals some danger results – Now this line has been laid in a great hurry with new men and under every disadvantage. Pray give us a moderate number of trains for the first week – surely 6 or 8 a day each way would do –

Yours truly,
I. K. Brunel

I shall meet Galton on Monday [the 28th]

Brunel's letter catalogued at Bristol as DM 326/21 refers to Galton's *first* inspection to take place 'on Tuesday or Wednesday', that is the 29th or 30th. Note that Brunel never gives 'Galton' the dignity of his Royal

Engineer rank, even when he could, with benefit to the rhythm of the sentence, have done so.

DM 326/21
Thursday, 25 August 1854
Friday morning

My Dear Saunders,
I returned last night but rather late and intended to have come up to you this morning but am prevented –
    Galton is to make his first inspection on Tuesday or Wednesday I shall try and make it to the latter – I think [...] is disposed to throw the whole responsibility on me – on my giving him a considered undertaking that such and such things shall be done –
    I think therefore you may assume that we shall be all right for the 1st.
    I do not see any one point at present likely to stop us but many that will be very close – more than several, still I think we may calculate on getting them all done – There has been a continuation of fatality about that Walker [...] which threatened positively to stop us but I have seen Mr Walker who has throughout been singularly accommodating and just so might like the opening. The new land has never been conveyed to him nor has he any agreement securing him his proper right so that he might have been completely cut off. I do not know where the fault is but as I have pacified him and given him my personal assurance – the lawyers had better not move till the opening.
    I saw a time bill at Birmingham with 20 trains each way of course this will not be – pray keep it to the nine each way for a fortnight or say till Monday the 11th.
    Where shall you be tomorrow – I should be in town and I shall not go down to Brighton till Monday.
    I have taken the signals of Joint Station into my own hands and ordered Bertram what to do.

Yours truly,
I. K. Brunel

On 25 August Captain Galton travelled over the BW&D, intending to travel south the following day. But on the 26th an iron girder bridge over the Winson Green turnpike road collapsed moments after a broad gauge ballast train, hauled by *Dreadnought*, a Gooch 0-6-0, had passed over it.

Brunel is now faced with the problem of replacing all seven bridges of that type on the line and having them erected. He brings from his Duke Street office, his trusted assistant, T. A. Bertram.

The bridge Brunel refers to in the following letter was a 63-foot 'tubular' span, one of seven designed by the BW&DR Engineer, J. R. McClean.

These letters (DM 326/22, 23 and 24) were written by Brunel from his lodgings in Birmingham when cholera was in full epidemic. During the final fortnight of August, Brunel believed he was suffering from the disease and was feeling 'very queer'. He believed he had had it for two weeks and had cured himself by working very hard; he was quite sure about this and very cocky about his survival (see DM 326/51 below).

DM326/22
Great Western Railway
Snow Hill Station
Birmingham

Saturday August 26 1854
6pm

Mr Dear Saunders,
I think we may get a bridge in the place of the other by Monday and I have told Galton who has been here all day (for amusement) but having said this I must now say a great deal more – upon a careful examination of the work I have come to the same conclusion that Bertram had already, that the bridge broke from no extraordinary cause and that if two trains met upon any of the other bridges of the same construction (there are 6 more) then the same result would ensue principally from bad workmanship and very bad arrangement of detail – I wish I could run down to you and discuss and re-plan all the measures and their consequences but I must give tomorrow to a close examination of the bridge as it is on some small mechanical details and workmanship that the question hangs. I would willingly leave you another day of comfort but I must do it without telling a positive lie and after all you will feel less annoyed by bolting the pill at once – we can't open under a month – this is from no squeamishness or over-caution of mine I would keep my mouth shut and risk much on silence as I have before now but it is no question of risk but of certainty. Before I go further I should tell you that I believe you will have a gentlemanly offer from the LNW to continue the working of the

Stour Valley until the mischief is repaired – Ledsam was on the ground and intimated his intention to write instantly to Ld Chandos to suggest it – so much for that – of course I have left every soul under the conviction that we should and were determined to open on Friday and have fixed with Galton to come on Friday and finally on Monday – but this is all a sham. I see in the ruins of the bridge which I was not unprepared for such workmanship and such bad details and contrivances that the bridge ought to have broken and I have every reason to believe that the others – all stereo-typed from the same design are the same – I am turning over in my mind the quickest and best remedy but whatever I may scheme a month is the shortest possible time.

Galton who is as kind and as little affected by it as possible says of course that after this he must send a double engine on both lines at once – I assented and promised to have it on Tuesday for the other bridges to the trains arrangements as I feel sure and so does Galton that they would not carry it [this makes no sense but it is what he wrote] – I mention this to show you that we could not open even if we chose to run a risk.

Poor McClean still believes that we shall make a push for opening a bridge and I shall leave him under the impression as his report may be more likely to induce the L&NW to make an offer.

I shall be home all tomorrow if you send any message – I am unfortunately suffering from another attack of bowel complaint which has rather disabled me today but I have no doubt I shall be all right in the morning.

I had ordered the Netherton canal bridge to be pulled up and sent down but have stopped it – there being a timber one in the Great Bridge branch that will do.

Yours truly,
I. K. Brunel

DM 326/23
28 August 1854

My Dear Saunders,
I have nothing new to tell you except that Maclean just called to say that he had seen two L&NW Directors who told him that their Chairman and Board were down at Holyhead that some telegraph messages had passed and that the communication I referred to would be made tomorrow.

I am going over all the bridges again tomorrow with Brereton – after well thinking over the question – and shall determine what is best and quickest to be done with each – in the case of 4 or perhaps 5 I think there is no doubt must simply remove the present one and substitute new, the others I think admit of additions that will make them right –
Poor [...] I have just heard is dead and I just hear that my next door neighbour the [...] Colonel Bush died yesterday after only 3 hours attack of real cholera – as you are in the country and out of it all I can tell you this without frightening.

Yours truly
I. K. Brunel

By way of supplement Gainsford's [one of Brunel's main assistants] *landlord died of a sudden attack this morning.*

My underlining highlights a unique event in Brunel's letter writing – an acknowledgement of the help he received from one of his finest engineering assistants. Brereton at that time was Resident Engineer of the Royal Albert bridge.

DM 326/24
Birmingham
30 August 1854

My Dear Saunders,
Brereton, Bertram and I have been at work incessantly – this bridge affair having involved a serious amount of labour – each bridge requiring examining and designing and putting out all the sizes of plates that will be required and skeming to get something like uniformity in the work required – Bagnall has undertaken to roll the iron – and I have just finished a preliminary list of work it will take them nearly 3 weeks to complete the iron – working entirely for us and we cannot put piling without it – and less than 3 weeks to complete the last girder after the last plate is delivered so that six weeks is the minimum – but I think it may if we are lucky be done in that time – if organising staff and putting one good man entirely [...] to say two bridges [...] so will be a great effort – <u>*Brereton will take it in hand and indeed without him it would be impossible*</u> *– I had no idea myself and you can have no idea of the*

amount of work that it has required – we must get all the iron and then get makers to make the new work – I shall try and put some at Swindon – and at Gloucester and at Chepstow for there seems little chance of getting much done here or of getting some workmen however we can only do our best.

Yours truly
I. K. Brunel

The following (DM 326/51) is the postscript of a lost letter written to Saunders – supposedly from Birmingham, and apparently in 1854.

PS. There have been several cases of Cholera rather near here. Hammond's old servant is just dead and several others I know – now in such times it is well to know a remedy and I can really quote my case. I had it you know for a fortnight more or less and during the meeting on Thursday was very queer and retired early after the meeting and a consultation of my assistants I found that owing to the time occupied in removing rails and other causes – there was not a chance of our getting the track in time for the B[W]&D – I set to work therefore seizing upon some of the South Wales and Cardiff and some South Devon's at Taunton and B'water and subsequently finding some B&E at Bristol – and sending off in all directions with orders to dispatch at any cost – I have deluged Bertram with almost more than enough – but no more than was required.

I was at first regularly floored and have been from that moment quite cured of cholera – now if you have an attack put Stevenson to announce a lot of debentures overdue or some other strong dose and you will be well.

Yours,
I. K. Brunel

Brunel appreciates the experienced track maintenance men employed by the contractor Mr Brotherhood. These are the men that laid the track in the first instance and Brunel trusts Brotherhood absolutely to carry out his contract promises without skimping.

(DM 326/38)
GWR Engineers Office
Paddington

November 30 1854

My Dear Saunders,
It is necessary to make some immediate arrangements for the
maintenance of way of the Birmingham & Dudley Railway – as
from tomorrow they must either make arrangements for
employing men themselves or continue the present sub-contractors
who have been borrowed from Mr Brotherhood. It would be in
our interest to let such a line by public tender until we have
ascertained more correctly the amount of maintenance necessary
and until the whole is more perfect but after discussing the matter
with Mr Brotherhood he is willing to contract for one twelve-
month from the present time at £5 per mile per week – for the
double gauge – which is in my opinion not only a moderate price
but the offer is in every way satisfactory and advantageous as we
know from experience that we can rely in every way upon the
performance of his contract and he would keep on the same
foremen and men who are now acquainted with the line.

Yours truly,
I. K. Brunel

The GWR purchased the Shrewsbury & Chester Railway (S&CR) and
the Shrewsbury & Birmingham Railway (S&BR) in 1854. The latter was
designed by William Baker and was constructed only as far as
Wolverhampton. The Shrewsbury & Chester had been designed by a
Scottish engineer, Henry Robertson. The line was 42 miles long and was
built in two years by two of the best civil engineering contractors in
Britain, Thomas Brassey and William McKenzie. The greatest works on
the line are also two of the greatest feats of engineering in Britain – the
Chirk and the Cefn Mawr viaducts. The former is 100 feet high with 10
arches, for a length of 283 yards, the latter 148 feet high with 19 arches
for a total length of 510 yards. The S&CR opened on 14 October 1848.
Robertson became the Engineer to both the companies when the S&BR
opened its service from Wolverhampton through to Shrewsbury on 12
November 1849. After amalgamation with the GWR on 7 August 1854
Robertson carried on acting as the Engineer of the route and Brunel
agreed to this. But then Brunel became concerned at what appeared to be
a division of responsibilities between him and Robertson. Brunel wanted
to know who was Engineer-in-Chief of the Shrewsbury railways, now
part of the GWR. At the same time he discovered that his salary was
discussed at a GWR Board meeting without his knowledge and this not

unnaturally, caused Brunel's to become agitated.

He wrote a letter to his devoted friend, Charles Saunders, headed 'Curiosity', but unfortunately that letter is missing. Maybe it was censored. But from Saunders' kindly and comforting reply, reproduced below (Rail1008/35, no folio number), it is clear that Brunel, in his letter, had taken an insecure view that there was some conspiracy against him, to deny him his proper status. The wording of Saunders's signing-off is unique, unprecedented. It is the equivalent of a big hug. Brunel's response to this is peculiar. First he denies that he believed he was being undermined, then goes on to suggest that even Saunders had joined in this conspiracy of silence. As Brunel's response to Saunders continues, the agitation and the hurt feelings surface again – and the handwriting, on a series of small sheets of notepaper, one of which is missing from the file, deteriorates from difficult to impossible to decipher.

London Terminus
Paddington
2 April 1856

My Dear Brunel
The answer to your note 'Curiosity' is simple and plain!

I must first deny that there has been to my knowledge any studied mystery or concealment whatever from you of matters appertaining to the two Northern lines and secondly I must remind you that your own professional delicacy prompted you to express a wish almost as soon as the Amalgamation Act was passed that you should not be treated as usurping the functions and duties which had belonged to Robertson as the Chief Engineer of both those lines.

When at Birkenhead and at Saltney with the Directors in September 1854 you alluded to the subject and when asked your advice about the improvements to the cattle pens I quite remember you repeating the caution about Robertson.

At that time and indeed almost ever since I know that the Directors have felt the difficulty in doing anything which could be attributed to throwing over Robertson as having been the Shrewsbury companies engineer. In requiring extension and improvements at Shrewsbury both in the Goods station (separate for the Shrewsbury & Chester) and at the Passenger station (Joint with both) he was consulted. You know that Robertson at your own suggestion and desire was made a party to the Low Level

Wolverhampton station in which you – as Engineer of the Gt Western – are, of course, conjointly also one of the Engineers.

The facts show plainly the light in which he has hitherto been regarded and altho' it is perfectly true that Robertson has had little to do beyond such consultation, he has been considered as retaining that position when required to apply to any superior authority over McIntosh who was appointed under him and who has always acted under him.

Now it is one thing to reserve knowledge and another thing to require professional advice and assistance and I am quite prepared to prove that, as far as I know, while the latter has never been exacted from you, the former has never been withheld. Some three or four months ago the question arose about the arrangements made with you in 1853 and among the matters the position you held under it – as to the Northern lines – was discussed. Mr Walpole thought it desirable to leave matters as they were for another year, seeing that the New Lines were under construction. I know that he was to have seen you and explained this. Whether he did or not I cannot say – for his sudden change into an Ecclesiastical Commissioner and MP for the University of Cambridge seemed to disorganise every plan or pre-arranged thought.

For all matters of general policy, even in the North, certainly for engineering purposes which do not necessarily devolve upon Robertson in the capacity of Consulting Engineer over the two Shrewsbury railways, I am satisfied that my Board have always and do now regard you as their professional adviser and friend.

It belongs to yourself to say candidly what you wish in any such matter and altho', of course, I cannot pretend to command success in these matters , you ought to have no doubt as to my willingness to take any friendly step which may conduce to a result such as you, with justice and propriety, desire.

In Locomotive or Carriage Department, I believe Robertson never had any authority & the only thing done has been to make Gooch a Senior to Armstrong & Gibson a senior to Mr Truss.

But surely, our course will be to say distinctly what you wish.

Believe me,My dear Brunel,

Very Sincerely Yours
Charles A. Saunders

Brunel, mollified, writes back to deny that he ever intended to give the impression that he thought he was being 'got at'. By the end of the decipherable part of the letter it seems clear that he does think he has been side-lined, not treated with proper respect. And it looks as if he has. This letter was written when he was up to his eyes in worry and feeling insecure over at John Scott-Russell's shipyard in Millwall, where the largest ship in the world was being built – his ship. In January 1856 Brunel suspected Russell of 2,500 tons of iron plate destined for the 'Great Ship' although plates rolled for that vessel might not have been suitable for any of the far smaller vessels which Scott-Russell's men were constructing. There was also Brunel's suspicion that Russell was 'stealing his thunder' as to the authorship of the ship. This feeling arose out words in an article written about the ship by a 'Times' journalist – words from which Russell vehemently disassociated himself. Isambard's huge worries over the 'The Great Ship', pile on top of the pressures he feels from his responsibilities for hundreds of miles of railway, much of which are still under construction – Westbury to Weymouth and Plymouth to Falmouth, for instance.

2 April 1856

My Dear Saunders
I never meant to imply any mystery was shown towards me as to any proceedings of the company – except what appeared (erroneously as I gather from you) to be a reserve in respect of any reference to my position. All that you remind me of as to my feeling with reference to Robertson is perfectly true and was not forgotten – or thought of by me – being a well remembered fact – but I had supposed that for sometime past Robertson had ceased to act in any way. If it is not so or if there is any uncertainty as to his position which would render my acting a prejudice to his position I should wish nothing to be done with regard to myself – most decidedly – but if he has ceased to act in any way – and it is clearly so understood – I should certainly wish that in my personal character as Engineer of the Gt Western Birmingham & Oxford there should be no distinction drawn between one of the lines of the GWR and another but I repeat that this way in which the Committee had settled all my affairs for me without speaking to me – either before or after he said he thought as you seem to have done that Mr Walpole had settled it all Mr W. never hinted at it and your note this evening is the first occasion in which anybody has

ever spoken something about the proposed Shrewsbury position and I said that I had not heard anything about it and that I did not think I was the Engineer in that case a few more words past [sic] which would arise only in the case of Robertson having ceased to be really or nominally the adviser of the S&BR and S&CR – in respect of those lines – and my question was put only because I had supposed that was the state of things – this state of doubt in my mind is the more excusable when I tell you that neither Mr Walpole or anybody else ever said a word to me about my position with the Company and by what I must suppose to have been a singular accident [...] I never knew of my position, my salary or any question relating to myself having even been discussed till I saw it in print in the Committee's report – You might have supposed that an intimate friend like Potter might have mentioned the conversation but strange to say although seeing him after he never told me a word of anything going on in that Committee and the first I knew of his own disagreement was the evening before I spoke to you about it – when I bullied him about the case ... [a page missing here?] ... to me about anything relating to myself*. You will easily see therefore that I felt singularly in the dark.

Yours truly,
I. K. Brunel

*except that I remember a week when the Directors asked me ...
[this note is incomplete]

In January 1852 Brunel was asked by his bosom friend Sir Benjamin Hawes, Chairman of the recently formed Australian Royal Mail Company to suggest ships for the work. Brunel consulted his friend, the naval architect and shipyard owner, John Scott Russell. Scott Russell, his design team and workforce were the best there were. Between June and November 1852 they designed, built and launched *two*, iron hulled, propeller driven, steam ships, almost as large as Brunel's SS. Great Britain – these were the SS. Victoria and the SS. Adelaide. They would have to stop off along the way for refuelling, an exceedingly costly procedure because other ships were required to sail with coal to Cape Town and Calcutta. Brunel was thus prompted to think of a steam ship large enough to go to Australia and back without re-fuelling. On 25 March 1852 Brunel made his first quill pen sketch of an 'East India Steamship' in his calculation book. 'Say 600ft x 65ft x 30ft.' He took his idea to John Scott-

Russell and the latter advised Brunel to offer the idea to the recently formed Eastern Steam Navigation Company. (ESN) The Directors approved and employed Brunel as their Engineer-in-Chief and gave the contract to John Scott Russell to 'design, build and launch' what would be the biggest ship in the world for 50 years after it was launched. Brunel was not the actual designer of this, his 'Great Ship' but Scott Russell and his team of ship building engineers. Brunel wrote the contract and gave himself the power to overrule the maritime professionals. Brunel was not a naval architect neither was he able to supervise tactfully. His first, highly controversial and damaging directive was to forbid the construction of a dry dock – on the grounds of expense. Scott-Russell had intended to build one so that the ship could be simply floated out and would have a place to return to for maintenance.

Brunel had built a dry dock in which to construct and launch the SS. Great Britain – how much more was one needed for the 'Great Ship'? Brunel then went on to ignore the advice of experienced ship builders in Britain and the USA and designed his own launching system which, he was warned, would not work. This seems to be another case of Brunellian self-deception. Brunel also forbade the use of cranes on the construction of the Great Ship. Brunel had hired the best team in Britain and then did not allow them to get on with their work. The necessity for his prior approval of everything slowed the work down and increased costs. When Scott Russell asked for money, Brunel refused it due to what he saw as a lack of sufficient progress in the work. The cost of iron was immediately increased when Britain declared war on Russian on 28 March 1854. Brunel, already suspicious of Scott Russell's lack of progress, now thought Russell was stealing money and iron. In June 1856, Brunel became ill and took to his bed. Russell sent him frequent reports on construction progress and from these Brunel realised an increase in the rate of construction. He was alarmed. He was not supervising, the work was proceeding more rapidly – they could not be doing the job properly. He sent word to Scott Russell ordering him to stop all work on the Great Ship until he, Brunel, was present to approve the details.

The physical pain he was now suffering and the many, many sleepless nights he spent agonising over his problems with Scott-Russell, the Great Ship and his various railway projects exacerbated his dictatorial attitude when dealing with even the most senior people – if he considered them to be 'underlings'. The atmosphere surrounding the management of the construction of the Great Ship became so bad tempered that the Directors of the Eastern Steam Navigation Co. had to minute an order to all their senior employees – which included Brunel –

to abstain from making personal, verbal, attacks. This letter, written by John Yates, the Secretary to the ESN Directors gives a good idea of the fury at top levels of management created by Brunel – whose fury in return can easily be imagined.

The Eastern Steam Navigation Company
(Incorporated by Royal Charter 1851)
13 Gresham Street,
London.
3 October 1856.

Dear Sir,
I only received your letter of the 1st instant on returning to Town this morning otherwise it would have met with an earlier reply.

I neither admit your assertions nor conclusions neither will I be deterred from offering an opinion whenever I feel it necessary or to be my duty to give one, and, were it not for the great respect I entertain for the Court of Directors, especially for the highly respected Chairman who framed the resolution passed at the last meeting in which it is stated 'That the Directors have a right to count on the utmost forbearance of all persons in matters partaking in any degree of a personal nature', I should probably replied to your present and previous letters in a very different manner. To the Chairman's doctrine I entirely subscribe but I cannot refrain from saying I feel strongly tat from your having failed in your attempt at a quarrel with Mr. Russell you appear determined, if it be possible, to seek one with me.

I will not however, be provoked, neither will I swerve intentionally from the faithful discharge of my duties to the Directors, whose servant I am and to whom alone I hold myself amenable. You have repeatedly put me down when I ventured to advise the Directors as something beneath their notice, a mere secretary. My right to advise the Board is perfectly equal to your own and whenever it has been my duty to advise I have done so in a respectful manner, without assuming the form of dictation which has too frequently been the case with yourself. I have no desire to quarrel with you but I will not be constantly subject to your misrepresentation or be trampled on by you or any man. I have always and frequently at very great personal inconvenience, endeavoured to the utmost of my power to meet your views and wishes in every respect And I assure you it is a source of painful

regret to me to find that I have been unsuccessful and that feeling
is greatly aggravated by the necessity for this correspondence.

I am,
Dear Sir,
Yours faithfully,
John Yates

In May 1858 Brunel was so ill that he went to the spa at Vichy to drink
the waters and did not return until September. In his absence the ship's
construction proceeded rapidly. In November he was seriously ill and left
for Egypt with his wife, Mary, his son Henry and a Doctor. He returned
in May 1859 to find that R. P. Brereton had completed the Royal Albert
Bridge, including the floating and lifting of the Devonshire span. Brunel
was taken across his wonderful design lying on a sofa on a carriage truck.
Brunel spent as many days as he could possibly manage, during his last
few months on this earth, supervising the fitting out of the Great Ship and
when he could not leave his bed he wrote exhortations to Scott-Russell
pointing out imperfections in the ship or asking to be invited to the first
steaming of the engines. Brunel's last visit to the SS *Great Eastern* as the
'Great Ship' was now named, was on Monday 5th September. At mid-
day, he stood, on deck beside a funnel to have his photograph taken. He
stood upright, holding but not leaning on, a cane walking stick, smiling
bravely for the camera. Shortly after the photograph he suffered a stroke,
collapsed onto the deck and was taken home. He died at 18 Duke Street,
with his family around him, on 15th September 1859.

So passed the most colourful, interesting, and perplexing engineer of
that or any other era. His personality was a mixture of passionate genius
and self deception, boldness and insecurity, artist, actor and engineer.
Physically small, mentally gigantic, that is – obsessed with the gigantic –
gigantically wrong sometimes, gigantically right at other times. In the
latter case he positively advanced civilisation – and mostly in ships rather
than in railways. Decisive and yet capable of changing his mind in the
middle of a job – the SS *Great Eastern* being the most unfortunate
example. Socially conservative, he was opposed to most government
controls – government should keep the working classes in their place –
maintain the *status quo* – and therefore also maintain the prisons, but
otherwise it was every man for himself to make the most of whatever
chances came his way and thereby rise through a hierarchy of merit. He
was very reluctant to agree to laws to control employers in their relations
with their workers. He thought that workers should be paid in cash for

their work but could not agree that employers had any responsibilities beyond that. He objected to the granting of titles and medals; the medal he was awarded – the French Legion of Honour – he never wore nor even asked British government permission to wear it. Brunel objected to the law and indeed the principle of patenting inventions. He believed patent rights hindered progress and he lost millions of pounds by refusing to patent his form of gun barrel rifling.

His entire estate was valued at £90,000 at his death. That was a great deal of money in 1859 but yet far less than the estates of either of his great contemporaries, Joseph Locke and Robert Stephenson. The former left £350,000, the latter £400,000. Like those two great pioneers of the railway, Brunel, had advanced civilisation with his railways. Unlike them, Brunel's works had cost a very great deal more money than theirs. Daniel Gooch said in his tribute to Brunel that 'great things are not done by those who count the cost.' But that was merely funeral rhetoric – Joseph Locke carried out great works more efficiently than Brunel and thus pleased his shareholders more. The judgement depends on the criteria adopted to decide what makes a 'great engineer'. One who does what he is paid to do – on time and within budget and therefore to the greatest advantage of his shareholders – or one who uses the shareholders' money to build but also to experiment, often against all advice – to complete years late and vastly over reasonable cost. Brunel was more concerned with his fame and the perfection of work even than with than making money for himself – or his shareholders. Bearing that in mind, Isambard Kingdom Brunel was a tremendous Engineer, like no other in his era, before or since.

INDEX